BE THE BOSS OF YOUR THINKER

By

Mark and Stephanni Myers Bishop

Be the Boss of Your Thinker

Photography by Mark Bishop

Published in the United States of America, First Edition 2024

ISBN: Soft Cover   978-1-73831-370-9
ISBN: eBook   978-1-73831-371-6

For discounted bulk purchases of this book for
your company, association, or conference, please
email: Bishop@BetheBossofYourThinker.com

For speaking, consulting, or interviews with authors,
email: public@BetheBossofYourThinker.com

To receive a free copy of:
15 Favorite M. S. Stark Quotes
A List of Unhealthy to Healthy Thoughts
Sample Creeds
Go to www.BetheBossofYourThinker.com/Request

www.BetheBossofYourThinker.com
YouTube @BetheBossofYourThinker
Facebook @BetheBossofYourThinker
Instagram @BetheBossofYourThinker

TABLE OF CONTENTS

INTRODUCTION: A GRAND HOPE FOR WILD HAPPINESS 1

CHAPTER 1: LIVING INTENTIONALLY 5

It's All How We Think About It. 8

Mark's Story of the Bees 10

Live. All. In. 12

A Good Life 15

Rise Above a Challenging Childhood 16

CHAPTER 2: UNHEALTHY OR HEALTHY THOUGHTS 19

Unhealthy Thoughts 19

Healthy Thoughts Create a Wonderful Life 20

Where Did the Story Begin? 22

Marissa 25

Expectations: We're Going to Get Wet. 27

Mark's Story When He Didn't Give Up 29

Keep Going No Matter What. 32

Create Personal Improvement Days 36

Make the Most. 38

An Inspiring Story of Courage 39

Make Love Not War 42

CHAPTER 3: B. S. BEAUTIFUL STRUGGLES 45

One of My Beautiful Struggles 45

The Suicide Disease 50

More Big Challenges 55

A Miracle. 60

Big Changes. 63

The World Needs More Sweetness 66

CHAPTER 4: HOW TO BE WHAT WE WANT TO BE:
A PERSONAL CREED 69

    Ideas to Write Your Creed 70

CHAPTER 5: DISCOVER OUR PURPOSE 77

    Live Intentionally 86
    Mark's Story of Kathy and Stanley 86

CHAPTER 6: LOOK FOR THE GOOD 93

    Mark's Story of a Motorcycle Crash 93
    The Rest of the Story 96
    Be Positive and Grow 98
    A Mirror or a Window? 103
    Mark Shares a Story: How Far Can It Be? 106

CHAPTER 7: I CAN DO HARD THINGS 111

    Mark's Trans-Canada Charity Bike Ride 111
    Tattoo Girl 114
    Swift Current 115
    Self-Talk 117
    End of the Trip 119
    Enjoy the Process 120
    Small Steps 121
    Always Something Good 124
    Hang On! 125

CHAPTER 8: THOUGHTS LEAD TO ACTION 131

    BEWARE!—Unhealthy Thoughts 137
    Healthy Thoughts 140

CHAPTER 9: THINK 145

    Mark Shares a Story of Upgrading Our Equipment: 150
    Change Begins with Our Thoughts 152

Who's the Boss? 153

I Bet $1000 You Can't Make Me Angry 155

The Wildest Ride, A Make-Believe Story. 156

Unhealthy or Negative Thoughts 162

Mark's Story of Autopilot 163

We *are* the Boss 165

Truth and Honesty. 168

Mark's Play in the Wind Story 173

We Can Change 174

Victim or Victor 177

The Tipping $$$ Principle 184

Pity Parties and Hard Times 185

Good Examples Abound 187

Mark's Pivotal Story at the Hospital. 191

Guilt 193

CHAPTER 10: WHAT WE SAY 199

Be Honest AND Kind. 200

Precise Language. 202

Gratitude 204

It's Just Opinion 207

Forgive or Forego 211

Humility 218

What is Fair? 219

When We Do Wrong 223

CHAPTER 11: DO 225

Chicago Subway. 225

Mark's White Rim Trail Story 228

Move Forward 233

Ideas for Taking a Break to Refresh 234

Mark's Story of Finding Success. 235

Mark Advises Us: Don't Chase Bears. 236

CHAPTER 12: SEIZE RESPONSIBILITY 243

    Own It! 243

    Skills 244

    Excuses and Blame 247

    Justification 248

    Not Perfect 249

    Honestly Stepping Up 250

CHAPTER 13: LOVING RELATIONSHIPS 253

    Agreements 255

    Disagreements 257

    Explore Rather Than Argue 259

    Made-Up Rules 261

    Life Can Be So Amazing 265

    The Gift of Feedback 267

    Abuse 274

    Empathy 276

CHAPTER 14: GRIEF 279

    Widow and Widower 283

    Stages of Grief Redefined 287

    Healthy Grief Stages 288

    Choose to Not Be Offended 291

    Guidelines for Healing 296

    Grief and Guilt 297

    Mark Shares a Story of the Day After Nola Died 302

CHAPTER 15: THERE IS ALWAYS HOPE 305

About the Authors 311

Be The Boss of Your Thinker

INTRODUCTION
A GRAND HOPE FOR WILD HAPPINESS

This book is written from our hearts with great love and a grand hope for wild happiness by living life fully. As we learn to Be the Boss of Our Thinker, we'll find joy despite what happens in our lives. Let us show you how Healthy Thoughts create a wonderful life.

This book contains the remarkably parallel thoughts, experiences, beliefs, and opinions of Mark and Stephanni. We tell some incredible life stories, amazing adventures, and fun personal parables. We openly share how we've made it through tragedies, grief, challenges, and hardships to remain ridiculously optimistic, cheerful, and enthusiastic lovers of life. People always ask what our secret is—it's Being the Boss of Our Thinker.

Our thoughts can be extremely powerful, which is why they are so important. Our life is largely forged in our minds. Our perspective, or attitude, is more important than the reality of our actual experiences in determining our responses. While we don't always have control over the events of our lives, we can be in control of our thoughts. A keen awareness of our thoughts, plus the courage to challenge and change them can lead us successfully through personal difficulties for a joyful life and to healthy relationships. No matter what.

To support healthy thoughts, we suggest you build a necessary foundation by being aware of healthy nutrition, restful sleep patterns, exercise, spending time in nature with plenty of sunshine, as well as healthy past times, attitudes, relationships, reading, friends, and your self-built community. Remember, your thoughts are created from all these influences.

Learning to change unhealthy thoughts to healthy ones is like any skill. It takes practice. Anyone can get better at it. Maybe start by simply being aware of your thoughts. Next, recognize if they are healthy or unhealthy. (See lists of both in Chapter 8.) Finally, practice replacing unhealthy, damaging thoughts with healthy, uplifting ones.

You will probably notice that our writing reflects our Christian life. We understand that others may not share our beliefs, and that's okay—but we make no apologies. We are not trying to convert anyone, but we believe we are having a spiritual experience here on Earth. Please focus on how we have learned to be aware of our thoughts and direct them to help us maneuver the world in a healthy and positive way. It is not only okay to disagree and have other opinions, but it is expected. Take away what may help you. That is the purpose of the book.

Then everyone will live Happily Ever After.

With our warmest wishes,
Mark and Stephanni

Note: Mark uses Canadian spelling while Stephanni sticks to the spelling of the USA. The gorgeous photographs are Mark's talent.

Miles and Memories

Well-worn accessories carry with them the patina of adventure. The same concept applies to life; Live Boldly. "Life should not be a journey to the grave with the intention of arriving safely in a pretty and well-preserved body, but rather to skid in broadside in a cloud of smoke, thoroughly used up, totally worn out, and loudly proclaiming, Wow! What a Ride!"

— HUNTER S. THOMPSON

CHAPTER 1
LIVING INTENTIONALLY

One Christmas I wrote my traditional letter. I raved about our many blessings, my great kids, good memories, fun (and free) activities we enjoyed together, and the numerous personal growth opportunities of "a wonderful year." I read it to my dear friend, Kathy, who had stood by me the whole time.

My BFF looked at me dumbfounded. "Are you kidding me? You had the worst year ever!"

I was shocked! Why would she say that? We'd been so blessed. Then she reminded me of just a *few* incidents of the previous twelve months, such as:

- I had gone through a complicated divorce when my husband drained our bank accounts and was institutionalized after a total mental breakdown.
- My children and I were homeless for a time and faced significant financial challenges.
- We lost nearly all our possessions in a terrible flood, followed by a windstorm (that swept our drying belongings to Oz), while I hobbled on crutches recovering from a painful accident.

- Now we were renting, but the kids and I slept and sat on the floor because we didn't have any furniture.

- I had been robbed at gunpoint three times on my night job at a convenience store.

- We were in desperate financial difficulties and food and clothing for my growing kids was an ongoing battle. Some days, we lost.

- A doctor informed me my seven-year-old daughter faced probable death, due to a kidney issue.

- My children had received numerous stitches required from several, different accidents.

- My daughter had been hospitalized with a serious concussion after a fall on the ice.

- We experienced a terrifying fire in our apartment, scorching my sleeping daughter's pillow as I scooped her up and away from the flames just in time.

All of this and more in twelve months. Yet, I had viewed it as a wonderful year. Intentionally aware, I centered on the good events and experiences. We had found a temporary place to live in a miraculous way: housesitting that provided a small income and supplied food for us. What joy! It sheltered us while I struggled to get back on my feet after an extremely difficult, unexpected, and life-changing catastrophe (that's a long story). My daughter lived through another dire prediction. We were saved from a house fire by divine intervention, and we quickly extinguished the flames. How could I not notice the many lovely wonders in life?

Our perceptions are generated by how we choose to interpret circumstances. Did I see the year as difficult because we were homeless, or as a blessed and wonderful year because we found a place to live? While keeping all the lessons learned, in association with gratitude for the positive outcomes in our life, my focus on the good colored my world lovely. Also, a naturally optimistic mindset influenced my thoughts, which I control. Fortunate to be born with a happy outlook, my continuous efforts to be aware of thoughts and think that life is grand, made it true for me.

Each thought we entertain adds to how our hearts and souls view everything we see, hear, and experience. I try to choose positive, healthy thoughts but sometimes negative, ugly, unkind, or unhealthy ones creep into my mind. But I am The Boss of My Thinker! I made those original thoughts, and I can change them. My thoughts are influenced by past experiences, reading, movies, conversations, or observations—even at a subconscious level.

I ask challenging questions when a thought occurs that could lead me down dark roads. Such as 'Is this true?' or 'Does this idea help or hurt?' or 'Does this concept reflect who my Creed says I am (more about that later)?' or 'Is this the way I choose to view life?' Each time I change my thoughts and intentionally think the way I truly desire, makes it easier to do so in the future and decreases the time I spend in harmful musings.

We have options to live in fear or faith. For example, fear that people don't like us or faith that if we love others our relationships will generally be strong. Sad things *do* happen. They make for a challenging hour, not a ruined life. We can cry in a dark room or go outside and experience the beauty of the world. We can make a truly bad incident much worse by how we deal with it. We can choose to remain wounded by another's words, wallow in self-pity, or be entrenched in 'why me, poor me' thinking—or not. Our thoughts can cripple us more than the original problem.

> *"Marriage is hard. Divorce is hard.*
> *Choose our hard.*
>
> *Obesity is hard. Being fit is hard.*
> *Choose our hard.*
>
> *Being in debt is hard. Being financially disciplined is hard.*
> *Choose our hard.*
>
> *Communication is hard. Not communicating is hard.*
> *Choose our hard.*
>
> *Life will never be easy. It will always be hard.*
> *But we can choose our hard. Pick wisely."*
>
> **—UNKNOWN**

It's All How We Think About It

Even if we're experiencing a large problem, we can have an easier time by thinking in a more positive/grateful way versus facing it with a victim mentality or a negative, self-limiting, 'poor me' mindset. We can always choose our response. We have options. Let's be intentional and scrupulously honest about how we view situations, what we can do to overcome trials, and even consider who we may become by developing strong, optimistic character traits.

We decide what our life will be like by choosing how we think about it. We can decide, despite experiences that happen, if our life is joyful or miserable. The way we think is the key. It's fabulous to know we are the Boss of Our Thinker!

Though Mark and I have had many challenges, our Big Picture View of life is one of wonder, gratitude, and joy. We choose not to dwell on scattered moments of misery as a reason to view our lives as a miserable existence. Our thoughts and outlook are geared towards gratitude and goodness; and as a result, we think of our lives as joyful.

But if we can't write the script the way we want it and stick to it, how can we be joyful? Doesn't everyone experience challenges, illnesses, hurts, setbacks, betrayals, and losses? How can those types of incidents result in happiness?

We're not saying we won't have times of sadness or difficulty, but the way we think about it will definitely make our souls healthy or unhealthy. We can choose to see life in the best possible, courageous way—as an amazing adventure, filled with opportunities to grow and learn but with challenges to overcome, OR we can see it as a nightmarish series of problems and disasters. The truth is that the same life can be viewed either way and be correct. It's all in how we think about it—our perspective.

We may insist we think about events *the* way anyone would think of them. If it's a bad deal, then we feel upset about it. We can only think positively *if* the occurrence is positive. How could anyone think of a 'bad' thing as 'good'?

Let's be aware of each thought. Is it a good way to think? We can challenge our thoughts by asking ourselves this: is thinking of this situation as miserable going to make our existence better or worse? Go for better. Worse is, well, worse.

We may not be able to erase all unpleasantness but can still enjoy our life as basically a grand adventure filled with all types of events, challenging ones, sad ones, surprises, romance, loss, suspense, overcoming, learning, etc. Life is a glorious time of opportunities for growth, as well as days with fun, laughter, love, and joy. Sounds like an interesting movie, right? And we can be the hero or die in the first scene and just hover as a sad ghost in the background.

Let's make the most of life. The good, the bad, and the ugly. Jump in with both feet. Let's not hold back in fear of getting hurt, or worried about what someone may think of us. Barely limping along does not make life better, just smaller. This is not a practice run; this is our only life! Be bold. Be intentional. And we'll live Happily Ever After.

Mark's Story of the Bees

My biking brothers and I had a lot of fun when we rode a particular pathway in Fish Creek Park, Calgary, Alberta, Canada. One springtime, a section of the trail became the domain of a nesting hawk. Periodically when we came through that area, you could hear the bird screeching overhead. With talons drawn out, it swooped down from behind to hit the lead cyclist's helmet. The mini pterodactyl would gouge your head, and your helmet would be knocked over your face. It really hurt when you were struck.

(What Mark doesn't tell you is that the guys always gave the 'honor' of being the lead to any new biker that rode with them. Hey, it's tradition. So, ride with them at your peril.)

One day, we were heading up that trail, and I led the way, when I heard the hawk screech. Fearing what would happen, I swerved off the single track and plummeted downhill fast as gravity got ahold of me.

I saw a tree stump and thought, *If I run into that with my handlebar stem, I'll stop.* I have used this technique in the past, so I aimed the front tire towards the stump and then I leaned the bike a little bit so it would hit the middle of the handlebar, expecting an abrupt halt.

But this stump had grown old and rotten, and it disintegrated, and I fell over, tumbling around in the debris. Unbeknownst to me, it contained a wasp condominium and I had just destroyed their multifamily unit, and they were not happy. I felt a sting and then another, and another and another, so I grabbed the bike and ran up the hill shouting, "Bees, bees!" My buddy, Brad Remington, who is allergic to bees, took off. I raced after him and WHACK! I still got hit by the hawk!

When I caught up to Brad, I had probably forty stings over my body and even under my jersey which I pulled off. Luckily, Brad had his bee kit with him. Over the next half hour, he used his venom pump to extract the bee stingers and I had zero ill effects. We had a fabulous bike ride and it ended up a great day, plus we had a fun story to tell.

So, the moral of the story is, Bee Prepared! (Mark wants the reader to notice what he did there; he thinks he's pretty funny.) Really, the moral is if it's your turn to get hit by the hawk, don't try to get out of it, take it like a rat. Stuff happens, think about what you can do to make the best of it and move on. Or maybe the moral is, sometimes when it looks like you're going to be hit by a hawk, don't make things worse and land in a bee condo. Or, that one bad thing, no matter how bad it is, does not equal a bad life.

Live. All. In.

Many of us may think every so often, or sadly, maybe every day, that life is just too hard. We get knocked down by one challenge after another, loss after loss, and we feel over-whelmed like we can't take one more thing. Mark and I think in those situations it's best to step back and look at all the good things in our life, at everything we have that merits gratitude. Even contemplating the trial we've just recently gone through by the fact we were able to get through it, by remembering people who came to our aid or noticing small tender mercies from God that seemed to show up when we needed them the most. We can even look at how it changed our perceptions or strengthened our character. We can always find some good in everything.

Realize life has a rhythm. Sometimes we go through periods when lots of difficult things are clumped together in a short time frame. When one challenge after another hits us, it can seem overwhelming and we may even cry 'This isn't fair,' or we may become angry at God, or so enormously sad and depressed that we wonder if life is even worth it. But know that the tempo will flow back. It always does. Don't expect periods when *everything* will be ideal. There will always be a few challenges, but they will usually be minor in the grand scheme of things.

> *"To have become a deeper man is the privilege*
> *of those who have suffered."*
> — **OSCAR WILDE**

We should take note of our individual strengths and ask ourselves; how can we use these strengths to help us through each trial. Conversely, maybe look at some of our weaknesses and say, how can we improve due to this situation? It puts a different spin on things and can help us not get hung up on a particular experience but instead, step back and see it as merely one portion of our entire lives.

Like everyone, Mark and I have tough times, and heartbreaking trials, after great difficulty, after another, after another, after another... But we bolster ourselves remembering we've gotten through rough times before. We try to choose a good attitude, are naturally optimistic and happy, look on the bright side of things, count our blessings, have good friends and families, and we notice tender mercies from God. But overall, we've learned to rely on our strength gained through hard times.

We're organized and stalwart and we think things through in a positive way. We've learned to outline our options, pick the best plan, and we muscle our way forward. Sometimes there's no way out but through. Eventually, things change, and we feel like we can fix anything. With enough work, enough muscle, enough gumption, and enough perseverance, we believe everything will be okay.

Then maybe something comes up that shakes our world to the very core, and it doesn't matter how hard we work, or all the rah-rah cheerleading we do for ourselves, and even our healthy thinking doesn't change it. It's hard to admit we have a limit in our ability, but sometimes terrible things will happen and there is no fix. Mark and I think there's great value in facing our vulnerability, and accepting we are merely human beings and that not everything is in our control. But what is always in our control? How we think and react.

Sometimes if we're particularly adept at getting through trials, we can lose that soft, humble side that can shine through when we are brought low. Maybe before the latest dreadful lesson, we may have thought that others need to buck up, keep going, and simply be strong, or we wonder at their despair over a seemingly small thing. After all, we've managed some big things.

Maybe we've even earned the reputation of being a Superwoman or Superman. But when we hit the wall, it can bring us a sense of humility, sensitivity, and compassion that is much needed in this world. When we mistakenly think coping is about strength and power and I-can-do-it, and then find that we can't bring a loved one back, heal a sick child, or restore a lost job, it may make us more sensitive and compassionate to others' struggles.

That former feeling of invincibility may have separated us from people who were battling with all their might. We can learn that sometimes we don't need rah-rah speeches or advice, instead people need love, understanding, and a hug. There is tremendous power in having another human being simply sitting by us in silence to let us know we are not alone. We can appreciate lessons learned, and strength gained, and even among ashes, recognize blessings.

But if we engage in unhealthy thoughts, like blaming another person for our problems, making lame excuses, or justifying bad behaviors, we can become angry or bitter that our usually successful, positive efforts are being thwarted. We can become upset and unable to accept the inevitable unpleasant parts of life, we may grow despondent or depressed from distorted thoughts running rampant through our mind.

It's our choice and depends on what thoughts drive our actions. We can do hard things in a healthy way, so we don't have a hard life. And we must continue this practice day after day because life will never be totally easy. It's not supposed to be. Accepting realistic expectations influences our thoughts.

A Good Life

I think of my life as one filled with full-on, wonderful living. I have been so blessed and have so much to be grateful for. I lived my childhood largely outdoors. I can remember so many hours running through the fields, exploring the woods, swimming in lakes or the ditch in front of our country house, and staring at the shapes of clouds moving across the big Oklahoma sky.

My older sister, Beth, was my best friend (she is still dear to me). We played with paper dolls, gathered acorns and twigs to make people, and dug deep holes just to dig. We rode our bikes miles down gravel roads, to swimming lessons, to the bookmobile, or random exploring. We would also sneak out the window at night, climb onto the garage roof, and talk for hours as we star-gazed.

On our weekly library run, I checked out as many books as they would allow. Then I would climb a tree, or a telephone pole, or find another spot outside and read and read and read. It was lovely to be able to transport myself to faraway places because it was scary where I lived.

Before starting school, I learned to read, finishing most of the classics in the beginning of my life. That gave me a fabulous point of view allowing me to think about things that happened with a mature–beyond–my–years perspective and made me realize I would be okay. I learned it is not what others do, I needed to be concerned about my own behavior. Although I didn't read Victor Frankl's Holocaust experiences until years later, I understood that no matter what challenges happened to me, I could choose my response and I wanted it to be a good one.

Rise Above a Challenging Childhood

Books made me realize there was a big world out there populated by good people as well as bad. Early on, thoughts formed in my mind that we were not responsible, especially as children, for what bad adults did to us. Those things didn't make *us* bad. I also learned to question where the story started. What had happened that made some grown-ups mean and angry or sexual deviants? What was their story? But to be clear, the story does not excuse bad behavior.

Instead, I thought I am free to grow up and be who I want to be. Nor was I defined by what other people said. My dad only wanted sons. After Beth's birth (the oldest), he left the hospital in disgust. Two years later, my dad told my mom, if it's a boy, call me. My grandpa took her to the hospital and there wasn't a phone call—I was born. My parents had five daughters.

My father became angry easily, and punctuated with plentiful swear words, he routinely railed against us cruelly: how we were worthless, we would never amount to anything, he would cut off his right arm to get rid of us (so oft repeated my sister calls it our nightly bedtime story). *And* there was The Belt or the board or a switch or barbed wire or whatever handy tool he found when his temper flared.

Not once do I remember being hugged by either my mother or father, or hearing them say they loved me or were proud of me, or thought I was clever, or cute, or special in any way. In fact, *quite* the opposite. I think because of the books I read, I realized, even though I was a young child, they were very broken people and I felt sympathy for them. I think objectively reading the backgrounds of villains in books, it helped me realize these people suffered greatly, usually due to something terrible that had happened in their lives. But I knew I didn't have to be like that; I could choose.

Often in classic books, the author featured the poor little abused orphan helped by a kind person and I wanted to be like them. I didn't become angry or bitter and did not let the abuse I suffered define who I was. I admit, there were times when I saw a friend's mom pick her up after school and watched them hug, I longed for that, but the realistic side of me knew it would never happen, and I would still be okay. Thankfully, Beth thought I was fabulous. Beth is incredibly sweet and kind and is constantly complimenting others. She did that to me for years (still does) and it saved me. Your parents are not the Boss of Your Thinker—YOU are!

Some extremely terrible things happened to me as a child, but I don't need to go into them. As I've grown older and witnessed people who are very broken from childhood incidents, I realized the enormously fortunate blessing of developing some healthy thinking patterns when quite young. I credit great writers. But it's never too late for anyone to learn to be the Boss of their Thinker.

When someone tells us we're worthless, or some other hurtful comment or action, we can be aware of our thinking and analyze our thoughts. So, the first question we can ask is: *What* am I thinking? Is that a healthy thought or unhealthy thought? Let's explore that.

Thriving

Nature illustrates that optimal conditions are not required to thrive. Healthy thoughts generate predictable outcomes. Choose gratitude, reap happiness.
"The highest possible stage in moral culture is when we recognize that we ought to control our thoughts."

— CHARLES DARWIN

CHAPTER 2
UNHEALTHY OR HEALTHY THOUGHTS

Unhealthy Thoughts

We could categorize our Unhealthy thoughts into 5 main areas.

1. **<u>We are NOT the Boss of our Thinker.</u>** In this category we think we can't help the way we think about a situation, it's automatic. We may believe everyone would think like this. We don't fully understand or accept that *we* are the Boss of our Thinker, not someone else. The truth is, we create our thoughts which means we can change them. That is empowering to know. Thoughts do not float around in the air and fall into our head. They come from words we have heard or read, experiences from our past, or behaviors we have seen modeled in real life, TV, or in a book. We may not even be fully conscious that we are continually taught lessons on how to think.

2. **<u>We become easily offended or angry.</u>** This may lead to feelings of revenge, or we may lash out with ugly words, or even acts of aggression. Anger diminishes our ability to think. Clearly, that would not be good in generating healthy thoughts. Most of the time, if we are not intentional about our thoughts and the consequences we want, our past unhealthy habits

may lead to quick, angry thoughts or taking offense when none was intended. When anger is directed at us, an angry reaction doesn't help.

3. **We think life is unfair.** We may think everything is harder for us than for others. We have an unhealthy 'poor me, why me' outlook. We can adopt martyr or victim thought patterns. We think in terms of comparisons. We think with a scarcity mentality.

4. **Extreme Thinking.** We may think in an exaggerated manner as if something or someone is much worse than it is. We may see catastrophic calamities in relatively minor events. We may use words like always, never, everything, or nothing. If something goes wrong, we blow it up in our minds to 'everything always goes wrong for me' or 'nothing ever works out for me' or 'she always (or never) does that' instead of being honest with ourselves.

5. **We Don't Own it.** We do not take responsibility for our thoughts, words, or actions but instead, we blame others, make excuses, or resort to justifications. However, we can't lie to ourselves. When we try, we are pulled into an unhealthy rumination on why it was another's fault, or make excuses that don't make sense, or engage in disastrous efforts to show we didn't have a choice, determined to push away the accountability of our thoughts, words, or actions.

Those are the five categories of Unhealthy Thoughts.

Healthy Thoughts Create a Wonderful Life

We could also categorize our Healthy Thoughts into 5 main areas.

1. **Be the Boss of Our Thinker.** Take responsibility for all thoughts, words, and actions. Focus on our part in the experience because that is where we can make changes for the better. This will help us live life fully. Own it.

2. **Be Honest *and* Kind.** Be both honest *and* kind in everything we think, say, and do. Keep in mind most things are opinions, allow others to have their own opinion without becoming offended or argumentative.

3. **Find the Good.** Practice the skill of being positive. Look for good in every situation, even if there are also bad parts. Maybe it will only be the opportunity to grow or learn from a bad example. The Scarcity Mentality falsely tells us about limits and makes us worry that someone is getting a bigger piece of the pie or even that we will not get a piece at all. The Abundance Mentality teaches that life is like a kitchen where we can make unlimited pies resulting in as many pies as we desire.

4. **Explore Options**. When challenges come, don't give up. Arm ourselves with as many options as we can. This will empower us to feel hope. Don't get locked into black–and–white thinking, or panicking because we don't feel we have any choices, or that we must choose between one extreme or the other.

5. **Gratitude.** Even on the darkest days, there is still some light, though it may seem dim. Be intentionally grateful and show appreciation often.

Those are the five categories of Healthy Thoughts.

These are not listed in order of importance. It depends on the situation and the person, so honest awareness and analysis is key. Recognize unhealthy thought patterns and replace them quickly with a healthy alternative. Of course, we may engage in more than one in a single situation too. In addition, we may use more than one healthy alternative to change our thinking.

- Be **<u>Aware</u>** of our thoughts.
- **<u>Recognize</u>** if the thinking is healthy or unhealthy.
- **<u>Change</u>** any unhealthy thoughts to a healthy one.

Remember **ARC**. **A**ware, **R**ecognize. **C**hange.

Instead of becoming offended by words from others, even ones that may feel hurtful, critical, or may even seem like an attack, ask yourself questions like this:

1. Is it true?
2. Do I want to change it?
3. What are my options?
4. What would be best?

Think each question over carefully and be scrupulously honest with yourself. This practical exercise may also help alleviate emotional or unhealthy responses.

Where Did the Story Begin?

When someone hurts us, calls us names, or in any way demeans us, understand it's a reflection of the pain, or jealousy, or spite inside them. Perhaps the first question is, 'Where did *that* story begin?' Now in a compassionate mode, so we don't get angry or lash back, we can ask ourselves, 'Is what they're saying true?' If it is true and we don't like it, then change it. If it isn't true, don't worry about it, forget it. Don't ruminate and make ourselves feel bad unnecessarily. Don't plot revenge. We are The Boss of Our Thinker. We can focus on the nice things people say to us (or we say to ourselves) or we can become very bitter by concentrating on unkind words spoken to us. It's our choice. Choose Better, not Bitter.

With my dad's negative criticism, I knew that wasn't true. I wasn't worthless. I believed I was a child of God. That alone gave me great value. Combined with deliberately living according to the values and beliefs in my Creed, I knew I was of great worth—like all people. So instead of having thoughts I was worthless, I was aware of what I was thinking and changed (ARC) unhealthy thinking to a healthy idea. I would not let my self-esteem be affected by his unkindness. I chose not to live my life in the misery of unhealthy thinking. Happy doesn't live there. I was sad he was not in a good place, and I felt compassion and didn't hold a grudge. I gave him grace. I also recognized that the world is *not* made up of perfect people and living in grace for others would help keep me soft and gentle but strong when dealing with difficult personalities. I accepted that it was not up to me to take on the complex task of straightening people out.

Despite all kinds of significant abuse, I looked for the inevitable good in life and in people. I also knew there were a lot of adventures and a lot of opportunities. I rode horses and played with the dogs and cats and held little baby chicks in my hands. I watched the noisy grunting piglets jostling for a place by their mothers. I chose to think of torrential rains, flashing lightning and booming thunder as awesomely exciting, not terrifying. I eagerly pursued learning. I discovered much I didn't know and felt excited to learn all I could.

I always earned good grades; I absolutely loved learning. I had an unquenchable curiosity about most things in the world. School acted as a refuge for me, and I wanted to be in everything. I joined drama, debate, student council, pep squad, and I studied several languages from an early age, and had the opportunity to travel all around my region in competitions.

My family also did a lot of traveling. My father was intelligent, curious, and loved to experience places he'd heard about. No one is *all* bad. I began working at only twelve years old as a waitress and worked full-time until I graduated from high school. My parents didn't help me financially, so when I chose to attend a university far away, and being too broke for a car, or a flight, I hitchhiked across the country, a teen girl alone. Fortunately, that worked out safely!

I married quite young (in my college sophomore year) and ten months later, had a baby. I felt enamored with this little boy and thought he seemed so fun, smart, and wonderful, that my excitement replaced any fear I had as a new mom. Having children proved difficult for me. I had complications every time and would be placed on months of bed rest. I suffered through horrendously awful morning sickness. Most of my babies had to stay in NICU for a while. Each time, the joy and happiness I had with each one of these tiny human beings made me forget all the unpleasantness of getting them here.

Once, I went into labor early and massive hemorrhaging endangered my life. We made it to the hospital 'barely in time' the doctor said, but sadly that baby didn't live. We also lost three other babies because they weren't correctly developed.

I could have had unhealthy thoughts and felt angry at what happened or felt life was unfair with a 'why me, poor me' attitude. But why would I make a difficult situation worse? I choose to be the Boss of my Thinker and find good in difficult circumstances. Although it was not easy, I had amazing growth, learned a lot about what was truly important, and had much gratitude for even small mercies.

My overabundance of energy blessed me as a mom, and I also had the ability to focus and power through the day with very little sleep. I especially needed that with my daughter, Marissa.

Marissa

During my difficult pregnancy with Marissa, doctors told me this baby also had some serious deformities. In my fifth month, they told me they couldn't find a heartbeat anymore and I would probably miscarry in the next couple of days. But she made it full-term. Right after her birth, I could hear one of the doctors whispering, 'Quick; wrap the baby in a blanket!' They only let me hold her for a moment before whisking her away. She looked so beautiful. She had lots of long, dark wavy hair, big blue eyes, and a darling little face.

I asked for my baby several times, but they told me she was undergoing tests. Finally, the doctor solemnly told me that my baby girl was not expected to live. How could I go through that again? Did I have a choice? He explained that most of her internal organs were either missing, in the wrong place, or not functioning. Her legs and feet were badly deformed. I asked if I could please hold her and he said it was probably not a good idea, but I insisted. He left and I sadly waited for her.

Later, two doctors, a nurse and a therapist came into my room to tell me the additional bad news about my baby. The list was long, with more expected to be added after additional tests (which proved to be true). They encouraged me to leave her there because trying to raise this child would be very difficult. They didn't expect her to live long, but if she did, they would put her in an institution. They explained "Most parents just tell everyone the baby was stillborn." The numerous medical procedures would seriously disrupt my life and the lives of my family. It would be challenging to be a good mom to my other children because of the time she would take, and it would be financially devastating. They also pointed out that most marriages fail when a child has serious problems.

I'd been through lots of hard things by that point, and I just thought, don't be ridiculous, I can do this. It seemed like their warnings were too big for that beautiful little girl. I demanded they let me see her, so they finally brought her from the NICU nursery swaddled tightly. I was determined to know what I faced. I started to peel the blanket back, but the nurse stopped me. I remember them saying to just leave the blanket on her, or at least I should take a tranquilizer before I saw her body. I told them I didn't need a pill; this was my baby; it would be fine.

Before they could stop me, I whipped the blanket off her and looked down at her badly twisted legs and folded-over feet. I remember saying, that's not so bad; I can do this. I could not give up this little baby; it would all work out. The doctors continued to discourage me from taking this journey, but I knew I would never forgive myself if I gave her up.

Soon they came to report additional discoveries. She couldn't urinate. The doctors could not find an external opening, plus she only had one kidney, and it was ectopic (in the wrong place). They declared: 'She was not viable.' While they waited for her to die, I held her as much as allowed and saw a lot of determination in those little eyes.

After a couple of days and many prayers, a nurse rushed in to tell me Marissa had a wet diaper! Armed with a long list of doctors' appointments, I took her home to meet her three older brothers.

When Marissa was three days old, and after painful manipulation, she had tiny casts put on both legs, from the tips of her toes up her entire leg to her hips. I can do seriously hard things, and she could too. And so, it began.

Expectations: We're Going to Get Wet

What are our expectations in life? If we go swimming, we are going to get wet. Expecting that outcome from the beginning makes a day at the ocean more pleasant. It is a bit silly to go to the beach and wade out into the surf and then get upset that we are getting wet. Expecting life to be easy, always pleasant, and just the way we want it, is the same.

We will get 'wet' in life. We may be challenged, hurt, betrayed, sick, lost, upset, or sad. Trials are a definite part of an earthly existence. But also, we will be amazed, happy, grow, learn, be helped, enchanted, loved, and so forth. All that + much more = life. Let's adjust our expectations. Our lives will have times of trial, and to let that bother us or make us feel life is unfair is like getting mad about getting wet when we go for a swim.

**Challenges are not obstacles along our way
—they *are* the way.**

Life is not just about the great things that happen, it's also about immersing ourselves in a variety of experiences that help us learn, grow, and live fully. We become our best selves by accepting challenges, and with fierce intention, tackling them. It is how we learn to understand others and compassionately connect and become better human beings.

- We are learning a little more every day.
- We get lots of chances.
- No one is grading us.

In a hard time, remember, no one else knows exactly what to do either. We just do our best. Don't worry about what we did long ago. Maybe that proved our best then. Now our best is better. In ten years, our best will be amazing!

If we get tired, learn to rest; not give up or quit. Keep going. If we were watching a movie and the intrepid hero lost his backpack over a cliff with the last map to Shangri-La, and it fell into the river, down a waterfall, and then disappeared out of sight, and he sat on a rock and cried, shook his fist in the air, and then slumped there looking sad, how long would we continue to watch before we wanted to shout, "Don't just sit there! Get up and do something!" Would we want the movie to end there? Doesn't it seem like there should be more? Let's be the writer and director of our life story. Move on to the next scene. And don't forget, we are the heroes. Act like it! And we'll live Happily Ever After.

Mark's Story When He Didn't Give Up

As leaders at a Boy Scout Camp near Waterton Park Townsite, Alberta, Canada, we decided to hike up to Crypt Lake. We took a boat over to the trailhead to begin what some might consider a rather aggressive hike. The cold lake is surrounded on two sides by glaciers, high in the Rocky Mountains. We hiked around the lake, slid down the glacier on slick rain-coats, ate lunch, and decided to catch the early boat back. That meant we had to hurry to the dock to not miss the launch.

We ran hard down to the water's edge. When we arrived, I could see the boat in the distance and knew I had a little time. It was a hot day and I decided to go for a quick swim to cool off in the glacier–fed lake. First, I emptied my pockets and stuffed a compass, my favorite pocket–knife, and other valuables into my shoes. Then, I stripped down to hiking shorts and waded in. Coming out dripping, I put my shirt on, gathered up my shoes, and walked out on the wharf.

Sitting, I dangled my feet in the water to wash them, then put on socks and grabbed the first shoe. I leaned over to shake the dirt out and the forgotten knife dropped into the lake. Distressed, I tied a rope to the wharf to mark the place where it fell. I got one of my Boy Scouts still in the water and said, "I want you to dive down to get my knife. Dig Deep." He tried and tried without success. It dropped much farther than I thought. Soon the boat came, and we had to abandon our recovery efforts. We crossed the lake back to Waterton Park Townsite and returned to our camp.

I taught my Boy Scouts that sometimes we must Dig Deep. We must push ourselves harder than we thought possible; we must hold our breath longer than ever before. We faced a lesson here for sure, and I didn't want it to end in defeat. We had to get that knife.

By morning I had a plan. Fortunately, that weekend my friend, Brad Remington, had also traveled there. I asked if he had a boat and he replied that he had his dad's. I said, "Let's go over to Crypt Landing" and I explained about my knife. I borrowed a wet suit, mask, snorkel, and flippers so I could easily make the descent. We climbed aboard for a choppy trip across the lake.

Reaching the dock, I dressed up in all the gear, went over the side, and attempted to dive to the bottom. But even with the flippers, I couldn't reach it before I ran out of breath. I tried it a few times and said, "I'm not getting there." Brad asked if I could see the knife and I responded, "No, but I know where it is."

I dove again. When I came up gasping for air, I saw Brad waddling out onto the wharf holding a huge rock. He said, "Let's tie this rope to the rock and around your wrist. I'll push it off, and when you get to the bottom, then you can grab the knife, and cut yourself free."

I enthusiastically agreed, "That's a great plan!" (This is why women live longer than men, Mark.)

We rigged it up and Brad said, "Okay, I'll shove the rock over the edge and…"

"No, no, no." I interrupted, "I need to psych myself up for this first."

Finally, he says, "You ready?" And just like that, I became a cowboy on an eight-second ride on a horse named Tornado. The rock's weight rocketed me to the bottom. I looked over and there sat my knife. I grabbed it, cut, then peered up and saw a teeny dock high above. *Oh my gosh, that is a long way. I had no idea it fell this far down.*

Kicking my flippers furiously, I got an idea. *I'm gonna' come up on the other side of the dock 'cause everybody is hanging over the edge staring down for me.* I emerged near the beach, took off the flippers, and crept along the pier to the guys. They were still searching into the lake intently, and it had been several anxious minutes. I stuck my head between them and said, "What are we looking at?"

In our lifetimes we're presented with challenges. Frequently we will need to do things that we haven't considered before. We'll need assistance and advice from others, or we may need to venture out of our comfort zone.

The moral of the story is: There's great value in digging deep to find a solution and giving more effort than we anticipated, or even more than we've ever given. We simply don't quit. Instead, stretch, dig deep, and figure it out. It's an attitude of 'git 'er done!' that results in wonderful growth and increased self–esteem.

Keep Going No Matter What

"It is not enough that we do our best.
Sometimes we must do what is required."
—WINSTON CHURCHILL

When we're having a hard time, don't give up; keep trying. Stay in motion. Advancing from a standstill is harder, so keep moving. Often with a little more effort and some creativity, things work out. There are many things we may consider before going forward.

First, be physically ready. Consider decorating our surroundings with items that feel good, with lots of light, and hopefully a feeling of nature. Sitting in an unkept, darkened room can be a downer. Strive to get sunshine, healthy food, lots of movement (especially walking), and adequate sleep every day. Do some breathing exercises.

When going through a difficult time, we can write about our feelings in a journal (start a Gratitude Journal), exercise, do an act of service, or get outside. We could call a friend (Brad Remington has the best ideas, lol), and if someone asks if they can do anything for us, be ready with some suggestions. What is it we wish someone would do? What do we need? Would anything make it better?

Do an activity or hobby we like. Sometimes we may not feel like it, start it anyway and give it fifteen minutes. Often that is all we need to get into a great state of mind and keep going. We are the ones in charge of our mood. Although none of this may change the challenge we are facing, we are at least strengthened to deal with it.

Finally, remember we don't have to do it alone. We don't get extra points for being a martyr. We don't have to 'over' suffer.

Let's look at some examples. Are we feeling lonely? Begin a new hobby (not solitaire) or take a class. Reach out with a phone call. Find someone to serve. Ask someone over for dinner or invite a friend to go out to eat. We all feel alone sometimes.

Feeling sad? Ask someone to watch a lighthearted movie with us or to accompany us on a nice walk outside. Are we sick? Maybe ask for a healthy meal or see if a friend can run an errand for us so we can stay home and rest. If we're doing something that makes us feel worse, like sobbing as we read old love letters after a breakup, STOP it!

Are we consumed by guilt? Fix it! If we've wronged some-one, swallow our pride, and go to them and apologize; try to restore what was lost or do whatever they may need to make amends. Once we've learned our lesson, done all we can to repair it, and resolved to change and be better, then it's time to move forward. Holding onto guilt is foolish. And unhealthy.

After we've worked with others in solving situations that made us feel sad, unhappy, or lonely, think of some family or friends that could use OUR help. Of course, pay back those people who have assisted us, but also graciously pay it forward. If we know someone who may be feeling lonely, invite them over or go for a walk and enjoy the outdoors together. Do we know someone who is feeling sad? Bring them some flowers or a treat. If we have a friend with a lingering illness, volunteer to read a humorous book to them. As we reach out, remember it is a two-way street. Let's take our turn, not just asking for help, but also giving aid to others.

Make a list of five people that are special to us. Now write down one thing we want to do for each of those people and start doing it. A surprising consequence is that serving others will make us feel better too.

Stay busy. A day of doing nothing often leads to unhealthy thoughts and moods; we need to get going and keep going. There's a saying that Jesus went about doing good, whereas in our lives, we may just go about.

Don't dwell on negative memories. Our best life is not heading backward. But also, let's not get ahead of ourselves. Life is unpredictable and living in the future or worrying about what *may* or *may not* happen can lead to anxiety. Live in the present. Learn from past experiences and plan, but today needs our attention.

If our mind is a mess and we don't know what to think, stop. We don't have to think about unpleasant things now, or ever. Be the Boss of Our Thinker. Give our minds something lovely to focus on. Place things in our head that we like to think about. For example: that great restaurant down by the beach, that perfect powder ski run, the hike in the mountains when we saw the baby hummingbirds, that kiss, the first time we held our child, a promotion at work, etc.

What do we intentionally seek? Are we knowledge seekers? Do we actively seek peace?

Do we hunger for adventure, love, or awe? Consider being a seeker of truth, light, freedom, or joy. Seeking is not casual or happenstance. Seeking is a yearning, a priority, or an earnest desire. **"By small and simple things, are great things brought to pass."**

What do we tell ourselves? Self-talk is important. Do not 'horrible-ize". Saying things like, EVERYTHING is a disaster! I'm soooo unhappy! I can't do it! *Nothing* ever works out in my life! Even using hyperbole like: This is the worst head-ache ever! The 'worst' compared to what? Those statements are likely false and make us feel unhappy, so don't indulge in saying them.

Be scrupulously honest in our speech, especially in our self-talk. Do not hesitate to ask in response to our thoughts, Is this true? If it isn't absolutely true, honestly reword it. If we say mean, bad things to ourselves we will likely not feel good. However, do not say something that is not true because it is 'good' for our ego. Be honest AND kind, especially with ourselves.

We must not indulge in self-defeating thoughts or behavior. What encouragement do we give ourselves? Even if we are going through a difficult time, think of this:

> *"If your path demands you to walk through Hell,*
> *walk as if you own the place!"*
> **—WINSTON CHURCHILL**

Think that things will get better, explore how to make that happen and have positive thoughts about our future. Being scared or nervous is okay. Move forward anyway.

Feeling lousy is hard. It makes doing anything difficult. But look around, some people are going through a heavy trial, yet they are still happy. How do they do it? There are many answers to that. But, if they can do it, so can we. We can be miserable in our circumstances, or we can choose to be happy despite them. We can write down our best advice for living a good life. Then read it and compare it to how we live.

Create Personal Improvement Days

Each day is a new chance to make life better. Practice controlling or directing our thoughts. Have a Day Without Complaints, a Be Positive Day, or Patience Day or maybe a Be Kind Day. Infuse the world with honesty, courage, and kindness or whatever virtue we want to cultivate. Read some articles about it, watch some videos, listen to a podcast, or find some quotes about the virtue we wish to focus on. Study it. Ponder. Write about it. Think about what that day might look like. Then make a plan and do it. Place some little reminder cards around the house or on our car's dashboard.

For example, on our designated Be Kind Day, we can read several articles about being kind, listen to a podcast on kindness, we can also contemplate kindnesses we've experienced (either to us or by us), and ponder how we will try to bring more kindness into the world, and we can wear one of those tee shirts embellished with the words: Be Kind. Then of course, deliberately BE KIND!

"Nothing Beats a Failure Like a Try."
—R. J. SMITH

If we find ourselves feeling defeated or lost, try again. But this time do it more like who we really are or who we are actively becoming. Count our blessings. Better yet, write them down. A Gratitude Journal can be especially helpful in elevating our mood; both in writing in it and later reading it out loud. Start eagerly looking for things to write about to encourage deep gratitude.

Create our Best Day. Include all the things we enjoy. Our favorite foods, our most comfortable clothes, the people we love, a beautiful sunset, an enjoyed pastime or hobby, or an act of service. Store it near the top of our memory to pull out often for review. Then, create another BEST Day. Rinse and Repeat.

Let's learn something interesting today. We can read or listen or watch something motivating or inspiring. Smile more. Watch a video that makes us laugh. Share it with someone else. We might be surprised who else needs to feel uplifted.

Perhaps we have a problem with anger. Let's tackle it TODAY. Examine why we are so angry. Often there is an underlying problem that is really the cause. Maybe we need to eat or get more sleep. Maybe we are embarrassed or fear we are not good enough. Maybe there is a situation that is upsetting us, and we are indulging in an irate reaction. Do we honestly think it's a healthy reaction? Do we need to be mad? Are we overreacting? Is that what we want for ourselves? How does this affect others? Is it going to make things better or worse? Remember worse is, well, worse.

Is there another feeling that would be more advantageous? What is our ultimate objective? Will anger get us there? Focus on the outcome we want and think of some possible means to achieve it. If temper is a problem, refocus our attention on cultivating peace or calm or another opposing attribute.

For example, we decide on this day to conquer our wrath by focusing on peace and understanding. We can read and study both of those virtues or listen to a podcast or watch a video that inspires or motivates us to develop calm reactions. Think about the positive results that will surely happen. What are our beliefs about anger? Do we feel more powerful? Do we think if we let something go, we are weak or like we might be taken advantage of? Examine those feelings and thoughts. Look forward to satisfaction in how we handle a difficult incident instead of the regret we've had in the past by allowing anger to rule. When we're upset, it's a setup.

Make the Most

Decide to Make the Most of any situation. During the Covid 19 lockdowns starting in 2020, I heard someone talk about making the best of the situation. What could we do during the lockdown that would lead us to a better life, away from fear, feelings of deprivation, or frustration?

My own business was shut down. I depended on conferences or trade show events that were suddenly not allowed. It greatly affected my income. But I still needed to Be the Boss of My Thinker. I decided being angry or moaning about how unfair it was or how much I might suffer didn't help. The anticipated money would still be gone, but why make something already difficult even more awful by thinking in negative ways about it? Would that unhealthy thinking make anything better? I didn't want those thoughts in my head. I intentionally thought of other activities the lockdown gave me the opportunity to pursue. I couldn't change the mandate, but I could change the way I thought about it.

We may only get one 'lockdown.' But the lessons learned, and the satisfaction gained by a constructive response will stay with us and strengthen us for future bad situations. Seeing it as perhaps our only chance to Make the Most of it and turn lemons into lemonade motivates us to think differently and develop the power to take a future trial and turn it into a blessing and we'll all live Happily Ever After.

An Inspiring Story of Courage

Many years ago, I witnessed a life-changing example of this. My friend, let's call her Joann, was in a very difficult situation, and I learned so much from her. It made me realize that we can't fix everything the way we would like, but everything is doable and the *way* we do it can be very important for us.

Joann's child was born with an exceptionally serious condition, though it took some time before they realized it. At around the age of three years old, instead of progressing, her son rapidly regressed. Months later, the doctors discovered what was wrong. They finally diagnosed him with a rare disorder that meant he would continue to regress to the state of a newborn, and then die. As friends and neighbors, we were all heartbroken for this dear sweet woman, her husband, her young daughter, and her son. We helped her all we could, but she shrugged off most offers and bravely forged through by herself. Sadly, her sweet little boy did die.

During this ordeal Joann became pregnant—before they found out that the disease was also possibly hereditary. When they received the test results showing that this baby too was affected and would also only live for a few precious, but painful years, my friend shared this with me. She said how grateful she felt. At first, I was shocked and didn't understand. Why would she want to go through that horrible experience again? Then she explained that she knew her son's life had mattered. That he lived it with dignity and joy in the smallest of pleasures. He had lived fully even in his diminished capacity.

She explained that she didn't feel like she had endured it well the first time. She pushed away help. She pushed away God. She pushed away her husband. She felt if she powered through it, not stopping to feel anything, just kept busy, that was the best way. Now she realized it wasn't.

She missed moments of joy like when she took him for a walk in his stroller, when he couldn't speak anymore but made sounds of delight in being outside. Immersed in her sadness, she missed the tenderness of the experience. She missed the closeness, afraid to love him completely for fear that it would make it more painful. Knowing that he would die felt so hard for her, she missed the wonder and love of that little boy.

She drew inward. She missed the bond that could have been felt with her husband if they had tackled the experience together. And the closeness she might have developed with so many friends who were willing to help but she refused to accept it.

"I felt like I had to do this by myself, like I was being punished and had to pay the full price in agony. I thought it was the only way I could get through this horrible thing. I've realized now that there are other ways I could have done it. I could have been a better friend. I could have developed closer relationships. I could have learned humility. I could have grown stronger as a person; more compassionate, more understanding, and more patient.

"I could have grown nearer to my husband and even God and let Him help me through, which would have taken more advantage of the atonement of Jesus Christ which I believed to be a gift to me. A gift that I seemed to reject because I felt such pain, sorrow, and confusion.

"But now, I have a chance to do this again and I can do it with great love for, and from, God and all those people around me. I can fully experience every emotion. Part of it will be difficult. I know that, but I missed a lot of what I could have felt and experienced the first time and I really want it all."

I felt moved and touched by her ability to think of the good and be grateful and look at other ways she could have dealt with her challenging, and sorrowful situation. I was in awe of her enormous amount of strength and courage, over–whelming courage, that she showed. Even today, decades later, thinking about it brings me to tears. I felt amazed at her wisdom and her ability to face life fully and bravely. It's a tremendously inspiring example to me. Good or bad, I also want to experience every bit of life in the very best, most healthy, loving, and growing way I can.

We will all go through challenges. We can choose to believe that challenges are orchestrated in our lives to help us grow. We can become better in so many ways as we travel along difficult paths. We can become stronger, more understanding, more loving, and even more compassionate to the trials that others face. Mark and I think that hard times are import–ant parts of life. We believe they can be a blessing to us. We realize it's not easy, but if we think of difficult things as a challenge *and* opportunity that can make us better, bring our family closer, teach us great lessons, and help us fully experience and appreciate every single part of life, then we've triumphed.

Make Love Not War

When a trial comes, what do we do? Is *fighting* the answer? For example, what does 'fighting cancer' look like to us? Is that giving too much negative influence to the many 'cancers' in our life? Maybe, we can shift our focus to 'loving.' Though we may have cancer or another challenge, we can love our warm, soft bed, and be grateful for the sun streaming through a window in the morning. Love our breakfast. Love those around us. Love our warm shower, the clothes we put on, and the music we play in the background or listen to with our whole being. We can love our bodies and the parts that work well. Feelings of love will bring us more peace and joy in the most trying of circumstances. We have so much to be grateful for. Fighting, hate, anger, and other negative thoughts destroy our emotional and mental peace and our physical health. The hippy slogan from the 60s could be resurrected. Be a lover not a fighter. Make love not war.

In this life we are all walking up a steep mountain and we can sing as we climb, or we can think about our sore feet and complain—whichever we choose. We still need to do the hike. Mark and I decided a long time ago that singing made a lot more sense. We can decide how we think of every experience. We want to live fully. We desire to experience as much as we can in this life. We view it as a smorgasbord with perhaps only one chance to try some things.

As we practice Deliberate, Healthy Thinking we can enjoy our treks around the sun, awakened to how glorious it can be. All of it. Even in difficult times, there is the potential to earn something: knowledge, gratitude, personal growth, compassion, humility, understanding, empathy, appreciation... The list is quite long. Enjoy the journey. One step at a time. Don't give up. Don't dwell on sorrow. Create a good life but be ready to have it interrupted.

Anticipation of a fun activity, visit, hobby, or an upcoming project can bring happiness and give us something to look forward to. Life is short. Let's not wait or put our lives on hold. If not now—when?

Road Less Traveled

Worthwhile seasons of life frequently exist on the other side of difficult. "The most difficult choice is the decision to act, the rest is merely tenacity. You can do anything you decide to do."

— M. S. STARK

CHAPTER 3

B. S. BEAUTIFUL STRUGGLES

A friend of ours, Will Gause, talked about a difficult experience in his life. His wife committed suicide. It, of course, created a very challenging time. They had a new baby and a young child, and it left him to raise his children while recovering from losing a spouse who had taken her own life. Many people told him how terrible it was, and what a horrible experience he had to go through. At first, he agreed and thought, *this is BS that I must do this.*

Eventually, he knew he could either be bitter or he could make things better. He chose to think of BS differently. He decided that BS would now stand for Beautiful Struggles. His struggles were beautiful because they were going to take him to a higher place in his mind. When he caught himself feeling self-pity, thinking life was hard, or even saying this is BS, he changed his thoughts to 'This is a Beautiful Struggle.' Then trials became a growth experience for him. He is, indeed, an amazing individual. We can all learn from Will to make things better and to stay away from being bitter. And we'll live Happily Ever After.

One of My Beautiful Struggles

I always thought of myself as a strong person. Like most people, I've been through some difficult times beginning in early childhood. Then in December 2014, Christmas morning, my late husband, Russ, and I drove over to pick up his mom to take her to a care center where my father-in-law faced the end of his life. He had suffered for several years from dementia and his condition had worsened where he could no longer be cared for at home. My mother-in-law had valiantly taken care of him but as she became older and frail, she finally had to accept that she couldn't do it any longer.

We were told he probably only had a few days left, which proved to be true. When we were almost at her house, I put my head back and closed my eyes because I hadn't slept much the night before. Suddenly there was a loud crash, an airbag exploded in my face and chest with the force of hitting a brick wall, and I screamed in unfathomable pain.

The next thing I knew, I woke up gasping for breath. My chest hurt, my face hurt, my knee hurt, and I had a horrendous headache. I felt disoriented by pain. I could hear my husband anxiously ask me if I was all right. There were other voices around me which I learned were paramedics. We had been in a terrible head-on collision. Our car was totaled. Later, we found out the reckless driver who had caused it, didn't have insurance due to numerous DUIs, lived in the United States illegally, and had quickly disappeared.

As the paramedics transferred me into an ambulance, I looked up at Russ's face and saw bloody cuts. I struggled to take deep breaths. I asked him how he was, and he said fine, but it wasn't true. He had also suffered several serious injuries. In the emergency room, I learned that my left rib cage had been torn away from my sternum, which was what caused the pain in my chest. My fractured left knee was badly injured and terribly swollen. We were the victims of a faulty BMW airbag which had been the cause of my concussion, massive headache, and dizziness.

I had numerous, very deep black and purple hematomas and lots of internal bleeding, so once they transferred me to a room, they started compression therapy to help reduce the blood clots. Russ had been treated and released but stayed at the hospital with me. That first night, I experienced very difficult, severe pain, waking up several times screaming from nightmares. The bad dreams continued even after they released me to go home. I couldn't walk, so they gave me crutches. I remember the terror I felt the first time traveling on the freeway. Cars zoomed past us so fast that I kept cringing from fear of being hit again.

In time, we learned that Russ had rotator cuff tears in both shoulders when they were slammed back by the airbag. His knee had smashed into the dashboard. Over the next fifteen months, he had surgery on each shoulder as well as his knee to repair the damage.

Meanwhile, my pain seemed to get worse and worse. The massive, deep bruises covered most of my body, so clothing had to be loose and soft. My knees, legs, feet, chest, stomach, and abdomen burned as if I were on fire. The unrelenting pain continued to spread until every inch of my body felt like I'd had gasoline poured over me and someone lit a match. I felt electrical shocks beginning in my knee but soon spreading to other parts of my body. In time, they were focused mainly on my neck and shoulders. I felt like the bad guy being tasered by the police. The jolts didn't happen all the time, but frequently throughout the day.

I also had random, phantom pains like someone ripped off chunks of my skin or stabbed me with a knife. I could sense the blade go in; I could feel it slicing the flesh. It felt so real I was surprised to not see a dagger.

My nervous system had created a torture chamber for my body. The agony felt excruciating, compounded by the fact I am allergic to pain killers. I visited several doctors, but no one could determine the problem. They thought I took a long time to heal from the car accident months ago, although I'm sure some of the doctors felt like I exaggerated, or it was all in my head.

I fractured my knee and had a torn meniscus. Yet it became even more swollen and discolored as the weeks passed. Strangely enough, soon both legs were swollen and became red and bruised-looking; my feet and ankles were enormous. The skin grew so stretched, I could barely stand the tight pain or the pressure in my joints. The taut flesh in my lower leg and ankle split open in places, but the bloody sores wouldn't heal. The pain became too tender for me to wear pants and my legs looked so hideous I started wearing floor-length, loose skirts. I had pitting edema; you could press a finger into me, and it would stay dented in as if my body were made of putty.

It felt literally like being burned alive 24/7. My body had turned into a pain factory. Even a gentle patting dry with a soft towel felt as if coarse sandpaper scraped off my flesh. A gentle breeze felt like nails being driven into my skin. Though the burning stayed constant, the other forms of torturous pain came and went without any discernable reason. After months of doctor appointments, I had no relief at all—in fact, it grew worse.

Six months after the accident, I went to a good friend of mine in Salt Lake City, a gifted chiropractor. Dr Hedstrom tried to help me with my horrendous suffering, and we noticed when he put ice on me, it felt like being burned intensely. He finally suggested I go to his friend who is an orthopedic surgeon since the treatments that would normally work seemed to strangely make matters worse. I also still needed surgery to repair my knee.

After listening to me recite the long list of odd symptoms and an exam, the new ortho doctor simply said, "I'm really sorry." He sighed heavily. "It looks like you have RSD, Reflex Sympathetic Dystrophy or some people call it CRPS, Complex Regional Pain Syndrome. Look it up," he said. "It's extremely rare; you'll find most doctors don't know much about it. You have all the symptoms, I'm sure that's what it is."

Well, I'd been to many doctors, and no one had mentioned this before. I remember writing it down thinking I would look it up later. I asked when we could do the surgery on my knee. He looked sorrowful, and explained, "Oh, we won't be doing the knee surgery now, that could make it worse."

What? I didn't understand an injury that would be made worse by surgery. I needed to make my knee better. I needed to be able to walk. A wheelchair or crutches were so cumbersome. "Then what can I do?" I asked. He opened the exam room door, but before walking out, he turned and said, "I'm sorry. There's nothing you can do for this condition."

"Wait, so it will go away on its own?" It had been a long time and the feeling of being on fire seemed to be getting more intense as it spread through my whole body. Desperate,

I asked, "How long will it last? Shouldn't it be gone by now; it's been months since the accident?"

Again, he said he was sorry. "There's nothing you can do; it will probably last the rest of your life." I heard what he said but it didn't seem to make sense, surely there's something somebody can do. I can't be like *this* for the rest of my life. I didn't think I could stand it anymore. I left feeling confused with a hundred questions swirling through my brain.

The Suicide Disease

At home later that evening, I looked up CRPS on the internet. As I read, I felt excited to see what I had been going through described the same as I had experienced it. I viewed photos of swollen dark red, or purplish discolored limbs that mirrored mine. At least now my experience had a name. *I'll study and figure this out,* I thought. The RSD.org website explains the condition like this:

"CRPS/RSD is a chronic neuroinflammatory disorder. It is classified as a rare disorder by the United States Food and Drug administration. CRPS/RSD occurs when the nervous system and immune system malfunction as they respond to tissue damage from trauma. The nerves misfire, sending constant pain signals to the brain. The level of pain is measured as one of the most severe on the McGill University Pain Scale.

CRPS/RSD generally follows a musculoskeletal injury, a nerve injury, surgery, or immobilization. It is important to know that research has proven that CRPS/RSD is a physical disorder. Unfortunately, it has not been unusual for medical professionals to suggest that people with CRPS/RSD exaggerate their pain for psychological reasons. If it's CRPS/RSD, the pain is not in your mind."

I finally had answers but unfortunately, the more I read the more despair I felt. This was considered the most horrible disease in the world and without a known cure. There were a few experimental treatments, but it was like playing Russian Roulette. They usually had no effect, some patients might be helped for a short time, but often people became worse, and it spread, so the gamble seemed daunting.

The McGill Pain Index ranks CRPS at the top of the chart, at 42 on a scale from 1 to 50—more painful than kidney stones, chronic back pain, childbirth, shingles, fibromyalgia, a ligament tear, chronic migraines, fractures, etc. Perhaps you've experienced one of those—once. Now imagine enduring that every day, all day with no end in sight. Then crank the pain up ten, twenty, thirty, or more notches. That is what CRPS feels like. Of course, physically it is mind-numbing, but it also takes an extreme emotional toll to face this monster. It is often called The Suicide Disease because such a large percentage of people suffering from it take their lives.

At first, I had tears rolling down my cheeks as I learned about it, saw pictures, and read heartbreaking stories of other patients. As the reality of my future sunk in, I started sobbing. This was a horrible life sentence. How could this happen to me? What would I do? I felt I had barely managed so far because I held onto the hope that this would soon end, and I would get better. But now being faced with the possibility that this would be with me for the rest of my life...

It seemed more than I could take in, in fact, I had to stop thinking about it; I felt so overwhelmed. But in the coming days, I alternated between despair and the hope I could find a cure. I often spent sleepless nights searching the internet. I learned about a support group on Facebook and joined up. It's a very rare disease and I didn't know anyone who suffered from it. At first, I learned a lot and it was sobering to know that all the experiences I'd been having were shared by others.

With morbid curiosity, I would click through the pages and comments, always ending up in tears. Russ urged me to stop reading about it. The outlook seemed so dark, he didn't want to ever talk about it, so I felt afraid and alone.

People on the support page would talk about struggling with deep depression and I read the most horrid goodbyes as they explained they couldn't do it anymore. Usually, within a day or two, someone would come on to their FB account to explain that the person had taken their life. These were people I didn't know, but because I understood how painful and frightening it was, I would break down and cry. I'm embarrassed to admit it, but I cried for myself more than them.

The pain of walking on my swollen, burning legs felt horrible but I eventually grew so used to it that I could use crutches for around the house or short distances, otherwise I rode in a wheelchair. My late husband would often push me if it was far.

I learned that most people with CRPS felt pain in one area. For instance, if you injured a wrist, you would have burning, searing pain, swelling, and discoloration in your wrist. I read stories of people who in desperation and out of their minds in pain, sawed away an injured arm or chopped off a leg.

Because I'd been injured in so many places, I had full-body CRPS which is very unusual.

I read of many possible medical interventions or potential cures, desperately searching for some relief. I visited a few more traditionally trained doctors; spending money without results. I tried all types of alternative treatments that friends suggested or that I learned of online. I did crystal healings, Tibetan bowl therapies, meditation remedies, acupuncture, acupressure, massage, and even multilevel marketing "miracle cures"—none of which worked.

Sleep proved very difficult; it felt too painful to relax. I would be awake for days until finally my body became so spent, that I would drift into a fitful, nightmare-infested state that lasted only a few hours before the excruciating discomfort woke me up. I remained exhausted. Sometimes, when alone, I would cry and feel sorry for myself. I had several Pity Parties, but they were not fun, so I finally refused to attend. With the constant pain and lack of sleep plus a reduced ability to move much, I ended up gaining weight which upset me too. I'd never been out of shape, and it demoralized me.

The electrical shock waves felt so strongly in my neck, were made worse by contact with electric items like my computer. Since I still worked full-time running my marketing business, that became a daily problem. Even when going through the TV department at Costco, I couldn't touch the cart because the electricity coursing through the metal would make me start jerking.

Since my body had become an enemy, I decided to focus more on my mind. I deliberately spent time thinking about my blessings. I had much to be grateful for. I decided not to make this horrible, painful part of life my *whole* life. I looked for the things that were good. For example, I owned my own small, successful business and it could be done largely from home. Often, I felt humbled by kind and caring clients.

For decades before, I worked in large, high-stress international corporations, and often had to meet with other department heads. If I had cancelled a meeting with other high-powered, busy executives at the last minute because I trembled uncontrollably or vomited from pain, it would not have been tolerated for long. Those days had moved at a hectic pace, and I travelled frequently. I had also supervised hundreds of people who needed answers quickly when critical issues arose. I now felt thankful for a flexible schedule and a small staff.

A wheelchair or crutches; sleepless nights; horrendous, constant pain; tight skin with ugly open sores; stiff edema; intense swelling; achy joints; electrical jolts; feelings of being stabbed and having my skin ripped off, and frustrating limits in my once full, active life persisted day after day, month after month, and soon, year after year. There were many times I told myself I couldn't do it anymore, but I knew I didn't have a choice.

I tried to have a good attitude. I tried to focus on what was good in my life. I tried to remember and count my blessings. I mustered up every bit of self-motivation and encouragement that I had. I had so many people tell me how strong I seemed, how amazing I was, what an inspiration. I would have people compliment me that I could be so cheerful and smiling through all of this. They had no idea what it sometimes took to cover up the tears inside with those smiles. I certainly didn't feel amazing or inspiring. But I sincerely wanted a good life. I wanted to be happy, and I tried my very best.

My life was not all doom and gloom. I wouldn't let myself think in an 'all or nothing' way. Despite the pain, I felt truly happy MOST of the time. The moments of despair were just that—moments. Not hours. Russ and I went out with friends and had fun. We traveled, and sought out live music, national parks, and anything that caused laughter. I enjoyed working with my clients and found my career interesting and challenging. And I became good at it.

Russ and I were heavily involved in working with men trying to transition from prison to life on the outside. He especially spent countless hours helping these men. I also became very engaged in the community. I served on several boards, chaired the local Chamber of Commerce, participated in Business Networking International, and volunteered as a mentor and speaker for Zion's Business Center and Women in Business. I continued my volunteer mentoring and presenting workshops with SCORE and helped numerous people with their business issues, even winning awards for my work. I donated hundreds of hours working with women and children in my church. I had a very busy and full life. Despite the agony of CRPS, Being the Boss of My Thinker made it possible to live Happily Ever After.

More Big Challenges

Two years after the accident, Russ felt like he wasn't recovering fully from his injuries and the three subsequent major surgeries. He still had a lot of pain in his shoulder, and he felt tired and physically drained inside. He went to the doctor who told him he needed to be patient, and since he was older it would take more time to recover.

A few months later, Russ went back again. The doctor did a few tests but told him to wait longer and he would be fine. He had experienced some problems with the pain pills after the surgeries. But even though he wasn't taking them anymore, he still suffered the side effects. The doctor prescribed something to help. It didn't improve at all, even when they increased the dosage.

Month after month, Russ felt awful. He grew weak and tired, lost weight, and made another appointment to talk to a new doctor. He missed work frequently and lost his job. Our life and health insurance were through his work since my small business didn't have benefits. I quickly made an appointment with someone for health insurance, and we opted for a high deductible, basic, catastrophic policy.

Russ made an appointment for more life insurance. The appointment time came, and he didn't feel up to it and didn't go. He talked to the insurance agent over the phone who would meet with him the next Tuesday when we would get everything signed. We'd always had life insurance and knew its importance.

Russ scheduled the doctor's appointment three weeks away, when we hoped we could find some answers to what was happening to him. On Thursday morning he received a call that the doctor's office had a cancellation and they asked if he would like to come in now. Russ said yes and left. After an exam they sent him over to a nearby hospital for some tests. In a few hours, he arrived back home. He'd barely returned when he called up the stairs to my office, "Hello, honey, I'm back. I'm making a sandwich..." and that's when I heard his phone ring.

I could hear him talking but I couldn't make out the words. A few minutes later he came to my office, sat down in his matching office chair, and rolled it over in front of me. Knee to knee, he took both my hands and said, "That was the doctor. I have terminal cancer."

I said, "Uh, that's not funny!" If you knew Russ, you would know why I thought for sure he attempted a very sick joke. He was an extremely witty and funny man who loved to tease and joke around.

"I'm being serious."

But still I said, "Are you serious? If this is a joke, it's not funny." The look in his eyes told me he spoke the truth. "But how can they know so soon? Maybe they made a mistake, they can start treatments, maybe..." Tears flowed.

"I have hundreds of tumors; the doctor saw them on a scan."

I felt such shock. How could this terrible thing happen to us? Didn't we already have a huge problem to deal with? The next day he had surgery where they took a slice of his liver for a biopsy to confirm the diagnosis. He had a very rare type of cancer: Neuroendocrine Tumors, Pancreatic Primary or NET.

In the next few days, we went through many heavy emotions: shock, disbelief, denial, and many tender moments when we held each other in silence as tears fell.

We called our agent and he said with a diagnosis of terminal cancer five days earlier, he wouldn't be able to get us life insurance. After all these years of paying, now when we needed it, it had become unavailable.

With a full schedule of treatments, Russ would not be able to work again. I thought, *I could still work, I have this business, I'm the main provider anyway; we'll manage.*

I was so naïve.

Now, in addition to my CRPS, I supported us financially, cared for him, and went with him to countless appointments, most about an hour's drive away in Salt Lake City while others were out of state. Since he had such a rare cancer, the closest oncologist specializing in NET was in Denver, Colorado (we lived more than ten hours away in Utah), though a few of the local oncologists could provide more routine care and treatments.

The additional stress of his diagnosis affected my nervous system and my pain worsened, but I kept my business running through twenty-eight months filled with his numerous surgeries, chemotherapy, radiation, a variety of procedures, infusions, and other cancer treatments. As well as the intensive care needed at home. Often, after being gone all day seeing clients, or sometimes days or weeks at the hospital with my laptop, I would come home or to a hotel room, and I'd work through the night. My sleep became even more restricted. I didn't know how I would possibly get through this.

In desperation I prayed and searched harder for anything I could find on CRPS because I knew I faced a pain-filled, monumental task of working long hours to pay all the mounting medical bills as well as the routine monthly ones, doing almost everything around the house, taking care of Russ, and spending countless hours at the hospital and doctors' offices. When we traveled out of state for surgery, we stayed a month at a time. We had wonderful family and friends who brought food, mowed our lawn, shoveled snow, prayed for us, and offered to help in any way they could. But I felt already at my limit, and I knew it would get worse. I needed to get better. I prayed for a miracle.

About a year and a half into our cancer journey, I sat at the computer one night studying CRPS and I saw something called The Healing Code by Dr. Alexander Loyd. I had checked out so many methods, but I had a feeling I should try this one. I didn't even have enough faith in it to spend money, so I immediately reserved the book at the local library. I'd read a little bit and it seemed rather ridiculous and far too simplistic to do any good against such a cataclysmic disease.

Soon, I checked out the book and started to read it. Chapter after chapter, but I still didn't understand how this could possibly work; it sounded so un-substantive. Instructed to simply put my hands near my head, as I listened to some music composed with complex, intertwined melodies and it would somehow take away this awful disease that people suffered from, died from, and committed suicide over. The very idea seemed ridiculous.

I had already tried so many other methods. I had also read about therapies other people with CRPS tried that failed. But the thought came into my head *'What do I have to lose? It's free; I don't have to buy the book, the music is on YouTube with a timer, why don't I try it?'*

A Miracle

With absolutely zero faith that it could possibly work, I started it. I knew I should probably try to be optimistic about it, but I wasn't. You can imagine my shock, when after doing the prayer and listening to the music for only a few days, I noticed a difference. After four years of my skin being discolored, it returned to normal flesh tones.

After a few more days, the swelling that I had suffered with so tremendously had gone down. The long-term edema completely disappeared a short time later. It miraculously took away the stabbing pains. The burning pain reduced significantly along with the feeling that my skin was being ripped off. Soon, both were completely gone. I couldn't believe it. The last thing to go was the feeling of being electrocuted. Three weeks after I started the Healing Code, I was in remission.

It seemed such a miracle to me, that sometimes even to this day, years later, it makes me very emotional to think about it. It proved a tender blessing to me and at the time I so desperately needed it. Russ's condition had become so bad at this point with thousands of tumors throughout his body and endless pain and suffering. He underwent more treatments, additional surgeries, and his body withered away, but now I could help without crutches or a wheelchair.

Plus, everything felt far easier without the debilitating pain I had suffered for four long years. Four years of my life. It was months before I could get up from a chair and walk across the room unaided and not marvel. I felt so grateful. I still thank God.

But as Russ's condition deteriorated, working, and caring for him became more of a challenge. I felt worn out. A common schedule for me entailed getting up early in the morning, going to the hospital, being with him while he had infusions and other treatments and consultations with doctors, then driving him home, helping him to bed, getting him food, medication, ice or warm heat packs, while desperately trying to catch up on missing the day of work. I would then often work till two or three in the morning so that my clients wouldn't suffer, and I wouldn't miss their tight deadlines.

During another trip to the hospital in Denver, I tried to work from a surgery waiting room but that day I faced a sobering realization. I had been told to expect the procedure to last several hours. But an hour later, I looked up and saw the surgeon approaching me, shaking his head with a grim expression. The surgery did not go well at all. Russ had a very close brush with death.

I had been so focused trying to juggle all the balls in the air, that I had denied the reality of our situation. My spouse was going to die. I had to come to grips with what that would be like. I would feel ravaged. It would seriously affect my mental, emotional, and even physical health. And what about my work? I couldn't put my clients on hold when they depended on me for an event that needed my immediate attention. I would not be able to endure the inevitable, frightening death of my spouse and then an hour later return an urgent call from a client as if nothing happened. It would be devastating in so many ways. How I had been coping—my organizational skills, ability to get by on very little sleep, and my energetic drive—would be nothing in the face of his death.

There were also serious financial repercussions I had to face. I neared retirement age, but our carefully and slowly acquired savings had been plundered. Cancer proved pricey. We no longer had life insurance. Medical Insurance covered a fraction of the total monetary cost. There were the travel expenses (which were huge in our case), extra meals eaten out, numerous medical procedures not covered completely by insurance, and all the missed work time. When you run your own small business, paid time-off doesn't exist. My income had definitely suffered from my reduced attention. I needed to greatly downsize our budget, or we would be financially ruined.

I felt guilty worrying about my financial future instead of sacrificing it all for Russ. Once a doctor, who suggested an expensive, experimental treatment, derided my questions about its efficacy and cost "Even if it is a small chance, are you more concerned about money than your husband's life?" In this case, a tiny percentage of researched patients had responded favorably but with a minute improvement for arguably a few extra, painfilled, miserable months. At the time, the doctor made me feel selfish and petty. Now I am appalled at his insinuation. Russ had terminal cancer. No amount of money would save him.

In the end, Russ insisted we try. So, we did. But it didn't help. The wasted money could have funded years of my retirement. A few months later, just before he died, Russ apologized as he confessed that he'd pushed for every expensive treatment knowing it would unlikely help. He admitted he didn't want me to have money after he died so I wouldn't be as attractive to another man. I felt stunned.

Emotionally as well as financially, I realized I couldn't keep up with all of this anymore and I needed to take immediate, drastic steps. Our large home and my career had to go. I wasn't sure how I would add to my already packed schedule to find time to put together my business financials, interview potential buyers, stage our home and get it ready to sell, search for a smaller house, and time the complicated buy and sale dance, without a left-footed where-do-we-live gap—all while maintaining any sanity.

Big Changes

Russ and I felt guided to build a home in St. George, Utah, about four hours away. If you have ever built a house, yes, the prospect is cringeworthy. Plus, now his condition had deteriorated so much that it necessitated me taking him to the hospital every few days. It became a ridiculously hectic time in our lives, but I must mention how loving, kind, and supportive our family, neighbors, friends, and even clients were. In two years, we never shoveled snow or mowed the lawn. We dined on numerous meals and treats prepared by loving hands. My adult children were amazing. I felt so delighted to see their good hearts and more evidence of what wonderful adults they were. Prayers on our behalf were abundant. We felt very loved and supported.

Before long, the business sold, and after a time-intensive transition, it was such a relief to me that I could finally simply focus on Russ's care in the little time we had left together—well besides moving. His condition did not allow eight-hour trips to check on the progress of our new home being built.

Meanwhile, I'm packing and paring down dramatically since our new home was so much smaller. Soon, our old house sold, and the moving van arrived with kind, good family and friends who came and moved us. Tyler Longman even took off work to drive the truck to our new place. He planned to have people help us unload in St. George. It was our first time seeing the new house and we loved it. Russ had become so weak by this point that one of our major concerns was finding him a place to rest in the middle of moving in.

We'd already set an appointment with the new oncologist, and we loved him and his staff; they were so kind and good to us. We went in every couple of days for treatments. Russ's condition deteriorated rapidly and though not unexpected, it was still devastating when the doctor placed Russ in hospice. We were blessed with some tender and miraculous, spiritual experiences that greatly reassured us both. We still faced another surgery to facilitate his final care at home. The Dixie Hospice nurses were so kind and gentle with him.

On a Thursday, a few weeks after moving in, Russ suddenly became paralyzed, and his emaciated body and organs began to shut down. He couldn't move, not even close his eyes or mouth, so the nurse taught me to place moisturizing drops in his eyes and swab his lips. I stayed by his side day and night, until Saturday afternoon, August 31, 2019. His lungs stopped working and I saw his panicked eyes as he gasped for breath. The nurse hurriedly gave him an injection. In deep sorrow, I held him and cried with my head on his chest as I heard his last heartbeat.

Even though we had known for over two years it was coming, his death still proved very difficult. I felt comforted that his immense suffering had ended. I believe in an afterlife and thought of his lovely reunion with his father.

Though grieving themselves, my fabulous children: Zach, Josh, Matt, Marissa, Spencer, and McKenna and their sweet spouses and adorable children surrounded me. McKenna took over my phone and the front door. Calls, texts, doorbells were constant, and with amazing finesse, she responded like a pro. She notified friends and family while my emotions ran high. I leaned on Josh as he gently helped me through funeral arrangements and difficult issues that arose. My sisters, Beth and Jan, my mom, my niece, Janna, my stepchildren, Nate and Melanie, and other family members came from great distances.

People were very good; so gentle and compassionate. It was a tremendous example to me, and I felt grateful for the lessons I learned through that experience. Even on the bleakest days, rays of light break up the darkness.

I remember a little of the funeral: Josh's tender vocal solo performance accompanied on his guitar, singing a song requested by Russ months earlier; a lovely song beautifully sung by my adult children; and the grandkids sharing a sweet tune, I Am a Child of God. But I don't have any memories of the cemetery.

After a couple of weeks, the last of my family left. I now lived in a new house in a new town without any friends or family nearby. I felt so alone. I had never been alone in my life. I grew up in a big family, then college roommates, a husband and lots of children. I lived solo for the first time. I felt so blessed when neighbors who were total strangers would come to my door and introduce themselves and bring me food, fruit, flowers and plants, and other acts of kindness. I received dozens of sympathy cards with touching messages.

At first, I wondered why we had felt so strongly that God wanted us to move to this place. Why couldn't we have stayed where we had family and friends? Wouldn't that have been easier? But as I walked into the remote desert next to my home, there was a great deal of peace and sacredness. I realized that for me, recovery was a solo journey. To heal I needed solitude. I gratefully recognized a tender mercy from God, who really knows me.

The World Needs More Sweetness

I learned many things through this experience that changed my thoughts. I discovered people really want to help. We need to think of ways to assist them to know what they can do. We heard 'Call us if you need anything' so many times. We usually said, 'Thanks, we're fine (what a lie). To the frequent question, Russ eventually adopted a standard answer. "Haagen Das, Chocolate, Chocolate Chip ice cream." Our freezer stayed well-stocked.

Russ was a big Utah Jazz basketball fan. When they were going into the playoffs, someone asked, "Hey, if there's anything I could do for you let me know." Russ laughed and replied, "Oh yeah, I'd like some playoff tickets!" Of course, he didn't expect expensive and very difficult-to-get tickets. He had asked for a ridiculously large favor as an obvious joke. But the next day, his friend knew somebody, who knew somebody, who knew somebody with the Utah Jazz organization, and we had playoff tickets! Wow!

When times are tough, ask for help and if someone offers, let them. If you tell someone you like licorice or honey crisp apples or whatever your favorite treat is, they'll be happy to drop it off. Even little things like taking a book back to the library or picking up something at the store. If you're feeling lonely, simply say, "I'd just like a little visit."

On the opposite side, if you know someone in need, think back on one of these hints or ask them about their favorite treat. Be specific, like "Hey, can I come by and take your car to get washed tomorrow around 4:00?" instead of saying, call me if you need anything.

One of my favorite sweet gestures happened a few days before Russ's funeral. A friend dropped off waterproof mascara.

Give help when possible and be humble enough to take assistance when needed—and you don't need a life-or-death issue to ask for it. The world needs more sweetness. Do a good deed daily. And offer what you can to fortify others.

Cloud Bubbles

Every individual has incredible potential. We're all exquisitely unique, like cloud formations. Life is full of so many interesting vistas to absorb and so much wonder. "All that is gold does not glitter, not all those who wander are lost; the old that is strong does not wither, deep roots are not reached by the frost"

—J.R.R. TOLKIEN

CHAPTER 4

HOW TO BE WHAT WE WANT TO BE: A PERSONAL CREED

It's not what's on the outside but what's inside that needs to be worked on. We know ourselves better than anyone, so instead of having others tell us what to do, let's listen to our true voice.

Writing and frequent reading of a Personal Creed influences healthy thoughts. Our Personal Creed is a powerful document that reminds us of the person we are striving to be. If we keep it short, we can remember it and reflect on it often. It's a long-term guide, not a detailed outline of our day. It is a place to write what is truly important to us and will vary widely from person to person. If we put a lot of careful thought into writing our Creed, the process helps us cement our priorities. This guideline can serve us for years. Though there may be times we wish to adapt it to fit our current situation.

Make it specific enough to influence us, but general enough to give us space to grow and learn. It includes values that we want to develop like kindness, empathy, or compassion, as well as goals we want to emphasize, like service, adventure, travel, or courage. Remember this is *our* life. Though it may be interesting or maybe even inspiring to read another's Creed, we need our Personal Creed to be unique and unequivocally *ours.* It is not a lot of pretty words that seem noble to impress others, but a reflection of us and the life we want.

In preparing to write it, we can deeply and honestly contemplate our purposes in life and how we want to live. Strive to create a Creed with a long-term perspective of who we are and who we aspire to become. If we are real, living as *we* are, others will accept us. It is when trying to be like someone else, or superior, or even inferior, that we make others uncomfortable, as well as ourselves.

We will grow in self-confidence as we are true to our uniqueness. The more we stay true to who we are, and who we want to be, the more peace and happiness we will have regardless of challenges. We become less reactive and more proactive when living the way we believe.

Let's think about some of the core values that resonate with us such as hard work, integrity, joy, stewardship, loyalty, or responsibility. What kind of person do we want to be? We can say we are a strong person in our Creed even if we don't feel that strength now. Write 'I am a strong person' NOT 'I want to be …' or 'I will be a strong person someday.'

We ought to strive for consistency in living our Creed, not only when it is easy, or things are going our way. Character is a gradual accumulation and repetition of many little thoughts, words, and actions over time.

Ideas to Write Your Creed

As we decide to write our Personal Creed, we may wish to take note of values, ideas, goals, or attributes that resonate strongly with us. We may also analyze a person who inspires us and try to discern the characteristics that attract us or that we wish to emulate. Think in terms of who we are actively becoming. For example, if we are gossiping, ask, do I want to be a gossip? Be positive, as opposed to listing traits we don't want, or engaging in negative talk. For example, instead of 'Don't gossip" think 'Speak well of others.'

Here are a variety of possible Creed ideas that we may accept, add to, or reject:

- Give others hope.
- Lift others. Use impactful, careful, uplifting, or kind words.
- If we want to feel the light, intentionally banish the darkness.
- Service to others makes us feel good.
- Be honest and kind to others.
- Be Family Centered
- Life's an adventure.
- Gratitude creates happiness.
- Heavenly Father and my Savior, Jesus Christ are important to me.
- Life is amazing and exciting; we never know what will happen next.
- There is always good.
- A secure financial situation can influence our relationships and our moods.

I share my Personal Creed simply as an example. This is who I aspire to be. You are different and your Creed should reflect that.

Stephanni's Personal Creed

I am a beloved daughter of God.

I see others as his precious children and treat them accordingly.

I turn my life over to a loving Heavenly Father; all
is well. I love and accept myself and others.

I know my purpose each day. I am Honest AND Kind.

With God, nothing is impossible; I can conquer all challenges.

I strive to return to live with God and my family,
with gratitude to my Savior, Jesus Christ.

I am blessed and deeply grateful. I am brimming with energy and overflowing with joy.

I am gentle to myself and others.

I am good, healthy, talented, safe, cheerful, and happy.

I am blessed with a brilliant mind and value learning.

I see things positively, looking for good
in people and all situations.

I listen and try to understand the hearts of others and

seek to do service with love and compassion.

I allow others their opinions; I am not offended.
I am courageous and speak the truth.

It's one of the best days ever! Good
things will happen to me today.

I feel light from God, and I trust that all He does for me is for

my ultimate good in His own perfect time.

My life is an adventure and full of miracles.

My life is simple yet joyful.

I have a blessed relationship with my beloved Mark,
and an amazing family, and dear friends.

I surround myself with beauty. I use
my time and money wisely.

I have opportunities to travel.

I seek joy. I feel joy. I spread joy.

When my oldest children were young, together we also created a Family Creed. During all those growing-up years, we would read this together each day, usually before our scripture study and family prayer. We found that it guided our thoughts and actions in our family and made family purpose and unity, as well as goals, more attainable. If it works in your situation, consider doing this. I share our Family Creed, again as an example. As usual, we each need to create one that is uniquely ours. It could be as simple as the Creed of the Three Musketeers: 'All for one and one for all.'

Family Creed

We believe in Jesus Christ and know that
if we obey his commandments,

We can be an eternal family.

We study the scriptures and pray together.

We seek truth.

We support each other and are helpful and cooperative.

We feel safe to share our feelings.

We strive to create a House of Learning,
a House of Fun and Laughter,

a House of Order, and a House of Obedience.

As good friends, we travel, work, and play
together, explore nature's bounty,

visit relatives and build lasting family traditions.

We believe that everyone is a child of God, and
we will strive to be good neighbors to all.

We will show love and kindness in all we do.

Mark's Creed

Stephanni introduced me to the idea of a written Creed a few years ago. What a great concept. I already had a clear self-image, but I had not written it down. This was a great way to review it purposefully. So, with a little bit of encouragement and effort, I put together my Creed. It explains who I am, and I've reviewed it a few times a week at least, and I know it's made a big difference in my world.

I think my Creed has assisted me to be in alignment with who I want to become and reminds me on a regular and frequent basis of my life's intentions. As I realize its impact and I've personally progressed, I've fine-tuned it. I weigh what's important, what I want, and what I value in my quest to be authentic. I believe it makes a huge difference to my happiness and towards my eventual and absolute purpose in mortality.

Mark's Personal Creed

I come from Divine Heritage and have been preserved to be on earth at this exact time.

I trust The Planner. I'm in alignment with His precepts and surrender to His higher purpose.

I strive to return to live with God, and my family, by being in harmony with Jesus Christ.

I delight in a fabulous life and I'm deeply grateful.

I'm brimming with authentic and positive energy.

People quickly recognize my overflowing and genuine exuberance.

I am gentle to myself and others.

I frequently laugh with abandon and encourage others to enjoy life throughout every day.

I'm kind, healthy, talented, safe, joyful, honest, sparky, and transparently happy.

I share my enthusiasm as I meet and speak with others.

I am blessed with a good mind, strong body, and pleasing personality.

I see things positively, looking for good
in people and all situations.

I enjoy learning. I listen and try to understand the hearts of others.

I seek to do service with love and compassion. I
am courageous and bold when appropriate.

I am wise through contemplation and experience.

Good things will happen for me; today is marvelous.

I feel light from God, and I trust all that He does for me is
for my ultimate good, in His own time.

My life is a magnificent adventure full of amazing miracles.

I live simply and joyfully.

I have a blessed and exquisite relationship with Stephanni;
our adventures fill our souls to overflowing.

I am endowed with wonderful family and friends.

I search for and uncover beauty every day.

I love life.

First, our Creed helps us understand who we are and what we want. Then, it guides us to think in healthy ways. It emphasizes *what* we should think about and *how* we should think about it. We can compare our thoughts to the ideas we believed when we created our Creed. As we affirm these beliefs, our thoughts will reflect those ideas. I usually try to read mine every day, out loud. This gives me a strong foundation for my daily thoughts. As we read the Creed to ourselves, it helps us focus our minds on not only the trivial or small things of today but on the direction we're taking long-term.

Now is the time to write your Creed, please. And then you'll Live Happily Ever After.

The Beauty of Light

Long after sunset, residual twilight provides this remarkable view of St. Mary Lake in Montana. Even a dim light illuminates the darkest of times. A simple smile can make a significant difference to someone. "The sole purpose of human existence is to kindle a light in the darkness of mere being."

— CARL JUNG

CHAPTER 5
DISCOVER OUR PURPOSE

Our life improves as we consciously seek and find meaning or purpose. We try to figure out what we want and go after it. Without purpose, our days will still be filled, but we may feel like we're floating aimlessly along.

I like to envision it as myself going down a river. The water is moving quickly and I'm in a boat with no motor and no oars, aimlessly going wherever the current takes me. I may end up in the weeds along the side or even go over a waterfall dashing onto the rocks below.

I could step it up a bit and bring some oars with me and try to row the boat the way I want it to go, but what if I use a motor and intentionally and effectively guide the boat where I want to end up?

When we have purpose, we're not floating along day by day waiting to see what happens; instead, there's intention in our lives. We can add some goals or make a to-do list which is like using oars, which certainly helps. But what if we have a 'motor,' or a purpose, that takes us where we want to go even when there's a strong current that is trying to push us another way?

The hours of our days will always be filled. But are we simply busy or productive? Are we doing what we really want with our time, the activities that will take us to where we want to go and who we want to become—or are we merely existing?

One way to find our purpose, or as Mark and I think of it, purposes, is to list our roles. For us now, our roles are (1) Child of God, (2) Spouse, (3) Parent, Grandparent, Sibling, Child, (4) Friend and Neighbor, (5) Outdoor Enthusiasts, and (6) Writers, Speakers, Photographer.

The roles and their order will change with each person. Make sure the way we live reflects what we deem to be most valuable. We may have other roles such as: Careers, Hobbies, Recreation, etc. You will probably have a purpose in each role. Roles can change or fall off the list. When I was busy raising my children, I didn't take much time for friends and neighbors, but now I do. My career was a role that took a lot of time until I retired.

Our following roles are simply included as examples. Yours will be uniquely yours. You don't need to agree with us or think how we do. You will probably have different roles and purposes. It's okay to have a different opinion of your purposes within that role.

Please know that we all have that 'funny half hour' and while Mark and I strive to fulfill our purposes in each role, we sometimes fail. Then we ponder what happened, recommit, and move forward again.

Role 1: Child of God

As children of God, our purpose in that role for Mark and me, is to follow His commandments, to love God, ourselves, and others, and to become our very best by following the example of Jesus Christ. It is important to us to read the scriptures each day and to pray to our Father in Heaven in gratitude for His tender mercies and guidance.

Role 2: Spouse

Our second role is to be a wonderful spouse. We were both married before and lost our spouses to cancer. When Mark and I married, our role changed to not pursue an individual life anymore, but a united one. Although we may have individual goals, overall, we are focused on what is best for the relationship, not necessarily what is best for us individually. However, we have found that they don't seem to contradict each other. Mark is extremely important to me, and we love spending time together. I truly love everything about him and adore him in every way. Mark is my closest friend, and I am extremely grateful for him. He feels the same about me. We spend hours talking to each other, laughing, and going on adventures. Still, we also have some things that we like that are done solo or with other friends. Our purpose in this spousal role is to shower each other with support, joy, happiness, and kindness, and to ensure that we feel immersed in love and acceptance.

Role 3: Parent, Grandparent, Sibling, Child

Our third role is as a parent, grandparent, sibling, and child. Our purpose is to stay in touch as much as we can and continue to build lovely memories in this role as well as with other extended family members. We would like to think we are also examples and guides, but our bright kids, grands, sisters, cousins, nephews, nieces, and in-laws, etc. often teach us.

My six children have been the focus of my life. They are strong, independent, responsible, kindhearted, good people, and wildly talented in so many ways. It's so fun now they are all adults to be friends with them. I genuinely love *and* like them, and we love to get together. Conversations run the gamut. They are well-read and intelligent, caring and involved in service, and adventurous world citizens, so there is always interesting discussion.

I also have eighteen grandchildren. All the fun without so much work! It really is great to be a grandma. I love listening to them tell me about their world. They are a talented, smart, wonderful bunch.

Mark's turn: I have four children. We have an amazing history together. My kids are each unique, fun, resourceful, and adventurous souls. Their independence has led them to entrepreneurial leanings.

There are currently nine lively grandchildren. They're all rambunctious, loud, fun, and easy to love. Their personalities and interests are unique and varied.

Stephanni's turn: My sisters are important to me, especially Beth. Through most of the hard times in my life, Beth is the person I call. We had a hard childhood in many ways. Beth was the oldest and I was two years younger, so our close age and our very similar interests bound us together.

I have three other sisters who are also very important to me, Debbie, Jan, and Donna. I love each one of them. They're all amazing women. Though my father died a long time ago, my elderly mother lives far away, but I still have a purpose of being a good daughter.

Mark's turn: I grew up with six sisters. Growing up, I was the pesky little brother to four older sisters: Dawn, Dyan, Judi, and Lu-Anne who performed as a song and dance troupe accompanied on the piano by my dad. I took my role as the big brother to my two younger sisters, Kori, and Misha seriously. I love them all and feel grateful to have been raised in a talented and loving family. My parents were great; they were devoted, kind, and gentle. My dad was an astounding musician, playing the piano by ear. He could hear a song and instantly make it come out of his fingers. My mom served in the Canadian military (in the women's army corps band— my mom actually did wear army boots, lol) and was in the European theatre in World War II for four years.

My parents and older sisters, Dawn and Dyan, have all passed, but as the only son, I feel a responsibility to honor the Bishop name and legacy.

Role 4: Friend and Neighbor

Our fourth role is being a friend and neighbor. This is a new focus for me, and I turned my attention to it more when I moved from the Salt Lake City area to St. George, a small city in southern Utah where I didn't have any friends or family.

Although before this I had always had friends at work and church, and knew my neighbors, and we often went out with other couples, I had been so busy with family and a career providing for them, that I had not placed much emphasis on friendships.

Being the only boy in his family growing up, Mark adopted many 'brothers' and doesn't know the meaning of the word 'stranger.' Many of his 'brothers' have joined him on countless adventures spanning decades. Along with his many long-time friends, he accumulates new friends every day.

Mark and I are both very friendly and outgoing and eager to meet people. In St. George, our home is in a brand-new housing addition, so most of our neighbors are also looking to make friends. It is a wonderful situation.

We also love living in Calgary. Both places we call home are full of amazing individuals. Mark has lived in Alberta for a long time, and I've been welcomed so warmly by his friends and neighbors. Even his late wife's entire family graciously invited me into their circle.

In making friends, the key is to remember to **Look Through a Window, Not a Mirror**. In other words, show interest in others as opposed to obsessing about ourselves. Let's get involved. Be kind and follow the golden rule. We need to be actively enrolled in creating the life we want; lives like that seldom come knocking on our door uninvited.

Mark and I understand that for many people, making friends is daunting. We're both friendly and fearless, and we love people, so we gladly make the first move—and the second, third, or however many someone needs. Having our very best friend constantly by our side makes life so wonderfully lovely. Mark and I have strong beliefs about our purpose in trying to make the world a better place—one person at a time.

Mark explains it like this: I try to encourage smiles, laughter, and 'feel good' to everyone I encounter. I regularly remove the focus from me and transfer it to another. I look for the unique or different and comment on it in a positive way. For over four decades, I've been riding and fixing bikes. When I'm out on the trails, I often see someone broken down. I'm a self-professed bike whisperer, so I stop and see if I can be of service. We have some laughs; I help them, and I bet they don't go home and kick the dog. Plus, it could lead to a valuable friendship.

We often do what I call a 'bump and run.' For example, when Stephanni and I are riding our tandem bicycle together, as we pass someone if I can catch their eye, I call out, "Is she peddling?" or "Hey, is she still back there?" They laugh and we all have a better day. Sometimes we get witty responses, and it makes it more fun for us all and in one short moment, the world *is* a better place.

Role 5: Outdoor Enthusiasts

Our fifth role is being outdoor enthusiasts by loving nature and appreciating the beauty and healing power of God's creations. We've always loved being outside and exploring. Mark and I live in two of the most breathtakingly gorgeous places in the world, Calgary, Alberta, Canada, and St. George, Utah, USA. They are vastly different.

Blessed are the curious, for they shall have adventures.

Up north, we've cycled, hiked, motorcycled, and taken long drives through the majestic northern Rocky Mountains, enjoying the numerous waterfalls, lakes, and forests. We've spent countless hours in the beauty of Fish Creek Provincial Park bordering our home, often racing around the winding network of bike trails, many of which Mark built.

From our third-floor balcony, we listen to music as we frequently watch our private, live Nature Movie unfolding before our eyes. At night we hear coyotes howling or owls hooting at each other across the valley under the moon and stars. We observe deer frequently, along with onery Canadian geese, bald eagles, bobcats, moose, and other animals. We've watched many coyotes, even ones chased by a deer or one climbing a tree! And there was a tug of war with a beaver—Mark won.

It is magical to walk through the forest in the middle of the night with snow falling silently around us. In 20, 30, or even 40 degrees below zero temperatures, winter birds flock to us and eat out of our hands. They predictively take the biggest peanut first. Mark calls me his Snow White Princess, but no Chickadees or woodland animals have followed us home to clean up yet.

We watch sunsets build to a crescendo and then softly subside. They fill the evening sky with bursts of astonishing color. We've walked or cycled for miles on a frozen Fish Creek marveling at the glacial blue-green of the thick ice topped by incredible, delicately shaped, ever-changing, magnificent frosty crystals.

Back south in Utah, we love to hike in red rock country, ride bikes through miles of gorgeous scenery on safe, off-road trails or across the desert, explore new places—especially state or national parks, go rockhounding, motorcycling or just walking our St. George neighborhood. With so many friendly people, it may take hours to walk a few blocks, it depends on who else is outside. Sunny St. George has phenomenal weather (okay, scorching hot in the summer, but luckily, we can escape north) and is an outdoor paradise.

The neighborhood borders the White Dome Nature Preserve which features the Dwarf Bear Poppy, a beautiful white flower that doesn't grow any place else in the world. We are at the edge of the Arizona Strip, a beautiful, wild, vast million-acre no-man's land with ancient Petroglyphs, mountains, slot canyons, cactus, lava beds, forests, miles of rough dirt roads, critters, and a glorious, dark sky. Mark and I love to look up from our old truck bed and view the Milky Way from horizon to horizon as we delightedly watch meteors and bask in the majesty of a glittering night sky. Well, until the bats swoop down and then Mark is outa' there! (He refers to them as flying rats.)

Being in nature is restorative and uplifting to our souls. Fresh air, sunshine, and lots of oxygen are invigorating and aid in more restful sleep. Let's choose the outdoors every chance we get to increase a healthy attitude and to live Happily Ever After.

Role 6: Writers, Speakers, and Photographer

Along with Mark's day job, our sixth role helps pay the bills. We love writing and speaking to all types of groups, either to share our ideas or to spin a yarn. We met when Mark was a speaker at a Widow/Widowers conference. We are both natural-born storytellers and have lots of crazy, funny, and sometimes unbelievable, but true, stories. We both appreciate words and the use of language. Writing is a fabulous way to organize our thinking and is a great mental exercise. I especially enjoy reading a well-written book when the author uses beautiful and precise language. Mark loves to write what he calls 'Whispers,' short, soft, uplifting encouragement accompanied by his stunning nature photos. They begin each chapter in this book.

Live Intentionally

Know what you want to do in life. Set some realistic goals but make them a stretch to reach. Let's not simply follow our dreams—chase them down! Completing our purposes gives us an amazing burst of courage to try more. When we are focused on personal growth it helps us avoid the disease of comparison.

We can do it! No constraints, especially none imposed by us. Keep going, even when we think we've hit the wall, remember—there is no wall. I believe we are the co-authors of the book on our life. God has let it happen; He has plans to let it unfold perfectly for us and then we write *our* part.

Our job is to build our best selves with all our heart, might, mind, and strength. The self we will love *and* like. If we don't like being a miserable person, create a happy person. If we don't like the scared person, build a brave one. We can imagine ourselves as courageous people. What would we be like? What do we need to change to become that person? Start now. Discover our purposes; who are we? Are we living like who we feel we are? Or do we sabotage ourselves?

Mark's Story of Kathy and Stanley

A friend and I decided to go on a motorcycle excursion from Calgary to the Mexican border following the Continental Divide Trail as closely as possible. We traveled through mountains and valleys for days, then one afternoon, after a razor-straight gravel road, we came into Pie Town, New Mexico, a place famous for pies. We pulled over at a restaurant, but it wasn't open, and we were unable to get any pie, so we continued through town heading east. We saw another place called The Pie 'O' Neer Café. The locked door had a sign that said 'closed.' We were disappointed that we wouldn't get pie in Pie Town and took out our maps and started doing some route-finding on an old wooden table on the porch.

An older Ford Explorer drove up and out jumped two individuals. The woman said, "Are you looking for some pie?"

We answered, "Yes, unfortunately it's closed."

She said, "Let me get you some," and disappeared around back. The white-haired gentleman with a ponytail introduced himself as Stanley and said, "That's Kathy, she owns the place." He told us some of Kathy's history. She had worked in corporate America in Dallas and ended up being moved by a Fortune 100 company to Los Angeles. She became disgruntled and decided to retire to Pie Town.

Soon, Kathy came around the corner and handed us two individually packaged pieces of pie in to-go boxes. We chatted with them for a few minutes, but they needed to leave.

I asked, "How much do we owe you for the pie?"

She answered, "You doin' the Continental Divide Trail?"

"Yes."

"Then the pie is free."

"Oh, do you accept tips?" She nodded and we handed her a large tip and said thanks.

She and Stanley joyfully got in their old vehicle and left to go to a birthday party for somebody in the neighborhood.

Their life looked simple and fulfilling and they seemed to be extremely happy. We ate our pies, and they were fantastic.

We could see a storm coming and were anxious to get back on the road. We headed towards a place called White Horse. There were round homes everywhere called hogans which didn't appear to have electricity or plumbing. Outside were satellite dishes and I think their TVs were powered by the batteries from their vehicles.

As we started south there stood a sign at the side of the road and it read, 'This section of highway is maintained by Simple Abundance.' We tried in vain to outrun the storm, but we got drenched. In my thoughts, it clearly came into focus that Kathy and Stanley and those individuals living in those humble round hogans did live in a modest, uncomplicated way. I considered how complex our lives can become and how it is an art to find happiness, fulfillment, and joy in the small things of life. A beautiful flower or lovely sunset, the gentle touch of a child's hand, a smile from somebody that we adore and love—all those things are so effortless yet incredibly meaningful. The moral of the story is to understand and implement the exquisite nature of Simple Abundance.

> *"If we are serious about growth, be serious about accountability. If we are serious about abundance, be serious about gratitude. If we are serious about intimacy, be serious about vulnerability. If we are serious about discipline, be serious about delayed gratification."*
>
> **— FADZAYI MAHERE**

It's quite lovely to have some ideas, plans, wants, desires, and dreams in our lives. We could plan a list of things to do before we die. We can choose the things we do each day rather than let the day pan out however it does—though at times, spontaneity can be fun.

Let's think about some of the things we desire to do; write them down. And then look at the items that we could do this year, maybe even look at the experiences that we could do on that list this month, this week, or even today.

Let's not allow ourselves to get caught up in doing things that we would never put on our list; they're not important. Don't be cheeky and say, well, we should take off vacuuming. Uh, no. Maybe acknowledge that we'd like our surroundings clean and safe.

I'm saying, don't drift through life. Be intentional about how we spend every hour of our days. For example: If we don't really want to watch a television show and we have a book that we've been hoping to read but others in the family sit down in front of the TV; try using some earplugs if we want to still be with them or go into another room. Try to avoid doing things that we later regret. Examine why we did them. Were we trying to be surrounded by our family? That's not a bad thing. Or did we give in because it seemed a lot easier to plop down and watch TV than to go into another room and get our book.

Maybe we're happier because we stayed with our family and watched the show with them. But if we regret it and feel like it would have been better if we had read our book, then next time, think ahead of what we will do when that situation comes up. Decide now how we will avoid it so that we don't lament later. Usually, our choices are deciding on good, better, or best things. Which can be more challenging than choosing between good or evil.

Be the light. I think it's great to have sparkly, wonderful people in our lives and I want to be one of those shiny beacons of light to others. I want others to see that life is good. It doesn't mean that it doesn't have ups and downs, but overall life is fabulous.

Fairy Garden

A few big rainstorms and the next thing you know, up pops a fairy garden. Patience and endurance after difficult conditions prepare us for a bright future in our metaphorical fairy garden. "We could never learn to be brave and patient if there were only joy in the world."

— HELEN KELLER

CHAPTER 6
LOOK FOR THE GOOD

Mark's Story of a Motorcycle Crash

After my late wife, Nola's, cancer surgery, we were informed that while it went very well, additional post-op treatment would be required. Notwithstanding the disappointing news, she continued to feel better and better, and stronger and stronger. Sometimes it's good to celebrate small victories. We looked at our calendar and timing allowed us to go on a motorcycle tour for a week or so. We had been enjoying a TV series called 'Diners, Drive Ins & Dives.' It seemed like a good idea to google 'DDD' locations and plan an excursion around a gastronomic adventure.

It felt exciting and fun to escape from the worrying world of cancer. We headed from Calgary to the west coast of Washington State and began our fantastically fun, food-fest, stopping to visit friends and family along the way.

The last few days of our trip were ideal: beautiful weather, amazing roads, light traffic, and we scooted along, chatting with the aid of Bluetooth communicators installed in our helmets.

This perfect day would soon be changed in a very dramatic way.

Traveling at about sixty miles per hour on a two-lane mountain road, we came up behind a semi-truck and waited for a safe time to pass. With no time to react, an oncoming car crossed the center line. I braced for impact. The hit knocked Nola off, and she slid down the pavement. I stopped but didn't get a firm foundation for the side-stand, so the bike tipped over and fell into a ditch while I launched into the cold river running alongside the road. I scrambled out of the water up a rocky embankment and rushed to her. By the time I got there, she sat on a rock looking a little dazed.

Note: When touring we ALWAYS wear Full Protective Gear.

Soon a sheriff's deputy arrived. Even though Nola appeared fine and felt good, he called an ambulance to transport her to the hospital. We arranged a tow truck to take the motorcycle to a local storage yard. The impact destroyed the left side valve cover and aluminum luggage box. The deputy and I chatted, and he said, 'I've attended many motorcycle vs. car accidents, and have never witnessed a happy ending like this.' He graciously offered to take me and our salvaged personal belongings to a hotel, which coincidentally was close to the hospital where Nola had been transported.

When we arrived at the hotel in Grangeville, Idaho, I loaded a luggage cart and entered the lobby. I provided the front desk clerk, Janet, with a credit card and informed her that we had been in an accident and my wife was being treated at the hospital. I asked if I could leave our things on the cart, so I could get over there right away. Janet replied, 'Don't worry we will take care of everything.'

I climbed back into the patrol car and thanked the deputy profusely for his consideration and kindness. He again mentioned divine intervention had guided the hand of fate that day and he felt honored and privileged to witness and be part of the story.

We quickly arrived at the emergency entrance, and they guided me to a treatment room where Nola rested on a white-sheeted gurney, chatting it up with the attending nurse. The mood felt light and friendly with spontaneous laughter. The doctor arrived and checked a one-inch round abrasion on the palm of her hand where her glove had worn through during the accident.

He then turned his attention to me and asked, 'How are you?'

I responded, 'Good, I think.' However, I had a small cut on my shin that needed some stitches. After a few signatures completed the paperwork, we were done.

The attending nurse then spoke up and said, "You don't know it yet, but you folks are in trouble here." She explained that there were no taxis in Grangeville, no rental cars, and no commercial flights. "You need to get to Lewiston to find any of those services. I get off work around seven and I'll be happy to take you there." I asked how far, and she said about seventy-five miles, one way.

Here stood a person that had worked twelve hours willing to drive one hundred and fifty miles to help us out. Wow! We were humbled at the kindness of her offer. As it worked out, I arranged for our son, Carter, to come from Alberta in my truck and gather us up the next morning.

We left and walked to a grocery store for snacks before our short trek back to the nearby hotel. We entered and were greeted by Janet. She said, 'Your belongings have been taken up to your room and are waiting for you there. Can I do anything else?'

Impressed at her thoughtfulness; we expressed sincere gratitude and went upstairs. Our clothes were hanging up in the closet, nicely organized. We were as far away from traffic and outside noise as possible. The spacious room looked clean and comfortable. There was even a hot tub.

Soon the phone rang. Janet said she had spoken with her husband. They had three vehicles, a truck and two cars, none of them were pretty, but they would be pleased to let us borrow one. I thanked her and let her know that we expected our son from Calgary in the morning, and we appeared to be well taken care of.

From the moment of impact until we were heading north again was less than twenty-four hours. But often, we reminisced about the good people of Grangeville. We'd felt snuggled by the kindness of strangers. Simple, old-fashioned caring had a lasting influence. We've done our best to pay it forward in any way possible.

The Rest of the Story

Nola and Carter slept, as I drove us back to Calgary for the next cancer appointment. I thought about the accident and what could have happened. While humbled to feel divine protection and clearly acknowledging the kindness and support we had received, I became melancholy.

Had I done anything to deserve that experience? I was an excellent rider with hundreds of thousands of kilometers under my belt without an incident. Why didn't I get some premonition or warning? What did I do wrong? Why did this happen and why now? Weren't we under enough adversity already; did we need this too?

At dusk, Nola spoke up and asked if we would make it to the border before it closed at 11:00 pm. My response was, "We should make it with about ten minutes to spare, *if we don't hit a horse.*" Within thirty seconds of saying that, I saw the faint outline of a lot of animals on the narrow road. I nailed the brakes, and maneuvered quickly, yet safely, through about six horses. No one said a thing. We began to get back up to speed when I distinctly had the impression '*Not yet.*' I slowed. In moments, there were two more on the right side of the road. After passing them I began to accelerate, when once more, '*Not yet,*' played in my mind. This time on the left side there were a few more horses. After getting by the animals and knowing that time was of the essence, we continued briskly.

Shortly after getting back up to speed, Carter and Nola gave me a questioning look and said in unison, "*If we don't hit a horse? Where did that come from?*" If we don't hit a deer, if we don't run out of gas, if we don't have a flat. Those sentiments would be reasonable, but horses on the road would be, to say the least, unusual.

We made it to the border with exactly ten minutes to spare. No further drama. It's interesting that as I silently berated myself for not being tuned in to potential dangers, I received what I considered to be a divine affirmation of not being abandoned or punished from on high.

Life is replete with Tender Mercies, those little messages that comfort and remind us of Godly influences. Be still and know.

This story is also about gaining perspective. It's about honestly and accurately evaluating situations, while abstaining from dishonest and inaccurate, exaggerated, *why me, poor me* thinking. Why did the motorcycle mishap occur? I now know why. An accident, that's why. Nothing more than that. It wasn't about me. It didn't ruin my life. It wasn't the worse thing ever. It consisted of simply a few frightening seconds followed by life-changing, uplifting experiences and encounters. The good far outweighed the bad.

We often see people who experience adversity and get stuck, doggedly hanging on to their difficult memories. This is the bigger tragedy because it's unnecessary and completely avoidable. The moral of the story is: We have a chance, maybe even a responsibility, to intentionally choose healthy responses to every situation. We can't change all life events; we can only devise the best way to think about them. It's essential to our happiness and joy that we select a method that is not impaired by exaggeration and negativity. Perhaps choosing true paradigms and perspectives is an essential way to 'Be the Boss of Our Thinker' and live Happily Ever After.

Be Positive and Grow

The most important relationship we ever have is the one with self. It is a worthy goal to like who we are. Being confident and comfortable with ourselves makes us feel at ease. This sets the tone for all other relationships. If we embrace our strengths and accept our weaknesses as human, we can easily love others. Conversely, if we are not happy with the way we are, we will struggle to be happy with one another. To save someone else, first save ourselves.

"People who shine from within, don't need the spotlight."
— ANONYMOUS

Everyone has positive and negative attributes and actions. Humans are a work in progress. Let's be gentle, encouraging, and helpful with each other as much as we can. Especially ourselves. Keep working to be all that we can be. If we want to improve any aspect of our life, learn about it, and then practice it.

Mark and I have had great lives, we are very blessed. It's not all smooth. Many hardships have allowed us the opportunity to grow, learn, and progress. Because we believe in a life after this one, we see every trial as temporary. Even if it lasts our whole mortal existence.

Let's not compare. There is always someone better *and* worse than us in every aspect. It doesn't matter. We're only trying to be better than we were and coming closer to the ideal we have decided for ourselves. Focus on the areas where we are aligned with *our* purposes and goals.

Know who we are, and who we want to be, but relax, we are still becoming. When we know better, we'll do better. An improved version of ourselves is more important than our career, our possessions, or how we look, etc.

"Self-awareness is our capacity to stand apart from ourselves and examine our thinking, our motives, our history, our scripts, our actions, and our habits and tendencies."
—STEPHEN R. COVEY

We may fear trying something new or making mistakes. Let's be willing to be temporarily uncomfortable so we can grow. It can be an impetus to try again or arrive at a better method of doing things. There is a benefit to uneasiness as we rise above failure. Fix any mistakes and the shame is replaced by the glow of success. And the sooner the better.

"Be not afraid of discomfort. If we can't put ourselves in a situation where we are uncomfortable, then we will never grow. We will never change. We'll never learn."
—JASON REYNOLDS

Sometimes, when we don't regularly achieve good things, the attention received after a tragedy may entice us to indulge in a bit of drama queen/king behavior. We may be tempted to hold onto the notoriety.

Let's attract the notice of others in a positive way. Excel at a hobby or sport, join a club, develop a talent, donate time, money, or effort to a good cause. That's a better way to gain fame. Plus, if you have been through (or are still going through) a Beautiful Struggle, focusing on something positive will help you achieve a healthier response.

Problems do not have to make us miserable. Oh, but they can—if we let them. Instead, we can think about a problem as the means to becoming better. We can think of it as a chance to adjust, figure things out, improve ourselves, and then it is a useful tool to become who we want to be. Overcoming a real challenge can bring a great deal of personal satisfaction and growth. With each failure, we can try to learn and profit from it.

"Do not fear failure; but please be terrified of regret."
— **DESHAUNA BARBER**

I am *not* saying that a negative, unhealthy reaction to a hard situation will never happen. Thinking in a positive, healthy way, like any skill, takes practice. There is certainly BS (remember, think Beautiful Struggles) that occurs that is sad, distressing, heartbreaking, challenging, or causes tears or profound grief. But we do not need to unduly remain in those feelings just because a normal part of mortality happens to us. It is our self-talk, our perceptions, our choices, to think about what is taking place in a positive light.

Let's not feel bad or judge ourselves harshly if the human being we used to be did something that we now could do better. We are a different person; we now know better.

"A smooth sea never made a great sailor."
— **FRANKLIN D. ROOSEVELT**

We'll always have a challenge we are trying to solve to realize our greatest growth and potential. And if life doesn't give us one big enough for the growth we seek—we can challenge ourselves. Learn a different language, take up a new hobby, try something that is hard. If we're shy, go meet three of our neighbors. If we are afraid of snakes, go hiking—or maybe start out at the zoo. Wink, wink.

When we're riding a bike, we focus on where we want it to go. Sometimes, especially when we're a new cyclist, we might see an obstacle in the trail, maybe a big rock, and BOOM the next thing we know, we hit it. That's because we're looking at that boulder and our bike seems to go right where we focused. It's the same thing in life. Watch and think about where we intend to end up.

> *"Pobody's Nerfect. If we're not failing, we're not learning, if we're not learning, we're not getting better."*
>
> **— M. S. STARK**

If we're complaining and whining or criticizing, STOP! Or we'll stay in a place where we can do more complaining, whining, and criticizing. Instead focus on thoughts that are pleasant, enlarging, motivating, uplifting, fun, inspiring, or thoughts that will help us reach our objective.

When hard trials happened and my children had to push through a challenge, I hesitated to jump in with advice too soon. If they faced some uncomfortable consequences of a choice, I tried not to fix it for them. If I made it too easy, I might be crippling them for the future. I often told them; **'I am more concerned about your character than your comfort.'**

Remember, we have lots of choices, let's not limit ourselves. If we are facing a problem, let our minds sort through possibilities. Adopt a 'Good, Better, or Best' mind-set. Don't stop with the first idea you think might work, though it seems to be a good idea. Keep going until you reach the very best solution. That's rarely going to be 'Stay in bed all day and cry'. Even if some claim that is normal and okay. Yes, that option may be easy to do, and it may even seem like the route we feel most like doing at that moment, but let's talk to ourselves about what's truly *best* for us. A 'Great, Long-term Choice' will make life much simpler instead of choosing what is easier for today.

It may seem a little bit difficult for us to get up and get going. But even a 'good' alternative that at least moves us forward is an improvement over feeling defeated by a situation or staying stuck. The momentum of doing *something* will often help us advance and then we can be in a position either to resolve the problem or maybe see new and better ways to help us manage.

A Mirror or a Window?

One of my favorite quotes is:

> *"Do I look at life through a window or a mirror?"*
> —M. S. STARK

I think this is vitally important for a healthy outlook. We can focus too much on viewing the world through a mirror and all we can see is ourselves and what is happening to us, or how we think, or what we want, or how we feel. Others' opinions which differ from ours may seem threatening to us. If others don't agree with us does that mean we are wrong? Of course not. We can be obsessed with worrying about what other people think of us or how they treat us. We can look at ourselves, and wonder: Am I good? Am I bad? Am I bigger or smaller? Am I more attractive? Do I have more money? And we make everything about us. We can become incredibly self-absorbed. That is a very unhealthy and unhappy way to live.

Self is a Burden.

OR instead, we can focus on empathy, concern, compassion, understanding, and cooperation and look at life through a window (as it were) and realize there are lots of people on Earth, not only us. We can again ask ourselves, which way of thinking is better? Which allows us to rid our mind of feelings of self-consciousness and anxiety? Which allows us to Live Happily Ever After?

Focus on Others

When we look through a window, we generally become less judgmental. We truly see another person, not on the surface but deep into their souls. For example, our parents were probably young when they had us. Don't expect them to be perfect and then hold a grudge against them for something they said or did years ago. It is healthier to be compassionate and forgiving if they made mistakes, or what we may consider a mistake. They probably did the best they knew how. Remember to think, where did that story start?

Let's see others with our hearts not just our eyes. If we can't see their goodness, it doesn't mean goodness is not there, it simply reveals our blindness to it. Why can we see the bad so easily? We need to have the courage to open our vision more compassionately.

It is tempting to judge others by their actions and results, but maybe judge ourselves by our good intentions—regardless of the outcome. Let's pretend we have a file labeled ME which is separated into different folders, each with its heading. And we're instructed to place each of our thoughts, words, or actions during the day under the appropriate subtitle such as Kind, Selfish, Complimentary, Critical, Uplifting, or Demeaning, etc.

Plus, we can't offer up an excuse for it but simply must put it in the correct place. When night comes, would we be happy with the size of each folder? Would we wish we had more in the 'Kindness' folder and less under 'Critical'? Let's be more aware of what we think, say, and do.

Do we strongly criticize someone, let's say on a social media platform, because of *their* political rant? And we feel totally justified when we do it because, clearly, *they* are in the wrong. Then the next week, someone (maybe even the same person) calls us out for *our* post about a new school policy that we think is too restrictive. How rude of them! How dare they! We decide to avoid them in the future, or not invite them to our birthday party. Or maybe we dash off a caustic reply online.

Do we stop to think that their public attack was the same thing *we* had done earlier? But it wasn't the same, we protested. It wasn't about politics; our post was about *the children*. They were wrong, we were right.

If we don't allow others to have, and express their opinions, why should we get upset when someone pushes back against our beliefs? But we were merely expressing our view, we cried. After all, it's a free country, right? Right. But for everyone, or only us?

In principle, they were doing the same thing we did. Simply expressing their sentiments. I'm not saying we can't civilly express our ideas but instead let's recognize when our actions are what we don't want someone else to do to us. Golden Rule and all that… And keep in mind, opinions are not facts.

The other person may very well also have 'evidence' for their conviction like we do.

Co-workers, friends, and neighbors all may see things differently than we see them. Remember, we are all human beings, works in progress. We all mess up. Do not expect others to agree with all our opinions. Their journey has taken them to different places—in body and mind. Do not expect them to live by (or even know) the rules we have made up for life.

Good can always be found in every person and situation. Do we keep our hearts behind a closed, locked door or is our love wide open so it can be returned? Think joyfully. Say wonderful comments to others. Praise generously and be honest and kind. Lift others, encourage, and notice even small improvements. We will feel the way that we treat others. If we treat others with kindness, we will feel kind and happy. If we are mean, even if we think they may 'deserve' it, we will feel mean and unhappy. We may try to change that by making excuses, rationalizing, or assigning blame, but it won't work.

Mark Shares a Story: How Far Can It Be?

I went on a bike ride with a group of friends through the mountains east of Kalispell, Montana to a place called Strawberry Lake. After we passed the lake, we intended to head north and drop into the town of Columbia Falls. In the first hour or two, there were a lot of trees that were down due to the winter snowpack. Our excursion took place early in the summer and the trails hadn't been cleared.

The route that we needed to take veered off to the left, obscured by some fallen trees, so we missed the junction, ending up in a valley taking us to a town called Hungry Horse. My friend, Damon and I decided that we wanted to go back, find the trail, and do what we had originally planned. "How far can it be?" I asked him.

"I'm in," Damon responded. "Let's go!" The other four guys went down to Hungry Horse and soon made it back to the cabin on Lake Blaine.

The two of us eventually found the obscured path, but it seemed like there were fallen trees every fifty yards or so. We had to lift our bikes up and over trunks and through branches and after a few hours, we got to a signpost that said Lake Blaine, the location of the cabin, but we really wanted to go to a place called Columbia Falls which we believed to be only ten or fifteen miles farther, so again I asked, "How far can it be?"

We agreed to carry on. The trail wandered and we didn't have much food; we were not really prepared for such a long trip. I think I had two power bars in my backpack and a little bit of water, and eventually we drank it all. We shared the food.

After a few more hours, we were so exhausted that we laid down on the trail amongst the rocks, went to sleep for about ten or fifteen minutes, and then resumed cycling. Soon, it was dusk but thankfully there remained some twilight. We kept going and going. We persevered. Our ride ended up being about thirteen hours and our other companions were ready to call search and rescue thinking maybe we were in trouble.

Sometimes we have significant trials, and we don't have many choices. There's no way out but through. We were in that kind of position. To this day, Damon and I talk about how incredible that was and how much of a bond it created between us because of the difficulty we shared and conquered. The moral of the story is this: I think there's a great deal of value in doing hard things, persevering, succeeding, and going well beyond our comfort zone. It causes our comfort zone to grow larger as well as our self-esteem, when we realize that we overcame a great challenge. I've done lots of hard things for the fun of it, including my bike ride across Canada.

Ice Caves

Clouds glow orange over Fish Creek. Bike lights illuminate Winter's exquisite icicle formations. Light enhances every circumstance. We appreciate those who add radiance to our world. "Hope is being able to see that there is light despite all the darkness."

— DESMOND TUTU

CHAPTER 7

I CAN DO HARD THINGS

When we succeed, tell ourselves, 'I did it! I can do hard things.' Spend time to reflect and remember past challenging accomplishments. We can be grateful we have been allowed the opportunity to surmount obstacles. Let's understand that every pain endured well prepares us to transcend future pain.

How we invest our time is important; it reveals who we are. The thoughts we think, plus the words we say, along with our actions define us. It is not imperative that we discover the whole meaning of life, find meaning in one day, or in one moment at a time.

Mark's Trans-Canada Charity Bike Ride

This is a story about riding a bicycle across Canada. It started through a chance visit with Vern Hyde, a long-term friend and neighbour, who had moved away from Calgary to Medicine Hat many years earlier. Our paths would cross from time to time and always resulted in an enthusiastic and joyful reunion.

Nola and I attended a Sunday Service in a small town north of Calgary; by chance, Vern was there too. He'd had a heart attack a year before and I knew of his desire to get back in good physical shape. He greeted me enthusiastically and told me he felt great, he then said: "I want to do something big to show my appreciation for health and recovery."

I said, "Okay I'm in; I'll do it with you."

He looked at me puzzled and said, "You don't even know my plan."

I replied "Yes, I do. You want to ride bicycles across Canada, I'm down with that."

He looked at me funny and he said, "How on earth did you know?"

I said, "I'm not sure." But I knew that's what he wanted to do. My response was a bit of a wild but educated guess as Vern had talked to me about cycling, bikes, and the riding opportunities around his home. He had become 'a keener' about riding.

We chatted about it further; his plan ended up being a little bit bigger than a simple ride. We knew a doctor who had started a project in Ethiopia called Canadian Humanitarian, a registered NGO charity. They had sufficient donations to run their program, however, they had not yet acquired enough extra funds to build an actual school facility. So, Vern and I decided to throw our hats in the ring and ride our bikes across Canada to raise enough money to build a school in Ghindo Town, Ethiopia.

With my late wife's recent treatments and remission from cancer, we too felt it appropriate to give back. It felt humbling to knock on doors, present our plan, and then watch as individuals and corporate donors committed their financial support. Our fund-raising activities were very successful.

The logistics of the trip went like this: A company donated the use of a one-ton truck for us to tow a large fifth-wheel trailer that I quickly named 'Shangri-La'. Calgary's largest bike store, Bow Cycle, and the importer of Surly Bicycles generously donated touring bikes to us at cost. We started at the Pacific Ocean in Stanley Park located on the western edge of Vancouver, British Columbia (BC).

Each morning, Vern and I would get ready and start riding east, toward the Atlantic Coast. Our wives would hook up the trailer, break camp, head east 100–150 km (about 60 to 90 miles), and find a place to park. If they felt like it, they would get on their bikes and ride back towards us. We would meet up, ride back to the trailer together, and have lunch.

After lunch, our spouses would drive an additional 100 km or so and set up the trailer for the night. The guys (Vern and I) would ride for a few more hours until we arrived at our campground. Frequently the women had started supper, and we would shower after the ride, eat, and then simply enjoy the evening. Note: I've done self-supported bike touring, so this set up felt like maximum luxury in comparison.

Our bikes were new, so they only required periodic tuning and simple maintenance. I took on that job. Vern and I rode bikes from morning until dark. Driving the truck and trailer, grocery shopping, meal prep, laundry, diesel for the truck, and propane for the trailer were the women's responsibilities. We all had our assignments, and the trip went smoothly. Mostly.

We began in early May 2012, and encountered five snow days, lots of rain, evil winds, relentless steep mountain passes, narrow highways with heavy truck traffic, and sections of road with disintegrating shoulders. We also experienced the creation of incredible memories, incessant laughter, an increase of personal fortitude by successfully dealing with hard things, beautiful scenery, chance meetings with unique individuals, and abundant generosity, which culminated in the building of a new school in Ethiopia. All because of a vision to bike across Canada. There were many experiences from the ride but here are four that delivered fresh insights to me.

Tattoo Girl

Traveling east of Sault Ste. Marie, Ontario proved terrifying due to the volume of heavy trucks and the extremely poor shoulders of the narrow two-lane, Trans-Canada Highway. (I consider this portion of the road to be a National Embarrassment.)

The horror stories we heard were dismissed and we forged ahead. After two perilous encounters in a short two-hundred-and-fifty-kilometer day (155 miles), we wisely left the Trans-Canada for a road less traveled. Eventually, we boarded a ferry boat that took us to The Bruce Peninsula in Ontario.

Our next day became blistering hot. We stopped at a roadside convenience store located near an intersection in the middle of a beautiful farming region. We cooled off in the air-conditioned building and purchased some treats to eat on a shaded porch. While we rested and enjoyed some protection from the blazing sun, an SUV pulled up and parked. Out of the vehicle came five middle-aged women, one of them had long dreadlocks, a tube top, lots of piercings and skin covered with tattoos; and some were quite large. I whispered to Vern, "Woah, look at that." I'm ashamed to admit I had quickly made a negative judgment call.

Vern popped out of his comfy chair and went directly up to the inked lady and began a conversation leading with, "Tell me about your tattoos." Their conversation proved friendly and engaging. Not too much time passed when she asked, "Where are you from and what are you doing here?" I eventually joined the discussion and found my quick judgement to be unfounded. We informed her of our mission to build a school in Ethiopia by raising awareness and money.

She became eager to help and enlisted her friends to unite and collectively they gave us five hundred dollars. These women were thrilled to participate. Vern's unjudgmental curiosity opened the door to dialogue and resulted in their buying into our mission and providing unexpected financial support.

The moral of this story is: don't judge the tattooed lady. I learned at that point, it's best to be slow to judge and be kind and gentle because overall people are great most of the time. Judge softly and carefully. I also recognized that I disappoint myself from time to time and I need to seek forgiveness and try to do better.

> *"Seek first to understand, then to be understood."*
> — STEPHEN R. COVEY

Swift Current

One of our most challenging and longest rides started in Medicine Hat, Alberta, and ended in Swift Current,

Saskatchewan. The day would be around three hundred kilometers (about 200 miles). When crossing the Canadian prairies by car the trip seems FLAT. Crossing by bicycle reveals some ups and downs—lots of 'em! Compounding matters, the expected soft wind from the west, quickly turned evil and became cold and rainy, with a driving, *east* headwind.

We endured the unrelenting, wet, frigid resistance of a ferocious gale for fourteen hours. By the time we crested a hill, and Swift Current came into view, instead of allowing our muscles to rest while we coasted down the last few kilometers into the town site, we were required to aggressively pedal down the hill to overcome the $@&#*€ wind.

A difficult, maybe even demoralizing day finally ended. It proved far more taxing than climbing up and over the Rocky Mountains in a snowstorm. We found the camping spot selected by our wives, but we felt too exhausted to do anything but the absolute minimum to get ready for sleep, no energy for lighthearted conversation, and even eating became a secondary consideration.

Now, getting ready for bed, I began to relive some of the unexpected and tough challenges of the day. Soon I became grateful for the difficulties, I realized the day's pain created mental and physical endurance that would serve us the rest of the trip.

I learned that concept previously, but it jelled with me that day and became a high watermark of understanding the value of pain, the value of suffering, the value of doing hard things that help us to be stronger and to realize that often if we have the right thoughts, pain will facilitate growth otherwise unobtainable. Learning how to traverse through the pain of life with nobility and grace is exceptionally valuable. I have a firm and abiding gratitude for difficult things.

The moral of this story is that when adversity strikes (and it will), we can choose to grow or to shrink. Here is how that works mathematically.

Pain + Why me/Poor me = Shrink
Pain + Gratitude = Growth

Growth and gratitude are inseparably connected. When we select appreciation for all of life's experiences, we progress. It's a choice. The choice is ours. Choose Wisely.

Self-Talk

As we crossed the Rocky Mountains, I thought that climbing up and over the Rogers Pass, the highest point on the trip, and on to Banff would be our biggest day of elevation gain. Once we had conquered the Rockies, we felt relieved about putting the most difficult section behind us. Never in my wildest imagination would I have considered that crossing the Canadian Shield in Ontario would be as arduous as it turned out to be.

About halfway through our Trans-Canada adventure, we entered Ontario and encountered a geological feature known as the Canadian Shield, a massive rock formation. There's very little farming, it's too rugged. The road going through the Canadian Shield is a few thousand kilometers of wiggling up and down a two-lane ribbon of undulating asphalt. A typical day would consist of climbing up about two-thousand feet, dropping down fifteen-hundred feet, up another fifteen hundred, down eighteen hundred, up twenty-five-hundred, and it goes up and down incessantly as it crosses that geological feature.

In comparison, climbing up and over the Rocky Mountains accumulated only around ten thousand feet of elevation gain in one day. Here, we could accumulate twenty-five-thousand vertical feet or more. That can be compared to riding from sea level to the top of Mount Everest in one day—day after day.

Two weeks of daily, huge effort; the climbing felt never-ending. We were strong, however it seemed slow going; we simply found a sustainable gear and would persevere. Before, when riding on the flats, Vern could follow behind me closely to take advantage of aerodynamics, and away we would go. On these big hills, he couldn't draft behind me because we were not going fast enough to create the vortex. Unfortunately, now he rode on his own.

I would certainly not sprint up the climbs, but I pedaled a little quicker than Vern and reached the top first. I usually found someplace to sit down and wait for him. I called every resting place 'The Couch,' whether a guardrail at the side of the road, some rocks off to the right, or a cliff where we could overlook traffic. I'd have a power bar and some water while waiting for a few moments for Vern to summit.

We developed a tradition that went like this; as he crested a hill, I would give him two thumbs up and ask, "You good?"

As Vern approached, he sang out "Made it!"

At the top of one particularly grueling peak on an unusually hot day, we gave our ritual greetings. Winded, he dismounted and laid down on a rock beside me on The Couch. Looking to the sky, he began to talk to himself *out loud.* "Wow, that was really hard." Answering himself, "I know."

"You know what, you did really good." A long pause. "I know."

"Well, you made it. It wasn't pretty, but you made it. I know."

"You know what, you've got this, you can do the next hill. I know."

He kept going on for a few minutes with this out-loud self-talk.

I sat smiling and impressed. Vern glanced at me to ensure I listened and then said, "I hate Mark. He's way too strong; he makes it look so easy." A short pause. "I know."

He laughed, and then we laughed together and simply rested until we both felt like getting after it some more.

A howling funny moment, but the moral of this story is: His talk sounded honest, and wonderfully soft and kind. The hill *was* hard; I don't remember one more difficult. I've never heard 'out loud' self-talk before. The entire experience encouraged and inspired both of us. Positive, personal conversations work.

End of the Trip

Our adventure across Canada took forty-two ride days finishing in Halifax, Nova Scotia. We surprised ourselves with tears from an unexpected mix of melancholy and jubilation. By the end of the trip, a steep climb or headwind conditions were inconsequential; our bodies were strong and would respond affirmatively to anything we asked them to do. I came to understand the value of pushing and doing difficult things that take us outside of our comfort zone, not only physically but also emotionally.

The moral of the story is: Improvement in our world often requires extra effort. Worth-while accomplishments are usually uphill from where we presently are. We must hang in there to make difficult situations work as best we can and simply do hard things until they eventually get easier.

> *"That which we persist on doing becomes easier.*
> *Not that the nature of the task has changed,*
> *but our ability to do has increased."*
> **— RALPH WALDO EMERSON**

Enjoy the Process

Even though I started riding a bike when I was a young child, my opportunity to understand the many nuances of cycling started as an adult when I met Mark. He patiently taught me step by step when I started riding with him on a gravel road in Snow Canyon State Park, and later around the St. George airport buttes or other southern Utah trails. On some tricky parts, he shouted, "Don't stop, don't stop! Be brave!" On more difficult sections, he would ride lead and call out, "You got this" or "I know you can do this next section, but if you want to walk, that's okay." The lessons continued in Canada.

Despite two bike crashes (one quite serious, which left me with deep fear and nervous hesitancy) with each ride under his gentle tutelage, I'm slowly becoming better. I know Mark is far more talented on a bike than I am (or ever will be) and that's okay. Let's not complicate matters by comparing ourselves with others. I am thoroughly enjoying my rides and I'm grateful for his coaching.

When learning a new skill, we can ask ourselves some questions. Do we want it? Why do we want it? Is it possible? Probably if others are doing it, that means we can do it. Remind ourselves that a new skill takes time. Even a skill like Healthy Thinking. Healthy Thinking will become a habit and get much easier with deliberate practice. Enjoy the process and notice how your comfort level gradually increases. Experts didn't attain that designation overnight. Mark has spent countless hours in the bike saddle. We may progress slower or faster than another, but it doesn't matter. Keep going, step by step. We'll get there.

Don't be a prophet of doom or tell ourselves that life will never get better. It changes. Even when a problem seems overwhelmingly big, we usually don't have to do it all at once. Break it down and take small steps forward and we'll Live Happily Ever After.

Small Steps

With my daughter, Marissa, we faced many major decisions, countless doctor visits, and I've lost track of how many surgeries and medical procedures she has had. She came into this world with multiple deformities and malformities. Most of her internal organs were missing, ectopic (in an abnormal place or position), deformed, or didn't function correctly. Her feet and legs were seriously twisted, and there were other problems with her ears, neck, and heart.

During her first year when I faced life and death issues with her, I still had three other preschool children to raise. But truthfully, it became more complex when my oldest, Zach, started kindergarten because I lost his usual help with his brothers. For the first two years after Marissa's birth, we returned to the hospital or clinic every two or three days, spending many hours or sometimes days at a time. We didn't live near family, so I led a parade of four young children to most visits.

The treatments she endured were horrifically painful and caused vomiting and diarrhea for my little girl. Since we returned every two or three days, Marissa never had a chance to fully recover before we were back for another session. As if that were not enough suffering, mistakes by medical professionals added to her misery. At only nine days old, a nurse accidently severed Marissa's teeny leg almost in half while removing a cast with a saw that "wasn't supposed to cut her." A few years later, during a surgery on her ankle to remove a large, misplaced, metal pin that had worn a deep, painful groove into her bone, the surgeon failed to pull it out straight and accidently shattered several bones. Other errors caused more serious results, like cardiac and respiratory arrest from the wrong anesthetic. On three occasions we were told of her imminent death.

To make matters worse, our insurance refused to cover most of her care since her conditions were rare and without standard protocol, so any treatments were considered experimental. Our medical debt skyrocketed.

She often struggled all night in pain. Innumerable times I lifted her tiny body from her crib and discovered bloody sheets that needed to be changed. There were mind-numbing, sleepless nights pacing the floor holding her in my arms as she cried. Her casts, from toes to hips, weighed almost as much as she did, and the combined pounds made my back ache terribly. I lived on meager minutes of sleep and with the constant medical appointments, attending to the demands of her special needs, three active little boys, a part-time job, and a household to run; I often felt exhausted.

I found that if I thought about what would likely happen in the future, all the doctor visits, all the surgeries, all the pain, all the sleepless nights, all the things she would never be able to do, my other young children with their own needs, etc. I became overwhelmed. I had to break it down. There were times that I couldn't look at dealing with what needed to be done that month; it still became too much. Even trying to deal with the week's schedule seemed daunting. Most of the time, I didn't allow myself to think about even the next hour—it caused some panic. In the hardest times, all I could manage was asking myself, "What must I do in the next fifteen minutes? Can I do that? Maybe. What else can I do but try?" and I moved forward. Fifteen minutes, fifteen minutes, fifteen minutes, and soon an hour passed. I made it, though I didn't think it possible.

When life gradually became a little bit easier, I could think about the next hour and finally, a whole day. I didn't worry about the requirements for that week or month or year. I took small pieces and I forged ahead. Sometimes I look back and I wonder how in the world I got through that awful time. Well, I did it in fifteen-minute segments.

I remember another situation, I had to find a quicker way to do something. I worked as an artist doing thousands of tole paintings and wooden crafts to support the family. But I knew I needed to get faster—not a little quicker but jammin' fast!

I wondered, did it have to be done through the method that I had been taught, the way that everybody else did it? That way seemed too slow. How else could I obtain the desired outcome? I examined the steps, thought about it, and tried to think of all the ways I could speed it up. As I analyzed how I did it, I realized that with some creative thinking, the process could be streamlined. I finally came up with an innovative system. It went so crazy fast, that soon, I accomplished in *one hour* what it had been taking me an *entire week* to do! My output and income skyrocketed.

Sometimes we must look at a single piece of the process. Take it apart and see how we can make small changes. Not only my crafts, but it can apply to anything. Don't be afraid to see something differently. If what we're doing is not working out, don't get hung up or discouraged by thinking we are a failure, believing there aren't any other options or other negative thoughts. There are always options. We want to concentrate on solving the problem, not beating ourselves up. Allow ourselves to expect more and believe that we can. We don't have to make huge changes; we can simply do small ones that will put us in a better place.

Always Something Good

I think we can see good in every situation even where it does not seem possible. We may think there's nothing good about what's going on—but keep thinking. There could still be sadness, fear, worry, frustration, etc., and the problem doesn't magically go away, but if we look for the good, we can experience some gratitude and growth and that makes us stronger.

For example, I had five severely deformed babies. Four died right away, one miraculously survived childhood but still faces many challenges. She had three older siblings and two younger ones. It took a lot of time and effort and much work to take care of this child with so many health problems. The other children had to pitch in and help, not only with her but with chores around the house.

As they observed the things that she faced daily, the pain she suffered, and her continued struggles, they became exceptionally tender-hearted. Once I read an article about a study that showed that siblings of children with severe physical or mental challenges were kinder and more compassionate towards others because of the experience of interacting with someone who faced serious trials day after day. It proved true. And I realized it had been a blessing in our family when at first it seemed like there was nothing good about the situation. My adult children are responsible, hardworking, incredibly kind, and extremely compassionate individuals who appreciate the strengths in their own bodies and minds, and who are also very patient with others who suffer difficulties. Aren't those lovely results that any mother would desire for her children?

Hang On!

We'll all have obstacles in our lives, and we could face them with depression, fear, frustration, confusion, anxiety, helplessness, or anger (or all of these!). Our attitude, our perspective, the meaning we assign to it, and what we do despite the issue, all enter in. We can have ruthless pragmatism and brutal honesty, not just pretending it's not bad. This isn't 'faking it with a brave face to the world' stuff. We can control our thoughts by intentionally seeking out the good in each challenge.

We can broaden our view. Let's step back and see trials as a normal and important part of our lives, not as horrible, out-of-place intrusions. Explore the ordeals with some questions. What can we learn? How can problems help us strengthen or acquire a virtue? Can we gain more compassion and empathy with others in a similar situation—or any of their struggles?

Use obstacles to test who we are. Be creative; look for new ways to do things. Understand that *we* decide what an experience means. I did not think my problems meant I was unworthy, or nothing ever went right for me, or that I had a terrible life. Does the perspective we choose make our lives better or worse? I knew I was worthy and strong, and certainly some things were difficult, but much of my life was wonderful. I'd rather exaggerate that my life was all fabulous than nothing ever went right. There will probably still be some fear, or frustration, but the negative feelings will be tempered, and we'll create a stronger foundation to cope.

Watch out for crazy self-expectations, rules, or fears that don't serve us well. For example: a false belief that we must be perfect, or others should be perfect, or thinking: this is the worst thing ever, I can't do this, or why is my life so horrible? Get rid of that unhealthy thinking and look for the absolute truth. Let's not be quick to judge an experience as bad or good, remind ourselves that there are usually elements of both.

How do we even decide if something is good or bad? Are cookies good or bad? Breakfast, lunch, and dinner of cookies may not be so good in the long run. Kids may think cookies for lunch are great. And as an occasional snack, they are yummy. But a parent with a long-term view wants their child to have some veggies. Life's classroom teaches us that everything is for our good. At the very least, it is a good learning experience.

Don't be quick to judge the value of our situation or experience. Example: I received an assignment at church to visit a woman who rudely put me off. Then ten months later, I had a private difficult situation, and she finally allowed me to visit her, and she led me to employment that proved to be a lifesaver. If she had opened the door to me earlier, she probably wouldn't have asked the introductory question of whether I worked, and likely I would not have revealed that I desperately needed a job.

We can believe that EVERYTHING is a blessing to us OR we can view life as hard. Which idea makes our life better?

Don't worry about our limitations; instead, capitalize on our potential. We can choose to fill our minds with happy thoughts and then get busy with worthy goals and pursuits.

Trust God. And his timing. God is never late. If we build a basket, God will fill it. And we'll Live Happily Ever After.

Don't foolishly fight against life. When we go swimming, we expect to get wet. Then when we do, it doesn't come as a surprise, and we accept it as a normal part of the experience. In life, we may wrongly hope it will NOT be filled with pain, sickness, difficult people, struggles, or disappointments. When those things inevitably come along, we won't be ready and could feel discouraged or think life is terrible or unfair.

We could feel like a poor victim. Don't forget those things are part of this glorious experience we call life. Why do we think it is supposed to be all fun and games? Look around, difficulties are the norm.

What emotions do we feed? Do we give more energy to good or bad in our lives? We can use the example of two plants. Let's say we have one noxious plant, maybe it's Poison Ivy and we have another that's exquisitely beautiful, like an Orchid. If we take the Poison Ivy and we make sure we water it and give it enough light and fertilizer and give it all the care it needs, the Poison Ivy is going to grow. Obviously. However, let's say we take the pretty plant, and give it little attention, a dark corner, and no water. It's easy to guess the results.

We choose what grows in our minds and what dies. If we want more so-called Poison Ivy in our thoughts, then we focus on the negative; we think about all the bad things that happen to us, and we expect more bad things to occur. Likewise, if we focus on the good in our life, and we expect more good experiences, and we notice more good, even trying to figure out how something that might seem bad could help us out— then goodness will grow. Feed the positive.

'Try to stay positive,' we hear in a cheerful voice that makes us want to scream, 'Well try having cancer and staying positive!' Would we prefer they advise us to, "Stay negative" with a morose tone of voice? Which mindset will be healthier for us to adopt? Either way, we'll still have cancer, but do we need to make ourselves OVER suffer?

Character

Years ago, something traumatic happened to this tree, leaving a scar and eventually revealing a visually interesting and remarkably strong character. "Endurance is not just the ability to bear a hard thing, but to turn it into glory."

— WILLIAM BARCLAY

CHAPTER 8

THOUGHTS LEAD TO ACTION

"Happiness is when what we think, what we say, and what we do are in harmony."

— **MAHATMA GHANDHI**

The foundation of life is Free Will. We are free to choose. But let's understand that the things we Think, are reflected in the words we Say (even in self-talk) and impact the actions we Do. We must be extremely cautious with what we think because those thoughts will affect every part of our lives.

Let's not be out of control. Choose wisely what we think, say, and do. Be keenly aware of our thoughts especially. That is where we will be able to shift. If you are trying to break some habit, you will not be effective until modifying the way you think about it. Permanent change takes place at 'Think' not 'Do.'

Our emotions are not out of control feelings that just come over us. They are a result of what we choose to think. If we don't believe this, let's think now of some memories of a happy time. Remember the details. We will probably soon have a smile on our faces. Those thoughts make us feel happy. Often this process happens so quickly we are scarcely aware. Our thoughts come from our experiences, the words and ideas we have overheard or read, and situations we've seen around us. Our mind takes in information day after day and then we form thoughts, even some we may not consciously remember. The accumulation of all those thoughts is the basis for our thoughts of today.

We can misinterpret all the different data and base our thoughts on former input we misunderstood. As we experience more events, our thoughts can change, and we can interpret our lives more accurately. For example: As a little girl, I thought my grandmother and great-aunts were a very drab and sad bunch when they were young. Why? Because in all the old photos I saw of them, they wore dull, black, or gray clothing. I worried and wondered what was wrong. Later, my grandmother, who studied a picture, said, 'I remember loving that blue dress as a girl.' I stared at the image and for the first time, I realized the photographs were so old they were in black and white. I laughed at myself and felt relieved that they had pretty, colored dresses and were probably just fine.

It is important to be aware of our thoughts and challenge them. We can ask questions like: 'Is this completely true?' 'Why do I think that?' 'What meaning do I give it?' Or 'Is there another way to think about it?' This exercise ensures that unhealthy, habitual, or immature thoughts do not stay stuck in our heads.

We can choose not to be overwhelmed even when we have large obstacles or big upsets. Controlling our thoughts and resulting emotions can help us take a new look at a situation. We can actively seek opportunities in every situation to find good. For example: How could this help us develop into a better person or understand others with more compassion?

Let's see each obstacle as an opportunity to practice and perfect a certain virtue we aspire to such as: patience, courage, humility, resourcefulness, reason, justice, creativity, etc. Hurdles are so frequent; we will almost always be faced with how to deal. Do we let ourselves fall apart as we wallow in self-pity, or will we advance over them with healthy thoughts and a determined attitude? Then with each incident we become stronger, and we're blessed to overcome challenges that grow our character.

Do we believe that when we suffer a trial, it is somehow fantastically worse than when others face the same thing? Let's not excessively languish in becoming a tragic figure, playing it out like the forlorn heroine in a melodrama.

Sometimes people say, 'I can't snap out of it; I'm in a funk' or 'just so sad.' But we can choose to get out of it. There's a process. The first step is to think: I don't like what is happening. We can wonder, have others successfully endured this? If so, then, we can do it too. We are not a special case; it is not worse for us. Next, remember we are the Boss of Our Thinker. We can choose how we respond. And finally, decide what a healthier, more helpful thought, or word, or action would be instead. Be deliberate.

We may think our situation cannot be controlled with this process. Perhaps something has happened that we especially don't like or seems way too big, and we feel responding with anger, fear, unforgiveness, or self-pity is the only way to deal with it. Slow down. What are our options? For example, do we really think that in the long run, anger (or some other negative reaction) is going to make things better or worse? Take a deep breath. Read our Creed. Then move forward based on our ideal character and in a way that will be best.

Let's be keenly aware of our thoughts. If we lash out, that is self-sabotaging and is also destroying our peace. Self-destructive thoughts are not healthy. If we find ourselves reacting in negative, self-defeating ways, STOP, and ask ourselves this: How's that working for us? Where will this end?

Keep in mind that in the heat of a situation is the instant we should bring out pre-contemplated values and aspirations. An oft-recited Personal Creed comes in handy for this. If this is the first time we've thought about triggers and our reactions, we may have some regrets about how we handled it. It is important to spend moments each day considering who we are and how we want to be.

Some pre-planning and exploring how we want to live is a far better investment of our time than hours of playing on our phone, or the computer, or watching TV. This is why reading our Creed daily, or at least often, activates our mind to think good, positive, healthy thoughts that keep us on track. Then we will know the type of responses our better self would make ahead of the time we need them.

It may be difficult to think that we can really control our thoughts like that. Especially if we've lived a life where we're just very reactive to outside stimuli. But it is totally possible—and even necessary to live life intentionally. We can direct our mind. We can choose to stop thinking about something that is unhealthy and harming us or others and can begin to think about something that's going to make the situation better.

Obviously the more we think about this and the more we practice, the better we will get at it. We may believe our reactions are just what happens, that it's not a matter of thinking at all. If someone insults us, we automatically get mad. But in there, although it may be lightning fast, are many possible unhealthy thoughts: how dare they, oh this person is attacking me, this hurts my feelings, how will other people judge me? But if we've already decided that we're not going to be an offended person and we have practiced a healthy, belief-driven thought about it, and practiced it some more and thought about it some more, and prearranged a beneficial response instead, then we will find that those emotions we deemed automatic and out of our control are totally governable by our thoughts.

For example: we can train ourselves to react in a healthy way when someone insults us. We can ask ourselves, what has happened to them that they do this? Or we can decide not to be offended but respond with something positive and nice. We can think, is this true? Are they trying to hurt us? Why? Are they feeling insecure and mistakenly believe putting us down will raise them up? Or we can laugh and exclaim, 'Ouch, I think that hurt a bit. Did you mean to do it?' And, of course, there is my famous Momism:

"Be grateful it was done *to* you and not *by* you."

It's important to learn how to challenge our thoughts and replace them with healthier ones very quickly. For example, someone may say something like, 'Oh you're late—*again!*' with a slurring, demeaning emphasis on the word *again*. We may feel insulted. Perhaps we remember other times this person has been condescending to us. Maybe we *are* late a lot, and it bothers us so this voicing of criticism hurts a little more than we would like to admit. We may even feel like *anyone* would be insulted and offended by what this person has said. Or we remember a time *they* were late, and we didn't say anything but were inconvenienced, and it seems an unfair payback.

All these thoughts can flash through our minds very quickly. But we can take the fuse out of fiery thoughts and replace them with healthier ones, slowing down our reactions so we can really understand what we're thinking, and then, challenge that thinking when needed. Ask ourselves, 'Is this the way we want to be?' It can be very helpful; but of course, if we haven't written a Creed and we don't clearly know how we want to be, this will be more difficult.

We may even think *we can't help it.* But we can help it; we can decide the type of person we're going to be and stick with it. Being prepared for the situation if someone insults us can leave us feeling strong when we think: *I'm not going to let another person control my emotions.* We may say to ourselves, *In the past, I became quickly offended and angry when someone said something that I perceived as an insult. Not anymore.*

Is what was said true? Yep, we were late. Then OWN IT! We can ignore the slur and respond with a laugh and say, 'Oh, you are so right. I hope I didn't ruin your day.' And mean it. This honesty will make the rest of our day so much better. No need to stew about it or ruminate about a cutting, revengeful answer you could have given. By the way, those do not make us happy.

Emotional instability is not healthy. Try this experiment. If we want to be happy right now, what could we think about that would make us feel glad? If we want to be angry right now, what could we think about that would make us mad? If our thoughts can make us feel an emotion, we can also make ourselves NOT feel one. We can Be the Boss of Our Thinker! We control it. Now, it may not be easy to do at first; but it can be done. Just believing that gives us fabulous new power. And this is where Happily Ever After lives.

> *"Greatness is best measured by how well an individual responds to the happenings in life that appear totally unfair, unreasonable, and undeserved."*
> **— MARVIN J. ASHTON**

BEWARE!—Unhealthy Thoughts

We have a choice to think in a healthy way or we can certainly think in unhealthy ways. It is an option. Be keenly aware as we clearly identify unhealthy or negative attributes, motivations, words, actions, or feelings. Realize we can steer clear of them. They start with non-growth thoughts. Use these and you will shrink. Be aware of your thoughts and learn to mentally place your thoughts in one of two lists. 1. Healthy or 2. Unhealthy. If we are having unhealthy thoughts, saying unhealthy words, or engaging in unhealthy actions, we can strive to replace them with healthy ones. Change takes place in our thoughts long before we speak or act. We discussed these categories of thought earlier.

Unhealthy Thoughts

1. **We Are NOT the Boss of Our Thinker.** In this category we think we can't help the way we think about a situation, it's automatic.

2. **We Become Easily Offended or Angry.** This may lead to feelings of revenge, or we may lash out with ugly words, or even acts of aggression. Anger diminishes our ability to think.

3. **<u>We Think Life is Unfair.</u>** We may think everything is harder for us than for others. We have an unhealthy 'poor me, why me' outlook. A victim attitude.

4. **<u>We Engage in Extreme Thinking.</u>** We may think in an exaggerated manner as if something or someone is much worse than reality shows. We may see catastrophic calamities in relatively minor events. We may use words like always, never, everything, or nothing. If something goes wrong, we blow it up in our minds to 'everything goes wrong for me' or 'nothing ever works out for me' or 'she always (or never) does that' instead of being honest with ourselves.

5. **<u>We Don't Own it.</u>** We do not take responsibility for our thoughts, words, or actions but instead, we blame others, make excuses, or justify ourselves.

The following negative thoughts, words, phrases, or actions could be in each of the above categories. Plus, they could be in more than one.

Rude	Mean-spirited	Jealous
Raging	Fearful	Defensive
Bitter	Cheating	Arrogant
Angry	Lying	Contrary
Easily-offended	Victim mentality	Comparisons
Over-indulgent	Scarcity mentality	Sarcastic
Close-minded	Need to always get our way	
Blaming	Refuse to hear another opinion	
Stressed	Put ourselves or others down	
Why me, poor me	Justifying feeling victimized	
Martyr	Making excuses for bad behavior	
Unfair	Playing the part of a drama queen or king	

(Mark wants me to add 'Sourpuss,' 'Grumpy,' and 'Stick in the Mud')

<u>Be vigilant against these defeating choices listed above. Unhealthy thoughts will cause unhealthy and uncomfortable emotions or feelings, and usually lead to unkind words and regrettable actions.</u>

Healthy Thoughts

Below are growth options. Be keenly aware of them. Incorporate these courageous, positive, effective, and powerful Thoughts, Words, and Actions into your Creed and Life. Using this list as a foundation for our day will uplift, strengthen, and boldly make us a better, stronger person.

We also categorized our Healthy Thoughts into 5 main areas.

1. **Be the Boss of Our Thinker.** Take responsibility for all thoughts. Focus on our part in the experience because that is where you can make changes for the better. This will help us live life fully.

2. **Be Honest _and_ Kind.** Keep in mind, most things are opinions, allow others to have their own opinions without becoming offended or argumentative. Be honest, you can't really believe your own lies anyway. Dishonesty leads to more unhealthy thoughts.

3. **Find the Good.** Practice the skill of being positive. Look for good in every situation, even if there are also bad parts. Maybe it will only be the opportunity to grow or learn from a bad example. The Scarcity Mentality falsely tells us about limits and makes us worry that someone is getting a bigger piece of the pie or even that we will not get a piece at all. The Abundance Mentality teaches that life is like a kitchen where we can make unlimited pies.

4. **Explore Options**. When challenges come, don't give up. Arm ourselves with as many options as we can. This will empower us to feel hope. Let's not get locked into black and white thinking, panicking because we feel we don't have any choices,

or that we must choose between one extreme or the other.

5. **Gratitude.** Even on the darkest days there is still some light, though it may seem dim. Be grateful for even the smallest blessing.

The following positive and Healthy Thoughts, words or phrases, or actions could be in each category. Plus, they could be in more than one. Let's intentionally incorporate these uplifting characteristics listed below. Healthy Thoughts will lead to Healthy and upbeat emotions or feelings and usually cause us to be kind and honest in our self–analysis and the way we treat others. Healthy Thoughts lead to Healthy Actions.

Responsible	Disciplined	Resilient
Accepting	Hopeful	Empathetic
Peaceful	Loving	Learning
Growing	Improvement	Boldness
Energetic	Service	Happy
Goal-oriented	Enthusiastic	Giving
Courageous	Kind	Honest
Understanding	Compassionate	Strong
Open-minded	Aware	Cheerful
Grateful	Caring	Helpful

(Now, Mark wants me to add 'Sparky' and 'Cyclist' and 'Howling Funny' which could be used to describe him.)

Memorize and practice these attributes listed. Be coura-geous and deliberate about making these more of an auto-matic response.

We can become familiar and internalize these two lists and think carefully about the ramifications. Where are our strengths? In which areas may we feel weak? Let's be keenly aware of our thoughts, speech, and actions.

Let's keep these two lists in our mind. Maybe print them and tape them to our fridge. Being acutely aware of our thoughts puts us in control. Otherwise, a thought comes into our minds without us really being firmly conscious of it happening. In other words, We Are *Not* the Boss of Our Thinker. We're Out of Control. We are not attentive or mindful. We are engaging in stinkin' thinkin.' Don't forget, the way we think is our choice. We can practice analyzing our thoughts and then mentally placing them on either the healthy or unhealthy lists.

Likewise, unhealthy thoughts often create a bunch of match-ing thoughts, words, and deeds. Be vigilant in recogniz-ing how we categorize our thoughts. Are they negative or unhealthy or are they positive, healthy, and uplifting? Remember it is our decision.

When we categorize a thought, word, or behavior in our mind and know which list it comes from, even if it is from the nega-tive list, that's great. We've taken the first step to eliminate negative or unhealthy thoughts from our life just by recog-nizing it. Step two is to replace it with a healthy thought.

<u>ARC</u>

- Be **<u>Aware</u>** of our thoughts.
- **<u>Recognize</u>** with absolute truth if the thinking is healthy or unhealthy.
- **<u>Change</u>** any unhealthy thoughts to a healthy one.

Remember **ARC**. Aware, Recognize. Change.

Once our thoughts become good, positive, and healthy, our words and actions will automatically follow suit.

"If we can't find kindness, be kindness."
— **M. S. STARK**

Exercise, especially outdoors, keeps blood and oxygen flowing through our brain, and when we combine working out with restorative sleep and healthy foods, that vital combination is foundational for healthy, clear thoughts.

Gateway to Narnia

We think these arched trees look like an entrance into a lovely, magical world. But we can't escape the reality of mortality. Fortunately, the inevitable adverse conditions we experience may provide learning opportunities. "When you lose, don't lose the lesson."

— DALAI LAMA

CHAPTER 9
THINK

Since our thoughts are the wellspring from which flow our words and actions, let's take a closer look at our vital thought process.

Thoughts are extremely powerful. The more we realize how powerful they are, the more powerful *we* become. And we are the Boss of that power. We can change our thoughts. In an instant even. Knowing and believing that idea can make our life how we dreamed it would be, even with trials and challenges.

> *"The way we think will influence our life more than anything that happens to us."*
> **— M. S. STARK**

Sometimes our thoughts are untrue, mistaken, or not healthy, and can be influenced by past, or current, or even future fear, anxiety, self-doubt, worry, or other insecurities. However, with awareness, we can challenge our thoughts.

For example, we may walk into a room full of people at a business meet-and-greet event. We don't know anyone there and we feel a bit nervous. A woman looks over and then frowns and turns away. We may think *this is going to be awful. Why did she frown at me?* We may even look down at our clothing wondering if it is too casual for this gathering. Several quick, unhealthy thoughts can create damaging emotions, and we want to bolt. What we see is correct, but how we choose to think about it, or interpret it, can be inaccurate.

We could ask: What do we think hurt us? What is the meaning we are assigning to what is happening? Can we see that we are making assumptions and adding our own ideas about what is truly going on? This means we have changed the truth, but only in our minds. Is our skewed way of thinking about it negative?

We can Be the Boss of Our Thinker and challenge the negative thoughts. Is it true that she directed her frown at *us*? Could her expression be because she expected a friend, looked up, saw us, and frowned simply because it was not who she hoped to see? We can glance around and realize our attire is fine and stop worrying about it. Be flexible, it's not as if we can do anything about our clothing now anyway. We can quit thinking about ourselves period and look for someone that is standing alone and focus on getting to know them. After all, isn't that the purpose of the gathering?

When we analyze our thoughts, we can ask questions. Most importantly, decide 'Is that absolutely true?' Let's strongly resist mind-reading, jumping to unjustified conclusions, or making baseless assumptions. The potential for a mistake is far too high.

In the business event example, we likely wish to appear and feel confident and friendly. Imagining that a disturbing facial expression is meant for us will likely make confidence more difficult and hinder us from being friendly, and hence unsuccessful in making new contacts. Does that unhealthy thinking make things better or worse? The answer is obvious.

Let's say she *was* frowning at us. What would a healthy reaction be? Frame a positive option in our minds. Maybe she recognizes us as a formidable competitor, and she is worried about possible future business contacts who may meet us. Let's remind ourselves that we do not know what others think. We are *not* mind readers. Remember, we can't control others' thoughts or guess them, so try not to even go there. Not only is it useless, but it is most often incorrect.

In many situations, there are a large variety of ways to think about it. Let's direct our thinking to positive, uplifting, beneficial thoughts. Let's not worry about what others may do; focus on what we will do. That is where our power is.

Let's plan to intentionally rev ourselves up on our way to the meeting with thoughts that build confidence. Decide to focus on others and banish any thoughts that will make the event nerve-wracking. Trade them for positive self-talk like practicing our elevator pitch or thinking of questions to ask in pursuit of getting to know people so the event will be a success for us.

The exercise of being aware and analyzing our thoughts as a practical observer intent on our best interest is vital. See ourselves as the Boss of Our Thinker, not merely a person at the mercy of wild, random thoughts flitting through the air and dive-bombing into our head.

Another tactic to get through a potentially stressful assignment is to make it a game. As soon as our thoughts improve, the stress dissolves. Instead of being fearful or nervous, tackle it with a whole new attitude.

For example, when my son, Josh, worked door-to-door sales, he had a lot of slammed doors and some very rude people, which made it discouraging. Then he chose a better way of thinking about it. He made a game of it.

He challenged the other salesmen on his team to see who could have the most slammed doors or the most people swearing at them. Of course, they were not to do anything to encourage it. But suddenly, they felt they had scored 'points' when a door slammed shut instead of taking it personally and feeling discouraged, angry, or even overwhelmed. That made knocking on the next one easy.

If they met with a bad reaction, they scored points and had a funny story to tell the others later. But if they garnered a good reaction, they made a sale. It had become a win–win no matter what. Our mindset makes all the difference.

> *"The happiness of our life depends upon the quality of our thoughts."*
> **— MARCUS AURELIUS**

There are consequences to the thoughts we choose. Our thoughts can make things better or worse. It matters how we think about things. For example: we can be driving along, and another driver cuts us off. Now we have a choice. We can either let this experience ruin our day and we can ruminate, get angry and frustrated, feel victimized by what this other person did, or we can choose to think differently.

I like to think that maybe that guy was on the way to the hospital to see his mother who is seriously ill, and he wants to be there in time before she dies. And then I find that I feel compassion for this person who's in such a hurry and I'm hoping he can safely go fast enough to get there in time. Now I doubt his mother is really in the hospital. Maybe he's late for an appointment, maybe an important job interview and something happened and caused him to be delayed.

Maybe he doesn't have a good reason. Maybe he's driving fast because he likes to drive fast and thoughtlessly weave in and out of traffic. It doesn't matter to me. We could think this isn't safe, he could cause an accident. But an accident hasn't occurred (no point worrying about unreal situations). Also, is there anything you can do about that? I don't know what the cause is, and I probably never will, so I can choose to think of it in a more benevolent manner that doesn't upset me and lets me easily and quickly drop the whole matter out of my mind.

Or, I can continue to ruminate and get angry and frustrated, or even infect others by telling them about this awful person and how he cut me off and how wrong that was. They could go home and kick the dog. And there's a little bit of a 'poor me, why me' attitude in there, that we know is never healthy. See, we can make the exact same situation either an okay one, or even a compassionate experience, OR we can make it one that leaves our blood boiling for the rest of the day. Which do we think is healthier for us?

Mark has a great story about having the right equipment. The best piece of equipment we own for all the storms in our lives is our Thinker.

Mark Shares a Story of Upgrading Our Equipment:

On a hike with Austin, my youngest son, when he was thirteen years old, we were in the Rocky Mountains near Field, British Columbia. We arrived at a location called the Burgess Shales that overlooks the beautiful, deep-green, Emerald Lake and the President Range, an absolutely gorgeous place. At Burgess Shales, we were searching for the world-renowned small fossils found there. It is a popular hiking area and as we were looking, a couple walked up, and we had a conversation with them.

We discovered they were from Quebec which I had already guessed since they spoke with strong French-Canadian accents. They explained that they had put all their treasures in storage and sold everything else and were hiking all the Rocky Mountain trails they could in six months. I asked when they had started and learned they began in May. I shuddered a little bit internally thinking, *oh man, the Rocky Mountains in May is very unpredictable as far as weather goes.*

I asked, "Where were you for the May Long Weekend?" which is a Canadian holiday at the end of May, and they said they were in Waterton in southern Alberta. I remembered that on the May Long Weekend that area got about five feet of snow. Knowing that, I gasped. "Oh no! You were in Waterton! Oh, my goodness, you've seen your share of bad weather!"

The man said, "There's no such thing as bad weather; only bad equipment."

Joking and being kind of flippant, I asked, "Oh that's an interesting way to think about it. How was your equipment?"

He looked me straight in the eye and said, "We needed an upgrade."

I laughed because I knew that was code for 'We were miserably cold, wet, and uncomfortable.' I didn't think much of that until we were driving home a few days later. I pondered the statement 'No such thing as bad weather; only bad equipment.' What a profound mindset.

For example, if we have an outdated computer and it doesn't work the way we want, then we upgrade. We should do the same with our attitude and thought quality—improve the equipment. If we're not managing well, if we fall apart easily, or have stinkin' thinkin'—then change. The equipment is our minds, our attitudes, and our preparations for life. We need to upgrade it by looking at things in a healthy way.

We can avoid unhealthy reactions like self–pity, anger, depression, blame, despair, sadness, anxiety, hopelessness, lashing out, revenge, betrayal, gloom, or giving up. Don't indulge in something on this list or anything close to it!

It's easier to *prevent* meltdowns and feelings of being over–whelmed than to deal with it after it happens, so the answer is to think ahead of potential situations of what we could do so we become stronger. The way we face obstacles and challenges makes us Better or Bitter. We can't always choose what happens to us, but we can always choose our response.

> *"It is better to Prepare and Prevent*
> *than it is to Repair and Repent!"*
> **— EZRA TAFT BENSON**

Change Begins with Our Thoughts

We cannot permanently change behavior by working on what we *do*. We must change at the point of our thoughts. Mark worked with a friend for many years who smoked a lot. And then he decided to quit, and he did. For a day or two. Then he decided to quit again. And he did. For a few days. This went on for many years. He was a world-class quitter—as well as a world-class starter-upper.

Much later, he went to see the doctor who told him if he did not stop smoking, his condition would be irreversible in six months. This gave him cause to radically change his thinking and consequently when he stopped working on his behavior of smoking, but instead began to think about it as an eventual death sentence, he could finally quit. And he did. For good.

> *"Thinking is where we change, but then we need to add the Vision to see where we want to go, have the Passion to get there, and the Discipline to do what's necessary to succeed."*
> **—M. S. STARK**

We can expect that there will be pain and suffering, challenges, illness, loss, and many trials in our lives. We have a choice. We can drown in self-pity, asking 'why me, poor me.' That attitude shrinks us. Or, we can decide to have gratitude for the good things in our lives in the midst of trials. We can even look at ways we can learn and think about the situation differently, see people in a new, more compassionate way, and understand those who are struggling with difficulties. Everyone is having trials.

We can grow stronger to overcome troubles if we have gratitude for all the many things that are good in our lives. No matter what bad events are happening, there are lots of good experiences for growth.

Remember, 'Why me, poor me,' that's when we shrink. Gratitude, during trials, equals growth.

There is a story about a man who accidentally locks himself in the freezer car of a train. It's the end of the day, and he realizes he could die from the cold before anyone comes to open the door. He sits there shivering, obsessing about his desperate situation and finally passes out. The next morning his body is found. An autopsy determines that he froze to death, which confounds everybody. The car's refrigeration system wasn't turned on. The temperature never fell below sixty-one degrees.

Who's the Boss?

Our thoughts are powerful, but also under our control. This is a very important concept to totally accept and learn because there are so many voices in this world trying to make us believe that we're not in control of our thoughts, that they sort of come and we're at the mercy of them. This is not true. There's not a TV channel in our head and it's stuck and we can't turn it to another station or turn it off. We don't have to accept whatever little thoughts are flitting through our heads. All those thoughts come from us.

They may originate with something we've seen, or read, or something that reminds us of another experience we've had or maybe that happened to a friend, and we transferred that expectation onto ourselves. The incident that laid the foundation for this thought can be so old, we may have forgotten about it. The more we analyze our thoughts and are simply aware of what they are, the easier it is to take a more active Boss role.

Let's be intentional thinkers. We can make sure our thoughts are positive, uplifting, encouraging, and compassionate towards us and others. We create the content of our thoughts. We simply need to be *aware* of what they are so when our mind starts to go off all crazy, we can ask ourselves, 'Is this the way I want to think?' If it isn't, simply STOP IT! and think the way we intend. Think the way that will make our life happier.

I've heard people say, 'I can't help what I think.' Wrong. We can and must. I do it all the time, and it takes focus and practice, and it takes deliberateness, and most of all it takes the belief that we truly can control our thoughts. We are The Boss of Our Thinker.

Sometimes when we're in an argument, we may think this is going to be a win-lose proposition. Well, a nice way to end that kind of situation, and make life pleasant, exists.

Don't believe everything we think or feel. We can choose to think, *I'm mad and I can't help it! I don't see how else I can respond to this situation except being mad about it. In fact, anyone would be mad about this situation so the feelings I'm having are normal and correct.*

OR, perhaps in our Creed we have decided to control our temper and not get mad or offended. We have decided to forgo taking offense. Because we have decided not to get mad, we don't care if Most People get mad about it. We are not Most People. We can choose to calmly listen, explain, explore, and make it a win-win conversation.

I Bet $1000 You Can't Make Me Angry

This is a story of our friend, Hugh Vance from many years ago when $1000 represented real money. He made an earnest, public commitment to *never* lose his temper again and decided to put his money where his mouth was. If someone could make him angry and take away his control, he would give them a $1000 bill, which he always carried with him.

Hugh excelled at being The Boss of His Thinker—until a few years after he made his commitment. Someone cut him off in traffic and he got angry. He realized what he had done and followed the guy and motioned for him to pull over. The gentleman got ready for a confrontation. Hugh calmly explained that over the past many years he had decided to pay somebody $1000 if they could make him angry. Handing over the large bill, he said, "You did it, and I commit further to never get angry at anyone or any circumstance ever again. This is the last time." And he Lived Happily Ever After.

"Whatever begins in anger, ends in shame."
— BENJAMIN FRANKLIN

We must decide to control our temper no matter what. We can also choose to not be intimidated by a difference of opinion. Let's remind ourselves that we are dealing with opinions, not facts. Instead, we can be curious and not upset about another person's ideas.

The interesting thing is, no matter what we think or feel, we—and we alone—have the power to alter it dramatically, to maybe switch to the very opposite feeling we had to begin with. We can look and see if we own any of the situation, and often we do. When there are two opinions it can still be a win-win when we're The Boss.

The Wildest Ride, A Make-Believe Story

Imagine we're going to The Most Wonderful Amusement Park in the Universe. We can only go once; and for just one day. It's truly the trip of a lifetime. We meticulously plan, alone and with our friends, a few of whom will go with us. We've heard lots about this amusement park for so long, that we wonder if it could all be true.

As the day gets closer, we become more excited about all the adventures we'll find there. Thrilling rides that will tilt, twist, and flip as our hearts soar, our veins race, and our stomachs turn. As we talk to others about going, we hear more stories from those who've gone before. They tell us about the wildest rides: Libra, an enormous seesaw that teeters up and down in a delicate balance that toggles faster and faster until it seems to spin out of control as it rises to a dizzying height.

And Sagittarius, where we are harnessed into a bungee cord and shot like a giant arrow across a small lake. Oh, and Wild Leo where we zipline through a jungle obstacle course. We shudder at the rumors of real lions that could tear us to pieces. That couldn't be true, could it?

The more we talk to those who have been, the more excited we become about the different rides. We don't fully under-stand, but their sketchy descriptions sound fantastic. Though not out loud, we admit to ourselves that some seem a little bit scary. Others sound *a lot* scary. We worry, will we be brave enough? Will we be strong enough? Will we be able to persevere?

We cringe at the thought that we might be standing in line and then, when it's finally our turn, chickening out and running back through the crowd, head hung down. We vow we will not just ride, but we will ride with honor, and bravely enjoy every moment—even the biggest bumps and the sharpest drops.

Finally, the day comes, and we shout for joy. The Most Wonderful Amusement Park in the Universe is everything we thought it would be and more. A grand and glorious place with bright lights and various sounds and lovely smells and tastes. We can hear screams of delight—at least we hope those are happy noises.

We searched all over the park for Pisces, that's the ride we were urged to do before leaving. We decided it's a great place to start. What fun! It proved a bit scary, but so worth it in the end.

And of course, the adventure wouldn't be complete without Aquarius. Lots of water splashing as we climb up, up, up. Our stomach flips as we plummet, and we grip the hand bar. Just as we fear we're going to crash on the rocks below, the attraction zips to the right and a fountain drenches us! We laugh like crazy!

Gemini is a dual ride. Everything we do seems to happen twice. We spin wildly, and then before the spin is finished; we spin around again even faster. We go down, down, and then when we think we've almost reached the bottom we stop—only to drop again. Wow!

We spend our rushed day racing from one ride to the next. Knowing the time is short, we hesitate to sit down for lunch, so we eat standing in a line to Virgo. We see many people sitting on nice benches in shaded areas, hypnotically staring at a small device in their hands. We're puzzled at their lackadaisical attitude.

But after a glance at our watch, we decided we'd rest when we got back home. There's so much we want to experience!

Some rides truly test our courage to the very max. We're terrified, but we do them anyway. We discover after conquering other adventurous rides; we've become quite a bit braver. We amazed our friends when we even took the Scorpio—the fastest ride in the park—with both hands waving high in the air.

Several times as we race around the park, we pass the merry-go-round. It's beautiful no doubt, but it seems a little slow; maybe not quite what we had in mind. Should we take a quick ride? We only have one day. We want to make sure to have time to do all the things that we dreamed about. Finally, towards the end of the day, our checklist nearly completed, we find the prettiest carousel horse. It's lovely; the music, the lights…. But maybe a little dull. The other rides, though they tested us, made us feel truly alive. When we get back, we'll be able to say we took an amazing trip. Every part of it.

As closing time approaches, we see a ride we didn't think we wanted to try at all. It's Cancer. We approach it carefully with a great deal of apprehension. Before, we'd heard others who had already been here talk about it, but now we realize that often they stopped talking and waited until we passed by to continue.

Those who rode Cancer often grouped together. They seemed to stand a little taller and shone a little brighter. It left us with a tingly curiosity and a strange… Hmmm… It felt like fear. Maybe we could skip this one, but would we regret not taking the chance and everything that comes with it? Would we be left wondering what it would have been like or more importantly, what *we* would be like?

Taking a good look at the ride itself, it contradicts the rules of gravity. We see people tossed into the air and falling *up* before they disappear into yet another tunnel. The ride seems to be exceptionally long, and many parts are hidden from view. Peering at the anxious faces waiting in line, there's a hush over the crowd as they get closer to their turn.

Maintaining some distance, we view the expressions of those coming off, looking pale and drawn, and with a peculiar, but wise look in their eyes. We shrink back and clutch at our pounding heart. We remember our pre-visit vow to take advantage of all we can on this grand adventure. So, we take a deep breath and step in line. It makes us nervous to see a few tremble as they get out of line and pass by us with a look of dread in their eyes.

It's finally our turn; our last ride. We climb into a small train, and it chugs slowly into a gloomy, dark tunnel. When we emerge, we realize the other riders have split into different directions and we are alone. Our car lunges forward, careening towards a brick wall, and we fear the ride must be broken. But at the last possible second, we veer to the left. We jet into a dizzying series of spins; with such sudden drops we fear our stomach is going to empty. With intermittent spins, turns, and plunges into a terrifying blackness, it is impossible to predict what will happen next.

Then beyond anything we thought possible, the ride speeds up as complete darkness consumes us. We scream, "No, no, no! Stop the ride, I want off!" But we are isolated. Within seconds we are completely lost; we can't tell if we're up or down. Terror grips us. Miraculously, we think we feel a gentle hand on our shoulder. It's only for a mere moment, or did we imagine it?

Then we are tumbling around and around, wildly zipping down and down, and blacker and blacker…

Arriving back home, our friends and family anxiously greet us. Those who have already been to The Most Wonderful Amusement Park in the Universe excitedly pepper us with questions. 'Did you go on Aquarius? Did you get wet?'

We squeal, 'We got soaked!' We hear many people yell, 'Me too!' and we are instantly better friends. High-fives and a few knuckles.

Pisces? What about Gemini? With each question, we proudly and excitedly answer an enthusiastic "Yes!" Much laughter all around and nods of understanding. There is a deep and unexplainable bond. Future travelers beam at each other, caught up in the exhilaration, but they hang back a little, their countenances filled with curiosity.

And then a soft voice from the back of the crowd. 'And Cancer? Did you do Cancer?' Solemnity overpowers excitement and we calmly reply, "Yes. Oh, yes." And the voice gains strength and laughs, "Me too! Twice." And suddenly, there are cheers and hugs and more high-fives. We're so glad we went and thrilled we did everything, even the wild rides we didn't think we could do.

Then we hear a timid voice. 'I went, but I only wanted to do the merry-go-round. The other rides, well, they seemed a bit much. I'm kinda' afraid of heights. I decided ahead of time that I could always watch others doing them; it'll be almost the same.'

With a tinge of pity we think, *no, it wouldn't even be close.* We turn back to the shiny faces surrounding us and exchange knowing glances with the sparkly ones—our co-adventurers.

We feel quite differently than when we entered the park, and it seems we have new eyes to see. So many memories, people, and experiences buzz through our minds. It was all so worth it!

We bask in the wonderfulness of now being cheered, praised, and admired by others. And we have a deep admiration for those brave souls who feel so close to us now. The courage and strength to do all the rides have allowed us to join an exclusive group where we feel very comfortable.

Before we went, we had always hoped we could do it all with courage and satisfaction, but it's wonderful now that we really know what we're capable of accomplishing. We've learned we can do *hard* things.

Story Disclaimer: As with any allegory, the challenges referred to here can be transposed to include any major life trials. Mark and I both lost our previous spouses to cancer, and we are certainly aware of the high numbers of people who are impacted by it. But we also understand the variety of difficult troubles faced, some not related to any disease.

"Happiness does not depend on what we have or who we are. It solely relies on what we think."

— **BUDDHA**

Let's question our thoughts, impulses, and feelings, are they true? Do they make the situation better or worse? What can we learn from them? A bad experience can lead us down a different path. Our thoughts decide if the new path is awful or great.

Let's say we are driving down the road and there's an accident because there's a large pothole. We can continue forward and be angry and upset and hit the pothole too and make it worse or we can alter our route for a better outcome. Why do we resist alteration and allow a negative thought to keep us moving farther down the wrong way?

When things happen and we manage to escape negative thoughts and learn the lesson, remember:

"When we lose, don't lose the lesson."

— **DALIA LAMA**

Unhealthy or Negative Thoughts

Constantly evaluate: are our thoughts Healthy or Unhealthy? Don't resort to anything on the **Negative list** such as:

- Cutting someone down
- Gossip
- Anger
- Whining
- Feeling self-defeated

- I can't do it.
- Life is hard.
- This kind of garbage always happens to me.
- She/He knows how much I wanted this.
- I never get a break.
- This is the worst thing ever!
- I've never been so mad.

"I changed my thinking and that changed my life."
— M. S. STARK

Mark's Story of Autopilot

Our friends, Ryan and Shauna arranged for a trip in late February 2011. As we boarded Ryan's private jet, one of the pilots pulled me aside and asked if I wanted to sit in the 'jump seat' during takeoff. To me, this was a no-brainer. "Absolutely" I answered. They pulled out a fold-down seat and handed me a headset with instructions to be silent from taxi and take-off to clearing Calgary tower airspace, which would be about fifteen to twenty minutes.

When the time came, Chris, the pilot said, "Any questions, Mark?" I began to ask about the dials, instruments, and vast array of cabin equipment. One, large gauge had numbers that were consistently changing. I asked, "What is that?"

The response was, "Oh, that is the autopilot."

"Why are the numbers always changing?"

"Because, as we fly our trajectory is always being influenced by changing winds, barometric pressure, temperature changes, and so on, so to keep us at altitude and on course, the autopilot is constantly making minute changes."

That's a good metaphor for life. We are frequently off-course (unhealthy thinking), however with the aid of an autopilot (our healthy Self-Talk) we make corrections and do our best to stay on track. It's interesting that if we remained off-course over time, our destination would be different. A one-degree change, not one percent, but one degree—that is one in three hundred and sixty—will, over time, take us to a totally unwanted destination.

Sometimes we need to initiate a change in our lives. It's encouraging to me that making major shifts is not always necessary, because small ones, over time will deliver our preferred outcome. For example, inner-city Miami has a significant criminal element and is a potentially difficult and dangerous place. A *few* miles from Miami is an Island called Fischer Island, it's one of the wealthiest zip codes in the USA, and crime is minimal. It's a wonderfully safe and beautiful place to live.

Small modifications in trajectory can make a significant difference in our result. Sometimes we are hard on ourselves when we realize our path is not favorable. It's encouraging to know that all it will take are small adjustments. Or perhaps we *are* on the right flight path, we have simply encountered turbulence that requires us to buckle up and keep going.

The moral of the story: Honest self-reflection is crucial to determining the difference between 'time for a correction' or 'stay the course.'

One thing is certain, self-berating is destructive. There is no value in negative and critical self-talk. Too many have been derailed by this type of self-sabotage. Don't do it. It's like Chasing Bears, and that is a bad idea we will talk about later.

We *are* the Boss

We are not at the mercy of rogue feelings, thoughts, or emotions. Some say that we can't control them; all we can do is absorb them, but it's not true. Where do we think they come from? They don't flit around in the air and suddenly swoop in one ear and lodge in our brain. Remember, we create our thoughts, from past experiences, things we've seen, read, or may have heard people say, but we create them.

Sometimes a thought flicks to a feeling, to an emotion, to words, or deeds. It happens so quickly that we may not recognize that there was an initial thought.

The great thing is we have control over it. For example, if we think someone doesn't like us, we can challenge that thought by asking, 'Is that true? Has that person said or done anything to confirm they don't like us, or have we misinterpreted something?' We can take it a step further and say, 'We don't know if that's true, but even if it is, it's not something we need to worry about. We can't control what other people think, say, or do, only those things that *we* think, say, or do. It's also okay if someone doesn't like us. We must do things so we will like ourselves which happens when our values and actions coincide with our Personal Creed.

Perhaps someone might be tired and looks our way and thinks, 'Oh shoot, I forgot to get the chicken out to defrost' and so they have a look of concern or worry flit across their facial features, but we think it's about us. Most of the time people are not thinking about us, they're thinking about themselves. So don't allow a frown, because somebody forgot something, make us think they don't like us. It's probably not true. We shouldn't try to be mind-readers. We are generally dismal at it.

Thoughts do lead to actions but there is a moment, thank goodness, where we can choose. For example, if someone throws a ball at us, we think to put our hands up to shield our face. Yes, we thought to do it. But it seems to happen automatically. Many years ago, when we were quite young, someone threw a ball and we didn't know to put our hands up yet, so the ball hit us in the face. Soon we learned to think in a new way. Now that thought leads to action so quickly, we don't notice the preemptive, conditioned thought.

We can go through life thinking that life is an adventure, or we can think that life is plum awful. We can find justification for either thought. But which one do we think will make our life more enjoyable?

> *"We are the creatures of our thinking. We can talk ourselves into defeat or we can talk ourselves into victory. Look for the good and build on it. Don't be a 'pickle sucker.'"*
> — **GORDAN B. HINCKLEY**

We need to be aware of all-or-nothing thinking. A bad moment does not equal a bad day and a bad day does not mean a bad life. When we have something unpleasant happen to us, we should not indulge in dialogue like 'Nothing ever works out for me, or rotten things happen to me all the time.'

Let's look at that kind of thinking. First, the idea that nothing *ever* works out for us is simply not true. The belief that awful things happen to us *all* the time, again, is simply not true. Black–and–white thinking can get us into trouble because when we tell ourselves false and extreme stories, we may start to believe them. Consider what type of life that could create.

> *"Looking at the dark side of things always leads to a spirit of pessimism which often leads to defeat."*
> — **GORDAN B. HINCKLEY**

It is delightful to Be the Boss of Our Thinker. No one else can take that job, just us. We decide what to think and at any point, we can stop and say, 'This isn't making things better, this isn't making me happy, we choose to not think like this anymore. We want to think in a healthier way.'

Now it's very difficult to make a thought simply vanish leaving a gaping hole in our mind. It's much easier to replace it with a better thought. A quick and easy idea is to think about something we're grateful for. Oh, there is so much! We can also have in our heads a few very pleasant memories to fill that gap in our minds. Those thoughts will make us feel happier and remind us that we can Be the Boss of Our Thinker. Don't believe that we cannot control the thoughts in our heads because we can. Remember also that our thoughts are not permanent, or set, so we must stay aware. We can always challenge them, but it takes practice like any other skill.

Truth and Honesty

Just because we think it, doesn't make it true.

Once we went camping when my children were little. We drove far away from the city, and we set up camp on a lake on a beautiful evening. We had so much fun. Of course, we had the campfire, the hot dogs, and s'mores but soon it came time to retire. Before we went to bed, we noticed that the sky looked a little darker than usual, maybe more clouds than normal. But it seemed a nice evening.

Now I'm not someone who listens to the radio or watches television, so I rarely had any idea what the weather would be. I dealt with whatever happened. However, this time it probably would have been good to have checked before we went camping, after all, we were in Oklahoma, a tornado area (blatant foreshadowing). We put the fire out and climbed into our different tents, the older children were in one and the younger children were in with us.

We could hear the kids talking and after a while they got quiet; we realized they had fallen asleep. We started to join them in dreamland and as usual, my husband dozed off before I did. I could tell that the breeze had picked up and soon it became quite blustery, and rain began to fall. After a while, I heard the wind howling and then I could hear something that sounded like a train.

Strange. We were out on a peninsula by a lake and there were no tracks nearby. But I could definitely hear the roar of a train that seemed to be coming closer and closer. Suddenly the rain stopped, and the fierce wind yanked at our tents as stakes were pulled out of the ground. We were both wide awake now and we jumped up realizing that the sound was a tornado.

We fought our way out of the wildly shaking shelter, each with a kid tucked under one arm, trying to get to the older boys as the roar grew louder. As we stepped out, the wind whipped the tent away and we were quite alarmed.

In mere moments, the gusts accelerated to a point that I could barely walk forward, and we realized that the tornado spun nearby. The oldest two were peering out the door of their tent and we took their hands and dragged them out into the squall. We fought our way towards where we parked the truck but had to battle the wind to move ahead. We watched some of our stuff flying in the air and not too far from us, we saw the tornado roar past. We finally managed to get to our vehicle as things swirled around us.

The silence descended upon us with an eerie calm. The rain started up again and we were quickly soaked. Leaving the wet and shivering kids in our truck, we went back to gather our belongings, at least what was left of them. The tents were gone but we found them blown against some trees with sleeping bags still inside. Clothing and camp chairs were scattered around the site and some things were never found. We dragged everything back and threw it all on the floor in the back seat deciding we'd figure it out when we got home.

We were all drenched and cold and had gone through a very harrowing experience. We didn't talk much as we drove to our house, about an hour and a half away. Soon I heard the two oldest boys, about ten and seven years old, whispering to each other. I heard the younger one say in a quiet voice, "Don't tell Mom." Well of course that got my attention. Then the older boy murmured, "But what if she finds it; she's gonna' be really mad."

Now they had to come clean. I asked them what they were talking about. I received the normal kid answer, "Nothing."

"Boys!" I said in a no-nonsense voice. Soon, Zach hesitantly confessed that Josh had caught a tarantula. Of course, with my nature-loving son this didn't seem unusual, but since we were leaving the campground, I didn't see its relevance and I had no intention of going back for it.

"Well," Josh added tentatively, "I put it in a jar in our tent." We had grabbed that up; it had collapsed and was all wet, but it was now on the floor behind the front seats.

My next question was important. "It had a lid on it, right?" The long moment of silence supplied the answer I needed. Because I had seen the tarantula earlier, I remembered it as being very large, and fear churned in my stomach knowing that hairy beast shared the truck with us. Maybe still in the jar, feasibly inside the tent, but there lurked that unnerving possibility that it was not.

I pulled my legs up onto the seat and curled myself into the smallest ball that I could but every few minutes I could kind of feel something furry on my leg, or my shoulder, or my arm, or my head, and I would quickly gasp and shudder and try to flick it away, but nothing was there. I spent a very long trip thinking I could feel that giant arachnid crawling on me.

When we arrived home in the middle of the night, we found the jar in the tent, but it had filled with water, and the spider had died. The whole trip I felt quite sure I could feel its hairy legs on me. Thinking that it roamed loose in the truck certainly controlled my thoughts. Sometimes we can think or feel things, but it doesn't make them true.

"Self-awareness is our capacity to stand apart from ourselves and examine our thinking, our motives, our history, our scripts, our actions, and our habits and tendencies."
— **STEPHEN R. COVEY**

Is it true? That's a great question to ask ourselves when we are the Boss of Our Thinker. We must be brutally honest, especially with ourselves. Statements like "The whole world is against me" are simply not true. How difficult would that idea be to live with? The whole world isn't even aware we exist. Catastrophizing is self-defeating. Let's not indulge in any type of dishonest thinking.

We may think, oh, we know the *whole* world really isn't against us, but we feel like a lot of things are piling up in opposition to us. Well, then say *that*. Even if we know it is not true but simply an exaggeration made for emphasis, let's train ourselves not to misrepresent a situation. Because our mind and body hear our declarations and may believe them. Let's always be scrupulously honest with ourselves.

Besides, that exaggeration will make us feel worse. And remember, we want to feel better. Let's say things to ourselves that are true and encouraging. If we find ourselves saying falsehoods, STOP! Stop immediately. Don't indulge in self-pity. Be aware of your language and challenge it. We can restate it using a revised, positive, honest statement.

Refrain from lies like these:	Instead, Be Honest and positive, like this:

I've lost everything.

> This is a big loss, but I can count the many blessings I still have.

I can't do this.

> I don't want to do this, but I know I can. I must. I can ask for help if needed.

My whole life has changed.

> Some parts of my life are still the same. But I'm facing a lot of change, and I can focus on the positive ones. The change could provide personal growth.

I'll never get over this.

> This will take time to recover from, but I can do hard things. Others have done it and so can I.

I'll never be happy again.

> I feel sad now, but that's not how I'm meant to live my life. It's difficult to believe, but I know I can be happy again.

This is the worst thing that could ever happen.

> It seems bad, but I can think of worse things. I can make the best of it and move forward.

God hates me.

> God loves me. He wants me to grow and be my best self, a strong and compassionate person.

I don't have anyone to talk to.

> There's always someone who will listen to me, I just need to reach out. Maybe there is someone that feels that way too and I can help them.

Why does all the bad stuff happen to me?

> I've had some tough things lately, I guess everyone has challenges. It's part of life. How can I grow from this?

I can't get out of bed.

> I feel sad and want to spend time resting. Soon I will feel better and venture out.

Why me?

> Why not me?

I want to cry all the time.

> I am so sad and afraid. I miss how it was and it makes me cry. It's okay to be sad, but it is not healthy to stay this way. I will allow myself to feel it fully. Later, I will gradually recover and crying days will become less frequent. I want life to get better.

Notice that regardless of how we say it, the incident doesn't change, so choose a positive spin.

Mark's Play in the Wind Story

In 2003, when my son Austin turned thirteen, I wanted to get to know him better with a great father-and-son adventure. I decided on a ride around Ireland and had a custom tandem bicycle made. I thought that would be a better experience than individual bikes. We got a trailer that would hold our gear and equipment. It all came apart into sections so we could fit it into travel cases.

At one point, we took a ferry from the mainland to the Aran Islands. It wasn't a boat that took vehicles and we needed to offload the bike and trailer. The wind blew so strongly that it seemed frightening. Gusts brought in the rain sideways.

Everything we had, our camping gear, our clothes, camera, passports, all our belongings were on that trailer and bicycle, which probably weighed about a hundred and fifty pounds. At twelve feet long, two other individuals and I were holding it tight as we manhandled it from the heaving boat across open water to the dock. If it slipped, everything would fall in the drink, and I felt panicked about the gale.

As we battled to hoist it across, my son, Austin, leaned into the storm in an almost horizontal position because the wind supported him.

He called, "Dad, Dad! Look at this!" and I became irritated with him. I thought, *don't you understand how scary this is, we could lose everything in the ocean.*

Later, I realized I had missed sight of the trip. I thought, *where are we going to stay tonight? How are we going to get dry? How are we going to ride a bike in this crazy wind?* But Austin found entertainment and joy, where I solely looked at the difficulties that were only potentially staring us in the face.

The moral of the story: Grab a hold of your thoughts before they go into the drink and sink to Davy Jones! No, hold up, the moral is: When you're young and Dad is struggling to save stuff, and you don't have to pay for any damages, sure, play in the wind. No wait, the real moral is: "We can always find joy in the storms of life." Whew, finally nailed it! The third time's a charm. —Old Irish Saying (LOL)

We Can Change

It's good to take inventory of ourselves sometimes. Self-awareness is our friend. We might be afraid to look and see what we need to change because we struggle with feelings that we're not good enough. To go looking for more evidence of it seems incredibly counterintuitive. But it's very healthy to understand that we are a work in progress, like all human beings, and we make mistakes. This means that we all need to make improvements from time to time.

Learning to control bad habits or lazy thinking is a process. First, instead of feeling defeated by trying to gain more control and not quite making it, you could work on 'Spotting.' Let's strive to be keenly aware of our thoughts. Start 'Spotting' unhealthy thoughts. Be on the lookout and when we 'Spot' a harmful idea in our mind, tell ourselves, woohoo, we see it now! Even if we see it days later. 'Spot' our Thoughts!

Once we become good at spotting, then start replacing and overpowering the thought with an upgraded one. Soon we'll control it right from the first—at least sometimes. Victory!

The more enlightening experiences we have, the more empathy and understanding we gain. The more self-awareness we grow, the easier it is to make those small step-by-step changes to create healthy thoughts. We might profit from spending time thinking about what's inside us that we need to let go of that has led to unhealthy thoughts. Are there hurts, fears, failure, guilt, poor self-esteem, bitterness, anger, or are we holding onto sadness or a grudge? Do we struggle to feel good about ourselves?

Make a lovely list of what we want. If we have created a Creed, let's study it. Know what results we would like to see in our lives and then question what we could do to bring them about. Intentionally planned experiences that strengthen confidence, patience, courage, compassion, forgiveness, gratitude, etc. and it's simply a matter of replacing any negative feelings inside us with positive traits we've developed for ourselves. Then we'll end up being a better person with a healthier mindset.

If we are not currently who we want to be, change. Don't live with regrets. It's never too late. Don't sabotage Being the Boss of Our Thinker by trying to find reasons we can't do it. It may be scary to confront events in our past that we now realize could have been prevented if we had been the Boss. Move forward. Don't waste time or happiness beating ourselves up for not always having healthy thoughts in ancient history—that part of our life is over. Start now on our future with better thoughts.

For example, once a woman I didn't know needed a place to stay. She was a friend of a friend. We took her in, and she stayed in our guest suite. We made some space in the fridge and pantry for her food, a place for her bike in the garage, etc. She stayed with us the whole summer and then moved out.

About three months later, I received a letter from her in the mail. It surprised me to find some money inside. I quickly started reading to discover that while living with us, she took our food from the pantry several times without asking. I never noticed and wasn't at all concerned about this, but she had suffered with a very guilty conscience. She explained she had planned to come over and pay me back, but she felt too nervous. Now that months had gone by and thinking of how we had rescued her during a difficult time, she felt even worse that she had "repaid our kindness by robbing us" and felt too ashamed to drop by. She apologized for taking the cowardly way out by mailing it and begged for my forgiveness.

I called her immediately and told her "Don't worry, not a problem," and then complimented her on being brave and honest and for doing what she needed to ease her mind.

Even though I wasn't upset by the situation, it had haunted and tormented her. The letter proved a brave step, and my phone call restored the friendship we had started when she stayed with us.

The moral of the story is, let's not prolong suffering. If something has been bothering us (no matter how small) do what we need to clear our mind and end our worry, don't berate ourselves, and Live Happily Ever After.

Victim or Victor

One of my favorite questions to ask myself when struggling is: Am I a Victim or Victor? I don't want to live my life being a Victim. I want to be Victorious! I'm not saying that any of us want to be a target of a mugging or a theft or something like that, although that's true too. I'm talking about when we feel sorry for ourselves and throw lots of private Pity Parties. Sometimes we may even take them public.

Remember, we are on our journey, about our stuff, and we run on our time frame. Everyone else is on their individual journey, with their stuff, on their time. What they do is not our business and certainly not under our control. Let's stay in our lane and work on our stuff.

We may think other people are hurting our feelings and being difficult. Or we go through many challenging experiences in our life and say, 'See what's happened to me! Poor me, why me?' This type of thinking gives energy to being a

Victim. It also shifts our responsibility to someone else. I'm not saying that things don't happen to us when somebody did hurt us, through no fault of our own, but often we are a Victim because of what is in our thoughts, not because of something that in fact, happened to us.

Instead, regardless of events, we can see ourselves as Victor. We can march forward, not drown in tears. It's interesting if we examine our language. *"We take* offense," but just because it is offered, we don't need to accept it.

There is too much of this victim attitude, 'the poor me, this horrible thing happened to me' because if we look, no matter what, we can see good IF we want to find good. But if we decide that whatever occurs to us was horrible, awful, terrible and we're going to be bitter and angry for the rest of our lives about it, and there's nothing good about it, and this is not fair, or, we shouldn't have to do this! Then we'll find evidence of that also. Either way, we will have what we seek.

In our current society, I see far too much victimhood. There seems to be a need, even a desire, to be a victim. Some wallow in it, or cling to it, with the result being cankering of their souls. They recount stories of being hurt or offended and relive trials for months or even years. I've heard people competing to be the biggest victims. This is extremely unhealthy. Since when did being a victim become a goal?

Let's watch our conversations. Are we pouring out the story of how someone 'done us wrong,' every chance we get? Do we relish an audience where we can recite our woes? I am not saying we can never vent, but those types of dialogues should be short and rare. I doubt there is a good reason to tell our 'poor me' story to one person after another, after another. Think of what could be done as an alternative with that time that could propel our life forward instead of backward. Don't seek a cheap thrill disparaging someone either. We've all made mistakes, or said the wrong thing, etc. Do we want *those* tales spread around? Golden rule, you know.

Examine why we think it gives us pleasure to be the Victim. And if it is not pleasurable to broadcast it, but painful, why, oh why, would we do it? As we read this, are we fighting this advice, protesting our right to free speech? It's easy to get into the bad habit of criticizing or complaining.

Our complaining is a problem if we are sharing it for one of the following reasons:

- We need attention or validation and show little concern for the other side of the story.
- We use the story to get out of things or to push off taking responsibility.
- We forget that struggle is a part of life, and we are not immune.
- We use the story to manipulate to get what we want.
- We want others to take our side in the situation.
- We want to make ourselves look better.
- We are jealous of another.
- We want revenge.

It doesn't look admirable, does it? Why do we do it? Instead, how do we stay positive and rid ourselves of the habit of complaining or the need to play the victim part?

Here are some ideas to think about. What are the payoffs we might get from telling our struggles or offenses? Are the payoffs so great they are worth possibly losing the respect of other people? Think about the ways we might be seen as weak, complaining, or needy. Are there ways we can share our experiences with only our inner circle without coming across as a victim? Can we share our experiences in ways that will make us feel positive and victorious instead?

Do we find ourselves telling the same negative story from our past frequently? Do we feel the need to let others know about it? Do we tell stories to compete as the biggest victim? Why do we hold onto them? Is it who we are now?

I remember soon after my late husband, Russ, died, I met with a few widows. The first one asked me how long it had been since he died. I told her it had been five weeks. She said, "Oh my goodness, you're doing really well to be out." (I learned it was not a compliment.) She said she couldn't leave the house for three months; she just lay in bed and cried. The second widow immediately piped in, "Well, I couldn't go out for *six* months. I cried all the time and couldn't eat or sleep." Clearly, in their estimation, I wasn't much of a widow and the second woman handily won the Best Grieving Widow Award. Although I must say, it didn't look to me like she went six months without eating.

Do we tell stories to show that our life is bad, that no one cares about us, or to prove we have valid reasons why we are not happy, successful, or in a better place?

That reminds me of the story of my sister, Donna. She was not quite two years old, and my sister Beth and I were in the woods behind my grandparents' house. Donna toddled behind us, but she stopped when she saw this huge, red-ant hill just off the path. Insects covered it, crawling in and out of the hole in the center and she stood next to it fascinated. She watched these busy ants going all over and of course, in a few seconds, many of them had crawled on her feet and up her legs.

Soon, one of them bit her, and then another bite and another. She started to scream and when she realized there were ants all over her, she started stomping her feet to try to get rid of them and in her panicked state she ended up falling on top of the anthill.

She plopped right on top, and they immediately went into full battle mode and swarmed all over her. They were attacking her so much she couldn't think straight or figure out how to get up. Drowning in pain, her screams could be heard throughout the woods. Quickly we rescued her, but she had been bitten all over and cried and cried.

Sometimes people get into situations, and they can't figure out how to move on. They stay on the ant hill, immobilized with fear or with anxiety. This intense state can paralyze us from moving forward and taking care of the issue.

Can we replace these negative thoughts of past hurts with positive, wonderful stories instead, where we are strong, blessed, capable, fortunate, and whole?

Or do we need these negative stories to gather support against our 'enemies' or to justify ourselves in our lack of progress? Let's not blame others for the way we are feeling. We are responsible for our emotions. Ugly reactions do arise when we suspect we're wronged; but once they arrive, we have the power to process through them and choose a healthier mindset.

Is our perspective accurate? The universe is not an unfriendly, scary place that is out to get us. The universe is usually on our side, but it is a clever teacher, and we receive lessons that can be used for our good to assist us in becoming stronger, wiser, and more charitable.

Things don't Happen TO us: they Happen FOR us.

Can we choose to focus on gratitude instead of woe? Our blessings will always be greater. There's so much we take for granted: walking, talking, seeing, hearing, clothing, having food, etc.

It's not so much about us telling one person about a bad deal we received, but the way we feel inside when we rehearse our victim stories is very concerning. Those are not uplifting positive thoughts. We will not feel better. Remember we are trying to avoid feeling bitter for our *own* sake. We want to be happy in life. If we give power and energy to bad times, we will find more of them. Speak of good things. Lift and encourage others.

We can enjoy basking in the sunshine or notice how clean the world looks after rain. Or we can complain about how hot it is or curse the puddles. If our desire is to have a happy life, then let's do the work it takes to get it. Feeling like a victor comes when we seek and find every win in our day. Even small ones, like:

- Our shower had warm water. Wow!
- We have clean clothes to wear. Fabulous!
- Our toast came out good. Hallelujah!
- The egg seems a bit overdone. Great! We've learned not to over-cook it and will try again tomorrow.

Most of us can see, hear, walk, talk, think, visit with family or friends, work, travel, read a book, sleep, get outdoors, have food to eat, and so many wonderful triumphs. Life is amazing!

Perhaps it sounds fake or unrealistic. But I have seen that if we talk about being happy, focus on the good events that occur in our lives, see the positive in others and cheer them on, and genuinely love life and enjoy the day, we feel optimistic. The result? We will feel fabulous. It will help us be full of gratitude for everything good all day. We can notice what others do for us. Let them know how grand it made us feel or how much it helped us. Thank them profusely. Notice anything nice about people. Does their hair look good? Tell them. And we'll all live Happily Ever After.

When life seems upside down, some may squawk and whine and say it's not fair. However, it's interesting that we will even pay money to have an experience that's white-knuckle challenging, shakes us up on purpose, spins us around, and spits us out, like an amusement park ride or whitewater rafting. It's a chance to prove our daring spirit and bravery. When a problem hits us, what if we changed our viewpoint and saw the test to be intriguing like an Escape Room Experience where we are excited to figure things out and emerge victorious? And solving our problems is FREE! Fist bump!

Let's look at FEAR as: <u>F</u>eeling <u>E</u>xcited <u>A</u>nd <u>R</u>eady

It can be motivating to be around people who have been through hard things because they inspire us. Many of us love books and movies about people who've gone through tough circumstances because we're lifted and encouraged. We think, *wow, maybe we could do that*, or *what would we do in that position*? Yet when we have a chance to show what we would do in a tough situation, we may whine and cry about it and feel sorry for ourselves.

Perhaps we have a warped view of our whole earthly existence. Or we can choose to see it this way: It's not happening *to* us it's happening *for* us, and then life seems fabulous and exciting.

Let's not become frustrated and feel depressed or frantic trying to solve all our problems so *then*, we can be happy. Be happy now because we will always have problems come up. Problems help us grow. Remember last year's problems? We lived through them. We can do this! We're going to get wet; but we'll dry off—or possibly be handed a big, soft, fluffy towel.

The Tipping $$$ Principle

Years ago, Merry, a friend and client, told me about her philosophy of tipping. She felt poor and life was not going well financially. She had been an Olympic athlete, then an injury ended her promising career. But this woman is not a Victim. She is a Victor.

With a Victor mentality, she decided to elevate others and thereby, lift herself out of the doldrums. She thanked people for everything, and she gave them a tip. Not just waitresses or hairdressers. Everyone. She started handing out five-dollar bills. It's all she could afford—and that might be questionable if you saw her bank account. But she did it anyway.

Soon she tipped twenties. If something made her life better in any way, she celebrated it. Handing out money made her happy and it also made her feel successful. And she believed that you get what you give. A miraculous principle!

When I first met her, she was couch-surfing. Within a very short time, she ran a small, growing business that she loved, with more than a dozen employees, lived in a lovely little house, and owned a few paid-for automobiles for her and her staff. She made lots of friends and everyone wanted to do business with her. She became a Victorious Winner in life. She felt happy and upbeat and was enjoyable to be around. She won the gold medal in success.

Pity Parties and Hard Times

Sometimes we may feel the need to throw ourselves a Pity Party. Keep it short and try not to overindulge. Especially avoid the group Pity Parties. They tend to drag things out. Also avoid people who encourage us to have one—there are much better ways to spend our time.

Sometimes when we try to take the easy way out, we often make things harder in the future. By ignoring, blaming, making excuses, or not taking full responsibility for our actions, we usually make things worse. Let's prepare ourselves for what we want by taking steps today to get there.

- Build ourselves.
- Take on challenges for personal growth.
- Be stronger, just do it. Do it boldly!

- Realize what is possible within us.
- Build resilience.
- Ask ourselves, does this make my life better or worse?
- What we tell ourselves is important.

Unless we really, truly are, don't excuse ourselves by saying we're doing our best. We often limit our potential, stopping at Good when we could move to Better or Best. Mediocrity will take us to a dead end. Take the path to 'real' happiness instead. It often takes grand effort and a lot of self-honesty.

Understand what our best is. A widow may fall apart. She may say, 'I can't go on.' Not true. It is honest to instead say, 'I can, but I don't want to.' What happens if we don't want to? Tears can be exquisite. But not if they are endless. The despair we may feel has options. Can we look at the situation with different eyes? Maybe be grateful that we had a great love to mourn.

Do we let ourselves identify with our pain and hardship? Are we just the poor, sad widow? Or are we still a mother, a friend, a person with purpose?

Are we grateful for our health, and the beauty around us? Are there parts of our lives we can still be happy about? Do we refuse to do that?

Work on making the bad parts as short as possible, focus on emerging happy and healthy, think of our purposes, and get busy on them. We can participate in the sorrow but don't dwell on it or get lost in it. Don't get stuck there. That doesn't help anyone, most of all not us.

Do we still have vision and purpose? What is it? What does that mean in the choices we make today?

Good Examples Abound

When feeling defeated, call up a few inspiring people who seem happy. We may be surprised to find they also face some challenging times. They don't need to be therapists or have near-perfect lives. We can often learn from a good friend or family member or a good biography. Resist the urge to complain or tell our story; simply listen carefully. And then take their good advice or use an idea from below.

I must say I felt terribly impressed with the powerful counsel I received after a ten-minute exercise consisting of a few messages. A simple text and I received super fabulous ideas. It almost makes me want to have a problem to solve! Just kidding! I discovered I have amazingly smart and kind friends and family and I know where to go next time I'm feeling lost.

My message said: 'I'm writing a book about Being the Boss of Your Thinker. What do *you* think, say, or do, to cope with a problem in a healthy way? Any example stories would be great.'

SPOUSE ALERT!!! Check out Matt's advice for solving marital issues.

Matt: "I listen to music. I also separate myself from the situation with thoughts that shift my mind onto something I can envision that brings joy. For example, when my wife and I have a disagreement, I remove myself from the discussion by saying let's talk about this tonight after the kids are in bed. Then I picture and plan things that would be a lot of fun to do together. That puts us on the same team, and we can keep things in perspective."

Matt focuses his thinking on a healthy solution while building the marital relationship. Smart man! And listening to music—an excellent idea. Personally, I like to sit in a dark room, eyes closed, with fabulous, soft tunes, or go to an energetic outdoor concert, or jump in the car and crank up the tunes and take a ride out in the country. Oh, and kitchen dancing with Mark is so lovely. I immerse myself in wonderful music, forget my troubles, and then come back refreshed and ready to take on the world—like Matt.

Becky: "I mostly remind myself that I am doing things for me. I used to be intimidated to go to the gym because I always thought someone would judge me, but then I told myself, 'I'm not doing it for them, I'm doing it for me.' I think that applies in many scenarios. Sometimes I worry too much about what other people think and I try to check myself and remember the reason I am doing certain things."

Like Becky, I also think we get too caught up and worried about what other people think. Most of the time they don't care—*if* they even notice us. Plus, what other people think of us is none of our business. And it necessitates us calling on our Awesome Powers of Mind-Reading—which we don't have. So that's kind of silly.

McKenna: "That's a very vast question, it completely depends on the problem. Some problems don't have easy solutions. Like stuff we see on the news that keeps happening. I don't have a solution and there may never be one.

But if the problem is that I'm out of toothpaste and out of money, I'd tell myself I need to find something to sell for $5 so I can go get toothpaste.

I personally look at facts. There *are* tragedies in our world. But it seems like lots of bad things are happening because it's always in the news all day. But if the networks reported the good things, that's all we would hear about for the next twenty years.

I think about what type of world my kids are growing up in. But then I think of the number of people affected and it's small. My kids will be fine. I cope with statistics and rational thinking. It doesn't always work obviously, things can still be stressful, but generally this helps me. We do our part with what we can, without going overboard on every little thing."

McKenna has a 'practical, figure it out, solve the problem, and move on' approach. Done. I love it! She is also independent and resourceful. Yay, forget the pity parties!

I agree with her, the sensationalism of the Bad News Media is not supported by statistics as she mentions. It's blown out of proportion and gets way too much coverage which distorts how prevalent an issue is and can cause undue stress. We can chill out and look at the facts not the hype. There's so much good in the world—focus on that.

Spencer: "I always try to take a step back and think around the problem; come at it with a mindset of resolutions instead of complaints, anger, frustration, etc. I then think through the options of each resolution so I can truly pick the best plan. We can choose to stress ourselves out or deal with it and move on in a positive way."

I think it's important to note that Spencer ran on very little sleep when he kindly gave me this feedback. His wife had tested positive for COVID, and his young daughter and newborn baby were feverish and sick. The same newborn son who soon after birth experienced some concerning health issues and was still recovering. Oh, and Spencer worked on an intense consulting situation on the other side of the country for the week. Oh, and he's in the middle of some board issues with BACA (he is an active member of Bikers Against Child Abuse). Oh, and as Chairman, he's also facing a tense, upcoming HOA board meeting.

But amid all this, and who knows what else, he took a few minutes to respond to me. Read it again and you'll be quite impressed. This shows that even when things aren't going so great, we can still be helpful and happy.

Perry: "Well, here's one thought: when I am trying to achieve a challenging task and I catch myself procrastinating, I tell myself, 'Something is better than nothing' and I take a small bite out of the challenge rather than trying to do it all at once, which can feel too daunting."

Our friend, Perry, is right. Our self-talk can encourage us OR discourage us. Don't let a project or a problem develop in our mind into a monstrous impossibility. Move forward one step at a time. Something *is* better than nothing. Such wise advice.

I'm sure all these good people are in the middle of several situations themselves. But note their positive, upbeat vibe, and even though I think they're very special and I feel truly blessed to know them, we can all learn from their wisdom. I received all of this in just ten minutes!!! Plus, we can grow up to be like them. And we'll live Happily Ever After.

Mark's Pivotal Story at the Hospital

When fourteen years old, I recall stubbing my big toe on a rusty nail. We lived in North Vancouver, BC, and were preparing to leave on a three-week vacation soon. I have no idea if the ensuing illness came from that rusty nail but it's the only thing that comes to mind.

Within a few days, I felt lousy and extremely tired. Our intended trip included visiting relatives for Canada Day (July 1st), then continuing to Utah to camp and do tourist things with the intent of having a memorable family holiday.

We arrived at my grandparents' house in the tiny town of Raymond, Alberta. Still very tired, I found a comfortable, cool place in the basement to rest. I was well on my way to challenging Rip Van Winkle, when one of the adults inquired: "Has anyone seen Mark?"

"I saw him sleeping in the basement a few days ago," replied one of my sisters. Finding me after a short search of the tiny basement, they discovered I had developed a raging fever and my lower left leg looked red and swollen. They took me to the hospital right away. In addition to being sleepy, I had a fever of 106 degrees. Instantly, steps were taken to reduce my temperature, and then to determine the cause. Within a few hours, they transferred me to St. Michael's Hospital in Lethbridge, the largest care facility in the area.

Doctors soon diagnosed me with osteomyelitis, an infection in the bone. Some antibiotics were given to me to treat the infection and hopefully the fever as well. Shortly after this, my parents decided that they would leave me in good professional hands and reluctantly chose to continue with the original holiday agenda without Mark. Mom, Dad, and my six sisters packed up and left Alberta, on their way to Utah.

Within a day or two, there emerged conversation regarding surgery to either chisel out the infected bone or amputate. They decided to try the bone chisel method. About two weeks into my stay, Mom, Dad, and sisters detoured to Alberta on their way back to BC and came by St. Michael's for a few hours to visit me, before continuing home. They gave me the option to go back to a Vancouver hospital, but I declined.

Here is why. We had lots of friends and family in southern Alberta. I would have visitors every day. Grandma and Grandpa, aunts, uncles, cousins, and friends of the family would come in to check on me. People would drop in frequently and often ask if they could bring me anything. At first, I said no, because getting three squares a day meant I didn't want for much.

Fairly soon I recognized that they were sincerely asking if they could bring me something extra. I thought about it and decided to ask for things like Orange Soda, Potato Chips, Chip Dip, Red Licorice, etc. You get the picture. The nursing staff collected the loot each week until Friday evening, then we would watch a movie and have a fabulous party in Mark's room. I was transparent with the givers and invited them to come too. The likelihood of re-creating that scenario in North Vancouver seemed slim, so I opted to stay.

During that time, a support mechanism evolved that seemed, from my perspective, fantastic. I felt comfortable, reading, listening to the radio, breakfast, lunch and supper in bed, TV, and visiting in the evenings. 'Rinse, Repeat.' Life, while not perfect, felt good.

Eventually, a second surgery was needed along with a unique process to minimize the risk of reinfection. The second attempt worked. My bedridden stay in Lethbridge lasted over three months.

Upon my eventual return home, I stayed wheelchair-bound for another six months and often received kind and compassionate service. The entire process provided many lessons that proved very powerful and foundational for me. As a bedridden or wheelchair-bound fourteen-year-old, I began my journey to understanding that what happens to us is of little consequence when we choose to Be the Boss of Our Thinker.

The moral of the story: I learned that even in less-than-ideal circumstances my joy and happiness were largely due to my perceptions and thoughts about life. There are golden lessons to be extracted from our difficulties.

Guilt

I am surprised how often people are not able to function well because they feel guilty. Their mind is obsessed with an incident, and they ruminate on what they should have done. They are worried that a challenge they now face is their fault since they are convinced it is a result of something wrong they did in the past (or didn't do).

It is interesting to me how adults will twist something that happened when they were children. A woman's father became stern with her after she misbehaved. Later that night, she heard her mom and dad fighting and not long after, they divorced. Of course, they were planning it for a long time, but their daughter went through life blaming herself because she didn't do the right thing that day. It wasn't at all the reason. Not in any way, shape, or form did she hold responsibility for that break-up, and it had nothing to do with what she did that day, and yet she carried this guilt deep inside her.

What about Mother's Day (or it can apply to Father's Day too)? Some women hate that holiday. They feel so guilty because of all the talk and greeting cards about The Greatest Mom in the World and yet they don't feel like a great mom. They made mistakes. We all do. They think, *oh, my gosh, I'm the worst mother ever and I hate Mother's Day, it reminds me of what a bad mother I am.* So instead of having a nice holiday, they wallow in guilt and wish the day would hurry and end.

Who said the holiday celebrated being a *perfect* Mom? Stop that nonsense already!

Isn't it about how kids love their moms, imperfections, and all? Or how mothers love their kids, sticky fingers and all? We can choose to see it as a celebration of being grateful for our kids. Or giving birth. After all, nine months of pregnancy topped by labor and pushing a whole person out is usually no picnic!

Do these guilt-ridden moms propose that their imperfect kids hide away and cry on their birthdays? No birthday cards or presents for junior because he isn't perfect. Of course not. We don't celebrate the kid only when he's perfect, why should we think we celebrate Mother's Day solely if we are a perfect mother?

It's a wonderful day for honoring Mothers for all they do. Focus on the good. Most moms have lots of positive things. Even if Mom showed a fabulous example of what *not* to do.

(Okay, some say it's a day invented by greeting card companies to increase sales. LOL)

Or some women hate Mother's Day because of their awful mom. Then don't send her a card. The holiday is not all about her. We can still be happy. Be glad we turned out well despite her—or if we're still working on that part, view it as motivation.

There's a lot of other ways we can think. It's destructive to sit and feel guilty on Mother's Day, so why in the world would we do it? If we aren't doing a good job, let's change, step it up, even if our children are grown.

And don't try to be bad so we can look good. You know, the false martyrdom that for some gives a kind of sick pleasure. Fishing for protestations and compliments, Mom dramatically places the back of her hand on her forehead and wails, 'I feel so bad, I cried all day because I wasn't a perfect mother. I could have been better, and I feel so guilty about it.'

I am surprised how many people talked about the guilt after their spouse died, especially with cancer or something where they had time to deal with stuff they felt guilty about.

It doesn't matter who we did it to, or what it was, or when. Let me repeat: If we did something wrong, apologize. NOW.

Do whatever we can to fix it TODAY. Then don't do it again and move on.

Feeling remorse that motivates us to repent quickly is great. Wallowing in guilt does not help, not us or the person we wronged. Drawn-out guilt is not good. Endless guilt is pointless; it doesn't benefit anyone. Focus on the cure, not the disease. I don't think staying guilty is a healthy emotion, fix it, and move on. It doesn't matter what anyone else did. Even if they had a part in it. Don't worry about it. Fix *our* part, honestly and humbly.

Some additional comments on thinking. Do we remember feeling self-conscious at our first dance? At the time, it seemed very uncomfortable, but now, really, it's kind of funny. It's all a matter of how we choose to think about it—stepping back for a more enlightened and broad perspective. When we can bring that same distance and humor to any awkward situation, we can create a more benevolent way to think about it, which can bring calmness even in the very midst of a challenge. Our perspective, or the way we think, is so important. And then we can live Happily Ever After.

Golden

It seems like light gives everything that little extra.
Perhaps we can be a light and make a difference.
Smile. Laugh. Choose Happiness.
"I am happy because I'm grateful. I choose to be grateful.
That gratitude allows me to be happy."
—WILL ARNETT

CHAPTER 10

WHAT WE SAY

Words we speak stem from our thoughts. If our thoughts are honest and kind, our words will reveal that with honesty and kindness. When we are in alignment with our deeply held beliefs, we will have self-esteem. If we stray from how we believe we should think, speak, or act, then we will struggle with liking ourselves, we'll feel sad, angry, and uncomfortable, and waste time comparing ourselves with others, and maybe blame people or make excuses. For Mark and I, our self-esteem depends greatly on knowing we are children of God. We then feel confident as we align our values, found in our Personal Creed, with our actions.

As we view others being mean, a good question to ask is this: Where and When and How did their story begin? We seldom know the whole tale. Hurt people, hurt people. It is difficult to judge accurately so don't take things personally. It will rarely be about us. When we have peace inside, it is harder for others to ruffle our feelings or make us mad.

If we believe being snide or rude is wrong—regardless of what others may think about it—then if *we* engage in being rude or snide, we destroy *our* peace. Even if it is true, or the other person 'deserves' it, or acted rude to us first, the result will not change. We must always be true to ourselves. No excuses. If what we are thinking, saying, or doing can be explained with a negative word, label, or tag, then we are *not* being our best selves.

Our bottled-up, negative emotions tend to hurt us. We should openly express our *honest, positive, healthy* feelings. We do not need to worry about acting strong for others or that we need to protect them. Those who love us are here for us. They may not always say the right thing (whatever *that* is) but then, neither will we. Don't look for offense. Just talk through our feelings, careful to replace any negative, unhealthy emotions with positive ones. We can hear the views of others, but we don't need to worry about what they will think about us. With a discovery motive, stay on the principle, instead of making it personal. People think what they think. But when we do express our feelings, always remember this:

Be Honest AND Kind.

When we talk to ourselves or others, my main motto is to be Honest *and* Kind. Not honest *or* kind. If we can't be honest and kind, don't say anything. Honesty without kindness still hurts. Kindness without honesty creates false expectations or could limit us in the future. Personally, I'd rather be hurt by the truth than pacified by a lie. However, I still think it's best if we try to deal with others honestly and kindly.

Let's say we had a super tough challenge. Maybe our parent or other loved one died, or we lost our job. Are we stymied when someone asks us how we're doing? Do we tend to say something that won't make them feel bad or sorry for us? Are we tired of saying "fine" when it's a lie? Or saying 'lousy,' when that doesn't really cover it?

So, what *do* we say? Just how *do* we feel? Maybe the answer isn't always about how we are. Maybe we can start saying how our mind thinks. Like, we are sad about going to the funeral tomorrow. Or we're grateful to have friends like them look out for us. Or we have some worry, but we're working hard to find a job. Then we let them know what we're looking for. They may surprise us by saying their uncle has a large corporation and is looking for someone like us.

Maybe they say, they understand what we're going through, once they had a little financial setback and had to shorten their Hawaiian vacation from a month down to only two weeks. Even though we're wondering how to make our house payment, don't judge what people say. Just like we don't know what to say in a challenging situation, they don't know what to say either. But they are bravely trying anyway because they care about us. Focus on their caring, not their clumsy words. Different people will react in different ways.

If a friend confides a sad event to us, be open and honest, answer something like, 'I don't know what to say, but I'm here and I care.' Understand that others usually are not trying to offend us, so let's not *take* offense.

And if they *are* trying to be offensive? Then that's more reason not to be offended. In summary, if they did not intend to offend you, then if you become offended, you lose. If they *were* trying to offend you and you become offended, they win, and you lose. Either way, any time we take offense it is a losing situation for us.

Precise Language

Are we facing a tense circumstance? Do we say, 'It feels like the whole world is falling apart?' That is super stressful to think like that. The world is NOT falling apart. So, find another image to think about that is more real and less alarming, maybe a funny one, and shift to that thought if we're obsessing about a destroyed planet. Let's tone it down and tackle the problem at hand—the fate of the Earth is not our personal responsibility.

Let's be careful that the language we use is positive and makes us feel better. Don't say something if it is not absolutely true. Guard against saying things that are not only false, but the very words take away our power and make us feel worse. Learn to be intensely aware of what we say and when we notice some of the phrases below that are on the Unhealthy List, change them immediately for an uplifting, positive, healthy phrase. See the following for suggestions:

Unhealthy Language	Healthy Language
I can't.	I won't, or I don't want to, or I don't like this.
I can't.	I can do this.
I should …	I could …
It's too difficult.	It's going to take time, or I might need help.
It's not my fault.	I take responsibility for my part.
Why me?	I'm on a journey of learning.

It's a problem.	It's an opportunity for growth.
It's too painful.	I'm altering my perception, or I can do this.
Everything goes wrong for me.	It's a challenge, but also something good too.
Life is a struggle.	Life is an adventure.
I'm not satisfied.	I want to learn and grow.
If only	Next time
What can I do?	I know I can handle it in a good way.
It's terrible.	It's an experience.
It's so hard.	What are my options, It'll work out, or I can do it.
My life is terrible.	I have lots to be grateful for.
I can't handle this.	I will handle this in a good way.

No matter what comes up, not only *can* we handle it, but we most certainly *will* handle it. We must, it won't simply go away. However, it is up to us to deal with it in a positive, healthy way. If a difficult incident occurs and we sit and cry, realize we are tackling the situation—by crying. That approach may very well make it even worse—like Donna sitting on the ant hill. Let's ask ourselves, what other ways could we manage it that would be better? We don't have much of a choice but to do something, but we have lots of choices of taking a positive path through it or a disastrous or self-defeating way. Remember the situation will not magically disappear, so notice if how we are handling it is our very best. If not, then step it up!

We have weapons of reason that arm us to succeed and well-earned personal strength. We've done hard things. We can do it again.

Gratitude

Let's create our life, don't wait for it to happen. Notice things to be grateful for, don't delay until ALL things are good. Learn to notice the good—ALWAYS there is good.

We can look at our strengths with thankfulness and nurture them. It's folly to compare ourselves with a champion. We don't have to be like others. Be realistic about our weaknesses. It is not healthy to berate ourselves. If we make a mistake, own it, and then determine how we can prevent a recurrence in the future.

Another important point: there is always something worthy of our gratitude. However, for some, it seems like it's a lot easier to find something to whine about. When we express appreciation, when we think of what we're grateful for, and when we look for blessings, we'll Live Happily Ever After. But when we begin to complain and be critical and whine, we tend to be more miserable. Again ask, 'Is what we're thinking right now making life better or worse?'

If we get stuck thinking, talking, or crying in a negative, depressing way, then we must intentionally recognize what we are doing and change. Let's reach our optimal coping mode by thinking ourselves well, instead of thinking ourselves sick. We can combat negative, stuck, ugly thoughts with gratitude.

Seek to be keenly aware of how much we have to treasure, achieve an overwhelming attitude of gratitude, and live life fully and with zest, and we will be set up for sweet joy.

Don't dwell on trouble even if it's a memory or something we fear in the future. Sometimes we worry about something that hasn't even happened yet and may not ever materialize. I heard two powerful quotes:

"Worry is like praying to the devil."
It invites unnecessary misery into our lives.
"Worry is like shoveling smoke."
—how useless.

May I share a story that helped facilitate a more benevolent and hopeful view? Back in our Ultra Poor Days, I had a routine of making my children oatmeal each morning after I had worked a nightshift before taking the kids to school and dashing off to my second full-time job. Oatmeal every day was all we could afford. To make the limited timeframe work, I always waited until the 'resting' period of the hot cereal to race upstairs to wake my kids. We lacked beds (and most household items) so the floor sufficed.

One morning, after starting the oats, I received a strong urge to go get my kids. I didn't have the extra minutes to make a premature trip upstairs, so I ignored it. The prompting came again. I demurred, thinking I would soon be at the usual point, and I could break away then. Suddenly a clear voice told me to go—NOW!

I raced up the stairs. I opened the children's bedroom just in time to see my little daughter's pillow burst into flames. Screaming, I dashed in and scooped her up. We quickly put out the fire. Apparently, during the night she had rolled over several times, pushing her pillow against the electric baseboard heater, and the heat in the fabric and stuffing had built into fire. Fortunately, it only singed her hair, but had I waited any longer…

I was grateful my tears that day were from humble gratitude. So often tender mercies intervene. That type of thinking is better than hours of worry about what might have happened.

Are we having a bad day? Let's make two lists. Side by side. In the first column, write all the bad things in our life. In the second column, write all the good things. We will be surprised at how many good things we have once we look. We have so much to be thankful for. Who has not held a newborn child and marveled at the perfectness of each little toe? I wonder at tiny hair follicles, blood veins, minute fingernails, pores, lashes, and so many small parts. In perfect order and made to function in their various roles. Even at the birth of my child with multiple deformities, I felt awed at how many *more* body parts were right.

Abd al-Rahman III, the Emir of Córdoba, became one of the most magnificent Arab rulers of al-Andalus, the Muslim kingdom of Spain. Born in 890 A.D., he ascended the throne in 912. Considered a superb general and politician, he fought decades of battles in his long reign. He brought glory to his kingdom and declared himself Caliph—Commander of the Faithful—in 929.

He died on 15 October 961 after ruling for fifty years. Nearing his death at age seventy, he wrote a letter, supposedly for his successor. He wrote: 'I have now reigned above fifty years in victory or peace, beloved by my subjects, dreaded by my enemies, and respected by my allies. Riches and honors, power, and pleasure, have waited on my call, nor does any earthly blessing appear to have been wanting to my felicity. In this situation, I have diligently numbered the days of pure and genuine happiness that have fallen to my lot: they amount to FOURTEEN: O man! place not thy confidence in this present world!'

Isn't it interesting to consider that a powerful ruler with all the advantages and luxuries of his era, numbered his days of pure and genuine happiness and they only came to fourteen? To me, it seems as though he took the journey, but he missed the trip. He missed the obvious abundance of good. I think it's important to number not only the days of our happiness but be aware of the minutes and hours of pure joy and even those seconds that bring us to an incredible Happily Ever After. Gratitude is a precious key to happiness.

It's Just Opinion

Sometimes we have an opinion, but we confuse it with fact. We're much healthier in our thinking and happier in our lives if we don't think that all our opinions are facts. It's easy to say our favorite color is blue and allow someone to have a different favorite color than we do. But even something as simple as a movie or a song that we think is wonderful can find us upset, even feeling threatened, because another person doesn't agree with our opinion.

We will be much better off if we allow people to have their own opinions. We can challenge our thoughts if we start to feel upset and tell ourselves it's okay, we don't have to agree on everything. It doesn't mean we're a bad person if another doesn't agree with us. Nor does it mean they're bad. It doesn't mean they think we're wrong; it doesn't even mean that our opinion is wrong, it simply means they have a different opinion. And we need to realize their opinion isn't wrong either.

If we feel threatened by a difference of opinion with someone, remember, would we feel threatened if they liked blue when we liked yellow better? It is not a challenge to our existence; they're not saying that *we* are wrong. If we allow ourselves to think about that and just relax and remember it's not a big deal if someone has another opinion, we'll be a lot more cheerful.

I think it is healthier to assume that *most* things are opinions with a few facts mixed in. How do we define a fact? Perhaps something that has been repeatedly confirmed as true, empirically proven. But by whom? So, do we define it as something that everyone agrees on—*everyone*—and is there such a thing? Is there anything that everyone agrees on? How many need to disagree before a fact is overturned? Because there is always new information and discovery, which is why most scientists prefer to use the term 'theory' rather than 'fact.' We may describe it as something well-established over time, but that doesn't mean that it couldn't change later as more information comes out.

Years ago, I believed there were at least a few things that *everyone* would agree on, but I had an interesting experience that surprised me. We were in a buffet-style restaurant and a couple sat in a booth across from us, perhaps a husband and a wife who looked to be in their early seventies. With them, sat a darling little old woman, probably in her nineties, perhaps a mother to one of them. She looked kind but seemed very fragile and the two people showed great concern towards her. They were very gentle and would go get her food and it looked sweet to see them interact.

In the booth next to them, I saw five people, maybe in their forties. After a while, the older people got ready to leave. The couple slowly stood up waiting for the lady to carefully scoot over to the edge so they could help her get up, but she really struggled.

The older man and wife, still trying to help the elderly lady, stood in the narrow aisle preventing passage of a man from the other booth who abruptly rose to get more food. I expected him to offer to help. But after a few seconds and in a loud, irritated voice the man said, "If you're too old to get up you shouldn't even be here; I can't get out!"

The couple apologized and tried harder to lift her, which seemed difficult for them. Even though it delayed the man only a few seconds, more complaints spewed out. "Come on old lady, I don't have all day!"

I felt shocked at his rude impatience towards the sweet elderly lady. Surely, he could see that she valiantly tried to get up, it wouldn't take long, not a lot of time, not a big deal. She looked like such a cute ninety–year–old, but this man became mad and seemed to feel entitled to be able to dash out and grab more food. It seemed the idea that he might have to wait infuriated him so much he loudly took her to task for even daring to be out in public.

Many patrons stared at him in disbelief, but he felt so justified by his own opinion he didn't care. I remember the couple were both very embarrassed and their mom felt deeply flustered, repeating, "I'm sorry, I'm sorry."

I thought *everyone* would look at this tiny, elderly lady and not only think she's adorable and would be patient and kind but maybe even ask if they could help. I pondered it for a long time afterward. I know there are lots of varied opinions in the world, but surely in *this* situation, everyone would be patient and understand that she's a little slow—not a big deal. But that proved false.

It made me wonder and I watched for a few months looking for something that *everyone* would agree with. I never found it.

Why do we often feel threatened by a difference of opinion? We seem so insistent that our way of thinking is right, which would mean any others are wrong.

> *"Let me never fall into the vulgar mistake of dreaming that I am persecuted whenever I am contradicted."*
> **—RALPH WALDO EMERSON**

I recently read someone's post on a social media site saying that local university administrators were a bunch of idiots because of a recent controversial decision they made. A Commenter wrote, "You're being a bully!"

The Poster replied, "Why am I being a bully?"

C: "Because you're calling out someone in public and trying to make them look wrong."

P: "But aren't you calling me out in public and trying to make me look wrong? So, you're a bully!"

C: "No, I'm not a bully; you're a bully!"

That string made me laugh. Isn't it amazing that we can be blinded by our opinions so much we don't even see we are criticizing others for doing the same thing we did?

Wouldn't it be nice to be able to listen to someone with a different opinion in the same calm way that we would react if somebody said, "My favorite color is yellow." We're not threatened by it, we don't get angry, and we allow the other person to choose whatever favorite color they want.

"Some things matter, most things don't."
—M. S. STARK

It's okay for others to have another idea. It's only a personal preference. It seems people get mad or feel threatened or get defensive because they take it personally. Let's be curious and follow the old principle, 'seek first to understand.' There does not have to be agreement to remain friends. We can celebrate the differences. Let's not make a big deal out of nothing. No fighting about it, say, 'Oh, that's an interesting observation.' Be a peacemaker.

We can allow others to be who they are. It's not our place to change them, judge them, or compare ourselves to them. If we like the country and our friend likes the city, neither is right or wrong. Remember, opinions are fine. They are not facts. Let's not argue about them. And most things are opinions, not facts.

Forgive or Forego

Be open to the possibility that we are wrong, even though we feel sure we're right.

Seems like there's a new national dance; it's called the offensive polka. People seem to be offended by almost anything and everything. Let's train our minds to think in a healthy way and being easily offended is weak, self-absorbed, and unhealthy.

> *"People get addicted to feeling offended all the time because it gives them a high: being self-righteous and morally superior feels good."*
>
> **— MARK MANSON**

Here's a great lesson from Caru Das Adikari, the priest and manager of the Spanish Fork, Utah, Krishna Temple. He teaches that forgiveness is not as important as compassion. If someone does something cruel to us or causes us some pain, that is between them and God. He said if someone offends us, it should be like water off a duck's back. A sage or a spiritually oriented person is not upset by the actions of another. When someone does something that causes suffering, it is the responsibility of others not to be disturbed but to treat them with compassion. In Krishna dogma, forgiveness is not needed because one does not initially become upset when slighted or wronged.

We do not expect others to be perfect and never do wrong, even if it involves us. So, we *forgo* becoming angry with another who is simply being human, with imperfections. We give grace and wish them healing. We cannot be compassionate and angry at the same time. So have tender feelings towards others. Look for good in every situation. Keep in mind that most stuff is not about *us*. Caru finishes by saying, "Look at the other person and think about how our reaction affects the community and the world."

Let's not catastrophize. Don't worry. 'This Too Shall Pass' is a lovely mantra. If it won't matter in a hundred years, it doesn't matter much today. But don't carry it to the ridiculous; it probably won't matter in the distant future if we eat today—but have supper anyway.

Sometimes forgiveness might appear impossible. A spouse, coworker, or friend hurts our feelings or offends us. But we can say, what is this difficult thing preparing us for? We can do hard things; have that mindset. One way to do that is by reflecting on and remembering past tough situations and the way we overcame them.

We should be grateful we're allowed the opportunity to overcome adversity and each time we should be able to do better. Every pain we suffer prepares us for future pain; then we become stronger and able to handle it successfully. We can test our limits; see what they are and push them a little further each time. Forgiveness can seem insurmountable. In reality, NOT forgiving is a bigger burden.

A quick and sincere forgiveness also makes future offenses easier to deal with. In time, we can even forgo taking offense. That makes our lives the easiest; it is not letting others get away with stuff. It is the freedom to act as we believe, instead of being controlled by the actions of others.

> *"I value my feelings of freedom too much to get offended."*
> **—M. S. STARK**

I decided I didn't want to live my life offended. I can choose right now to skip the whole forgiveness process and forgo. In other words, I don't get offended in the first place. I don't think there's anything to forgive them for. If another person has done something wrong to me, it's their journey, not mine.

It's not ignoring what they've said or done. I've chosen to try to step back and look at it in another way. Maybe they're intentionally being mean to me. But if I choose to forego and not even take offense in the first place, well, I'm not any worse off.

We may say, but then that person could do it again! We let that person get away with it! I think there's a difference. I don't think that if someone is intentionally trying to hurt me—which again is sometimes hard to even know—I must continue to let them hurt me. I can enforce boundaries. I think my best option may be to examine my pride and walk away from someone lost on their journey.

If they are intentional, I have the choice to become offended or angry and out of control OR not. Now, which state of mind do I want? One of peace or one that I feel all bothered. I think it's simple to see which one is the easier path. I also take away their power to control me because I'm The Boss of My Thinker.

I admit that sometimes I get all bothered and it makes the situation harder for me. Later I see it more clearly, but I'm trying to get faster at Being the Boss. I don't want to go into that Big Ugly Part or become reactive. I can instead choose to think to myself things like this: maybe I've been misunderstood, maybe they're having a funny half hour, maybe their mother is in the hospital. Let's forgo the whole 'being offended and should I forgive them' part because we understand there's nothing we need to forgive.

I take it a step further because I believe in Jesus Christ and our Father in Heaven. I don't believe it's my place to be worried about forgiving other people. I think whatever they've done—which I don't know their whole story, I can't read their mind, I don't know what's in their heart—it's between that person and God, He can work it out. I have faith that God knows all, so I'll just turn it over to Him. I see forgiveness as something that God does with perfect knowledge of the situation. I don't have perfect knowledge of any situation so I'm just not going to get messed up into that forgiveness business; it's not my thing. I choose to simply forgo.

Remember my Momism:

'It's better that it's done to you and not by you.'

This is a great saying to think about when someone has done something that seems hurtful or if they've done something mean—because mean things do happen. But it's always good to think, I'm so glad *I* didn't do that. I want my conscience to be clear.

Unhealthy thinking sometimes complicates forgiveness. If we're harboring any negative feelings or emotions like being sad, lonely, insecure, left out, tired, opinionated, etc., it's easy for us to hear someone say something—anything—and twist it so we can be offended. If we're intent on seeing the whole world as unfair and out to get us, or if we are absolutely drowning in self-pity, we make it a no-win situation for us all.

If we find ourselves becoming offended or angry frequently, it may be an indication we need to work on ourselves. Those feelings usually come from inside not outside. We become what we think about most of the time, so watch our thoughts and Be the Boss of Our Thinker.

What about abuse? We must be very careful about defining what abuse is. Because somebody does something we don't like, doesn't mean they're abusive. If someone calls us out because we've done something we shouldn't have done and they're standing up for themselves it doesn't mean because it hurts our feelings, that they are being emotionally abusive to us. Just as we would like to be able to speak up and express our feelings with kindness, we should allow others the same consideration. Golden Rule and all…

Now a caveat: of course, if a situation is dangerous or truly abusive, or illegal, step away and get help.

A question that has always helped me a lot is, where did the story start? We don't know another person's full history or even their side of one incident. We don't know why they're like they are, or why they think the things they think.

A good follow-up question is, do we even know the *whole* story? In my life, I've had lots of accomplishments, but my parents have never said anything. I could win an award at school, or in the community or in business, publish a book, give a speech, etc. They never mentioned it and they never came to the award ceremonies. Even when featured in newspaper articles, my parents still never said a word, they didn't seem to care.

Years after my father died, I ran into a man who worked with my dad for a long time. He asked, "Are you the one that moved out to Utah?" and I answered yes. Then to my great surprise, he said, "Your dad sure was proud of you. He always bragged about the things you did, and he had all those newspaper clippings he'd bring into work and show everybody."

I never knew that my dad felt proud of me; he never said anything to me; no congratulations or praise. He never mentioned those things; he didn't seem at all interested. It made me sad to think that I spent my time in his life feeling totally unloved. I didn't know the whole story.

The only filter we need is if it is true or not. If we have a poor self-image, then we tend to imagine that others are criticizing us—even though they are not; we can distort what was *actually* said and jump to negative conclusions. We think they hurt us, but in reality, it is the way we choose to think about it that hurts us. Then because we're hurt (but it is only our perception), we choose to strike back and hurt them *intentionally.* Remember, hurt people, hurt people. We hurl cruel names and say mean things without any apparent concern about the damage we are doing or the deliberate pain we are causing. As if broken glass, or hearts, can be restored. We may not even seem to care if what we say is true. What a tragic cycle we create.

> *"It is difficult to catch a black cat in a dark room,*
> *especially when it's not there."*
> **— CHINESE PROVERB**

Insecurities usually lead to obsessing about things and negatively exaggerating their meaning and importance. That's not healthy thinking; it often leads to rage and ruminating. It is never about the *problem*; it is the way we choose to deal with it. In a dark world, have we been a light? Let's add new, positive, healthy thoughts to our minds and prepare to change.

Humility

Making a mistake is not a big deal. It might mean that we're one step closer to finding a solution to a problem. Researchers try numerous methods to resolve a question, yet ideas that fail are common. Being wrong about something is not the end; it doesn't mean that *we* are wrong. One error does not make us worthless in everything in life. Our blunder is not *us*.

To be healthy, have the courage to be 'wrong.' For some people the idea is very scary. With unhealthy black-and-white thinking, we think if we mess up, then it means that *we* must be a bad person. But we are okay, even when we make a mistake. We can still work on that one issue; we don't need to give up and feel like a complete failure. We can understand that as a human, we will make missteps. Everyone does. Fix it the best we can and move on. It's not a reflection of us personally. Let me emphasize this one more time. *We* are not a mistake—no matter how many mistakes we make. We are all enough.

Let's consider that it is not always what happened, but our interpretation of what happened and our limiting beliefs that guide our reactions and emotions.

Isn't it interesting that we want people to agree with us in our views and can even become a bit offended if they don't validate us, but if we're wearing a dress and another woman shows up wearing the exact same dress, we feel differently about consensus suddenly? We're dismayed; we don't want them wearing the same dress. Sometimes diversity is preferred.

It may seem a little contentious if, in front of others, someone doesn't agree with us. Maybe it feels like they don't respect us or maybe we even feel publicly humiliated. But Be the Boss of Our Thinker. All our thoughts are choices we make. We don't need agreement or to be too heavily invested in our opinions. Disagreeing with us is not disrespect. If we stay calm and act in accordance with our values, we have no reason to be embarrassed either. And when we do have a different perspective, if the time is right, we might simply explore instead of arguing about it.

Understanding can only happen when we can still discuss; we don't have to reach a consensus. It's okay to amicably end with different viewpoints. Remember all our opinions are usually based on past experiences: things we've read, things we've done, or things other people have done that we've observed, etc. Because none of us have the exact same experiences, we will often arrive at a different conclusion and that's fine. Agreement is not necessarily our goal, but harmony and understanding might be a healthy consideration.

Not being able (or even willing) to look at others' beliefs is limiting to us. Being curious and open-minded is a great way to learn something. Emotion without reason leads to distortion of thought. Black-and-white thinking, *one* point of view, and fear of being wrong, all limit our ability to be happy and healthy.

What is Fair?

An old but wise joke: There are only two kinds of 'fair.' County Fair and State Fair. Let's change our expectations and examine the rules we make up. Don't falsely assume our rules are universal and that everyone knows and should follow them.

When my children were growing up, because they were of different ages and abilities, they had different rules. For instance, the older ones could stay up a little bit later. If the younger ones were up too late (for them) they felt tired, cranky, and weepy the next day. They needed a little more sleep and at times they even needed naps during the day. Of course, they would complain, "This isn't fair! Zach doesn't have to take a nap; why do I have to take a nap?" I thought it completely just because it fit their situation and worked best for them. It was ridiculous to compare a three-year-old's needs to someone sixteen years old. Many situations do not need to be equal or the same to be fair.

Sometimes in life, we may think something we're going through isn't fair. But do we really know enough to under-stand what *is* fair? It seems like there's much heartache, sadness, disasters, suffering, and pain in life but as well there is great joy, happiness, elation, fun, and laughter. Maybe *all* those things are fair. Don't they all make growth possible? All those feelings and experiences can help us understand what it's like to really be alive.

> *"Being fully human is not about feeling happy,*
> *it's about feeling everything."*
> —GLENNON DOYLE

What if we could only choose one emotion or one feeling? Even if we chose a good one like happy to make life 'fair', would that really be for the best? Because sad things do happen. What if we couldn't feel sadness?

Does it do us any good, is life better when we bemoan and cry and complain that life isn't fair? Especially when it's a situation we can't change. I heard a widow say it's not fair that her children had to grow up without a father. For some reason, people think that their life should be the way they want it, for it to be fair.

Well, what about those whose parents are divorced who grow up without a father? Or what about those who have a father but he's not a very kind and loving father? There are all types of situations and maybe we think it would be better if every child had a father with them their whole life, helping them and being loving and kind and all the idealization of what a father means to us, but that simply is not how life works. We can't teleport either, darn it.

Again, remember my old saying 'Life is like going swimming, we are going to get wet.' Spending a lot of time swimming, while complaining, whining, griping, and feeling victimized because we're wet, doesn't make sense. How much nicer it would be for our mental health to simply enjoy all the aspects of swimming. Even the getting wet part.

What's interesting too is that we all might think 'fair' is very different. I don't question whether it's *fair* that on the day of our big outdoor party celebration, it's raining. Maybe we should be more precise with our language. Maybe it's going to be *inconvenient* we're going to have to figure out how to work around it, maybe it's not the way we had hoped it would be, but can we honestly say that because it's raining, it isn't fair? When did rain become fair or unfair? And remember, somewhere there's probably a farmer who is elated that it's raining; so, is the rain unfair? Maybe it seems that way to us because we have the party, but it doesn't seem that way to the farmer whose precious crops need it.

Say this to ourselves, "Things would be okay in my life if I had _____ then I could be happy." Fill in the blank. Or we could say, "Without _____ I can't be happy." Think about this; how did you fill in the blanks? If you get *that*, THEN what will you blame your unhappiness on?

"When life shuts a door—open it again. It's a door.
That's how they work."
—ANONYMOUS

Honestly, we may not like trials, but I can say truthfully, that I really enjoy being around people who have overcome enormous trials and kept going. They are strong, kind, inspiring, and encouraging to others. Those individuals seem truly, deeply alive, not just breathing. These are my favorites to spend time with. I am greatly encouraged when I see hard experiences make someone more compassionate instead of bitter or hardened. I remember they had a choice and could have gone either way. I ponder, when the inevitable challenges come to me, which way will I go?

"Resilience is all about being able to overcome the
unexpected. Sustainability is about survival.
The goal of resilience is to thrive."
—JAMAIS CASCIO

Life has challenges. What did we expect? We're going to get wet and can still choose to live Happily Ever After.

When We Do Wrong

When we do something against our moral code to someone, it pains us deeply. We now have a choice, even if we think they may have deserved it. We can either quickly do all we can to make it right: fess up, apologize, provide restitution, and not do it again OR we can ruminate on it, feel bad, make excuses, and twist it to try to shift the responsibility from us to our victim. If we choose the latter, we get horribly stuck. In a sad effort to protect our self-esteem and feel better about what we did, we may unconsciously spin out of control. We're caught in a whirlpool of justifications and lies in our vain attempt to escape responsibility for something we know we never should have done.

The reasons we give ourselves to ease our conscience don't work to truly convince us because they are simply not true. So, we may wildly try to make up another reason. Again, being based on a lie or exaggeration, it doesn't soothe our conscience either and so on it goes. We may, with enough time, even begin to believe our new version of what happened.

If you find yourself trying to justify something you did that's against your moral code, you may be caught in this vortex. Be honest with yourself and make it right to find relief.

Sadly, this doesn't always happen before a person dies or moves away. That results in not being able to settle things which may leave us with regrets.

Epitome of Fall

Change is inescapable; the coming winter will be beautiful.
We might as well enjoy and appreciate the inevitable.
"If you don't like something, change it.
If you can't change it, change your attitude."

— MAYA ANGELOU

CHAPTER 11

DO

Simple Consistency in our actions beats one Big Deal.

Taking steps day by day to be kind in small ways is better than wreaking havoc daily and then every few years, making one, grand, nice gesture.

Chicago Subway

I remember the first time I took the subway. Traveling in Chicago on a business trip, I felt nervous. I had never done it before; I grew up in an area that didn't have subways, making it foreign to me. I stayed at a hotel out by O'Hare Airport, and I didn't have a rental car since my meetings were on-site, but I wanted to go downtown. I decided to take the subway.

I didn't possess any personal experience with subways but had certainly seen subway scenes in many movies. I knew the general idea though the details were vague. I asked the concierge a few questions and he directed me to the nearest stop, a short distance from the hotel. Arriving at the subway station, I looked at all the maps on the walls and the color charts of routes and quickly realized that 'downtown' was not a single spot. I wasn't sure where to get off. I also realized that there were different lines, and I may need to change trains.

The more I studied the map, the more confused I became. I felt nervous about what might happen if I took the wrong train and got lost. I looked around but there didn't appear to be any subway workers to assist me. A swirl of foreboding thoughts crowded my mind and I decided that it was too difficult for me, and I should give up.

But I really wanted to go downtown because I had never been there before and didn't know when I would have another chance. So, I pacified my cowardice with the idea that I would try again tomorrow after I had a chance to ask more questions to the concierge. But for now, I needed to go back to the hotel.

As I walked out, I looked around me and saw people that looked like they were having a lot of drug and alcohol problems in life. They seemed to be barely managing. I began to worry about getting robbed or worse.

But then I thought, wait a minute, if *those* people could get on the subway, surely, *I* can do this. As I looked at a train that came in and hordes of people poured out the door, I realized lots and lots and lots of people figured out how to do this every single day. And I didn't think they were any more talented or smarter or capable than me. I decided if they could do it, I can do it.

I took another look at the map trying to figure out the system and soon boarded a train. I also told myself that the worst that could happen would be I missed my stop, must turn around, and go back. Well, that's not a problem.

I made it downtown fine. I didn't want to give up in defeat; I needed to simply do it. It wasn't long before I became good at subways. Over the years, I've traveled around the world and traveled on many mass transit systems. They all had much in common, even when the languages differed.

Let's not allow ourselves to make excuses that hold us back from what we want to accomplish. Do it! Persevere. Don't give up or 'settle.' If we get overwhelmed over a big project, break it down and focus on one piece. Sometimes saying, well, it's the best I could do, is an excuse for subpar performance.

It is possible for an outside force to prevent us from doing something. But what cannot be taken from us is our thoughts. Everything we do begins with a thought. No one can prevent us from thinking the way we want to think. In a new situation, it's best to adopt a can-do attitude. If we start to have negative thoughts, ask ourselves, is this making things better or worse? Why would we keep thinking that way if it's making it worse? Let's have the courage and strength to say no to negative thoughts and change our thinking to something more positive.

If I don't know how to do something, I read and study until I get it, or ask for help. When I'm afraid, I look at my options on what to do to change my situation. It's energizing to know that I can transcend most problems. I don't feel defeated. I don't make time to feel sorry for myself, that is not something that makes things better.

I learned not to be deluded and fantasize about easy solutions. For example, if we have financial problems, let's not think about winning the lottery, it's a waste of time. When we don't have enough money, start thinking about realistic solutions we could try. Make a whole list, explore it, think of all the things that we could do to better our financial situation.

Let's not worry at first about how to do them, simply throw down a lot of ideas on a piece of paper then look at those solutions and weigh the pros and cons of each one. What will take more time? Will we need additional resources? Decide the best option right now and then go after it with boldness and courage.

Sometimes it's easier to eliminate choices and then we can see a solution that we can try. If any of these ideas don't work, don't worry about it, move on. Keep in mind that failures lead to success. It's a wonderful thing to know what *doesn't* work because then we don't waste time on it.

Words have power, so don't say, I can't do it! That is probably NOT true. Remember if someone else did it, then there is a good chance that we can do it too.

Mark's White Rim Trail Story

While attending an industry only Bicycle Trade Show, I heard about The White Rim Trail. In conversation with some friends from Moab, they mentioned a young guy who rode the entire circuit as a day ride. They spoke of his unbelievable effort in awe and reverence.

The White Rim Trail (WRT) is BIG and challenging. The journey is a loop inside Canyonlands National Park, Utah. It's around 175 kilometers (110 miles) long with about 7,000+ vertical feet of climbing. It's traditionally a two or three day, 4x4 excursion. Bikes trips are usually organized for three to five days and supported by a four-wheel drive.

Hearing about that guy, I thought; if he could do it, so could I. With that thought seed planted, I looked it up, considered it, then committed myself to be, That Guy, too. I also talked about it and told people my plan, then asked around to see who wanted to do it with me. No takers. Are you kidding me? It sounded so fun.

In my world of Think, Say, Do; I only had one thing left; Do It. I picked a date in late January 2007, four months out, and began to prepare. I planned to make this grueling ride in winter. I remember as I contemplated my public commitment, I started to wonder if I could do it. At fifty-two years old would it be wise to take on something like the WRT as an unassisted, solo day ride? Absolutely!

I made a fitness plan and pushed ahead at full speed. My plan included *long* hours in a gym on a stationary bike. I increased my time in the Spin Bike Torture Chamber from a few hours a day and eventually put in many intense twelve-hour training days with only a few *short* breaks.

Physically I felt ready, emotionally I felt anxious. Truth be told, it intimidated and scared me. I often reminded myself, if 'that guy' could do it so can I! That sentiment seemed to calm me down—most of the time.

FEAR = Feeling Extra Anxious Really!

I carried a healthy respect for the WRT with me, laced with a portion of fear, on the solo drive from Alberta, Canada to Utah. I felt as ready as I would ever be.

Upon arriving in Moab, I spoke with some friends and let them know my plans; I would park at the bottom of the notorious Shafer Trail and leave the keys to my truck in a specific location. I would start before sunrise, and finish after sunset. If I didn't call them by midnight, they were instructed to please come and find me. I planned to ride the loop counterclockwise. So, the rescue team should take my vehicle and do the loop in a clockwise direction.

I drove to the bottom of Shafer, set up quarters in the truck and went to sleep. Waking up comfortably warm in a winter weather mummy bag at about seven am, I climbed out and quickly realized how cold it had become. Zero degrees (−20 C). The forecast had indicated a cold night, warming to above freezing by 10:00 am. Yet here at my location it felt CRAZY COLD!

I got up and ate some dried fruit, beef jerky, and some sort of power bar along with an electrolyte drink. Outside the air felt capital C Cold! Discouraged by my fear, I agonizingly decided to abandon my aspirations of a WRT day ride. Erring on the side of reasonable caution, I told myself, 'I'm out.'

That stated, I still wanted to go for a ride. Deep in the canyon, dawn finally approached. I put on my warmest gear, took a full Camelbak, two water bottles, some dried fruit, beef jerky and cheese, and started the ride to the top of the mesa, fifteen hundred feet up on a partially *ice and snow-covered, switch-back ascent.*

Climbing warmed my body to a comfortable level despite the cold. Easily conquering the dreaded climb, I soon felt great! The sun had come up, so I continued riding along my planned route. By mid-morning and forty miles in on the WRT, it had warmed up considerably and I remained strong.

I thought, *maybe this is still doable.* Maybe?!? Then came a thrilling, internal commitment. *I'm In! I can and will do the*

WRT after all. Excited to reverse my earlier heartbreaking decision to quit, my hand reached down to retrieve a bottle for a first drink but realized that it held a frozen brick. 'Now what?' Bashing the plastic bottle on my handlebars while zipping down a dirt road, I discovered it wasn't solid ice. Cold water. Bonus!

I came to a junction and instinctively turned left. At this point, the realization hit me that the printed map—lay back in the truck. *Darn! Now what?* Keep in mind, in those days we didn't have GPS on our phones. And down in the canyon there wasn't any cell service anyway. In preparation for the trip, I had poured over the maps and had a pretty solid recollection of the route. Double down, *I've got this, I'm still in. Besides, if there's trouble, my friends will come in like the cavalry to the rescue, all is good. Giddy-up little doggy.*

Soon the trail got tough. Up one mesa, then a sketchy descent down, sandy sections, and good, smooth, compacted ground. I stopped for a few minutes for calorie intake. Then pedaled past a few more junctions with signs put up by National Parks personnel. Relatively confident of my location, I still worried if I remained on the WRT. Had I missed something and taken an unintentional outlier route?

I kept pushing as twilight came into the canyons. Using a small camping headlamp, I readied myself for desert darkness. The bitter cold began to creep in once again. I felt tired and weary, but not physically exhausted yet. Mentally and emotionally though, my tortured soul second-guessed myself in a big way. It grew dark now; food ran low, and my energy lagged. In addition, I felt utterly alone. I had not talked to another person in over twenty-four hours. The man-made road, a few signs, and the occasional vapor trail of a jet passing overhead showed the only evidence of humanity seen all day in this vast desert.

For quite a while I had wondered why I wasn't back to my truck yet. Did I recall the map correctly? Being horribly lost or possibly off-course, would my rescuers be able to find me? What had I been thinking? All this played on a program in the back of my mind, eroding my self-confidence, belittling my preparation, and negatively impacting my resolve.

Now fighting fatigue, a deteriorating attitude, and pitch-black darkness, something glimmered in front of me. My dim headlamp revealed my route had brought me within a few feet of smashing into the back of my truck parked at the side of the dirt path. 'Made It!'

(Mark glosses over the incredible feat of a fifty-two-year-old riding the WRT, solo, in ONE day, in winter, without a map or backup jeep support. He is truly an amazing, strong adventurer and possibly a bit crazy—but in a very lovable way.)

Be strong, in every way: mentally, physically, spiritually, and emotionally. Inevitably we will be blindsided and make mistakes. Hard things will happen. Get ready. Be the Boss of Your Thinker! Let's keep going in the middle of difficulties. Second-guessing is counterproductive, it doesn't make the journey better. Do hard things intentionally. It will build strength and increase our confidence and ability to endure life's adversity.

We can create a support mechanism around us: friends, family, community, church, and work. We need to understand reciprocity. As we give time and energy to others, we are creating a safety net for ourselves if things go off-track. Take in all the information, make a decision, and go! When we get new details, changing our minds and recalibrating our direction might be appropriate.

"Good decisions come from good information."
— **M. S. STARK**

The moral to the story: Once we have completed our plans, Get Started! Perpetual preparation isn't valuable if we don't act on it. Discipline and determination combined with action will produce impressive results. Get off the couch.

Move Forward

One exercise to encourage us to keep going is this: Add the word 'almost.' It can motivate us to continue moving and push a little harder to finish—don't give up even if it gets difficult. *Almost* completing a task is not satisfying. Do it. Do it boldly. For example, we *almost* did the dishes. Is that any different than not doing the dishes? We have *almost* completed the quarterly report. Won't the boss still not be pleased? We were *almost* kind, isn't that unkind? Keep going! Don't settle for 'almost' Get'er done!

Consider the energy needed to accomplish our tasks. Everything is an energy exchange, not only do we need to be mindful of who we surround ourselves with, but also of the media we consume, who and what we listen to, the personalities we follow online, and the conversations we have both with ourselves and with others. Everything we consume affects our overall energy and well-being. Let's intentionally do our own thing. Spend energy wisely. Be Bold. Don't simply play along.

Sometimes we get stymied, blocked, stressed, or discouraged, etc. Taking a break often helps us come back feeling fresh and ready to tackle what we need to do. But don't quit. Perhaps one of the following may also help.

Ideas for Taking a Break to Refresh

1. Read a good book.
2. Go for a walk outside.
3. Send thank you cards.
4. Read some positive quotes.
5. Call or text a friend and express appreciation.
6. Write in a journal.
7. List good things about ourselves.
8. List blessings or things to be grateful for.
9. Sing.
10. Dance.
11. Talk to a friend.
12. Read a joke book.
13. Play games with friends.
14. Get a Massage.
15. View great art.
16. Take photos.
17. Find a new hobby or enjoy an old one.
18. Call Beth. (She's my sister. That's what I do. Oh, you don't know her? She'd talk to you anyway.)
19. Go for a long drive in the country.
20. Cook or bake something and share it.
21. Enjoy your favorite food.

22. Gardening.
23. Hug a loved one.
24. Hold a baby.
25. Play with a pet.
26. Fix, tinker, rearrange, organize, clean…
27. Forgive.
28. Go for another bike ride (that's what Mark does).

Use the following self-talk and find evidence for it: 'I can do hard things.' Reflect and remember past difficult accomplishments. Think about how we approached it. How we did it. How we felt afterward. Do not dwell on failures in the past, but perhaps we could analyze one to determine what we could do better next time. Test our limits, and even push them a little each time. We will be glad to see great results.

Let's not set ourselves up by thinking we can't Live Happily Ever After. Instead, decide to be happy and see how frequently we can manage it.

Mark's Story of Finding Success

In my early twenties, I decided to further my education and needed to earn some money. I learned about some specialty, industrial lubricants that could be used on farms in agricultural equipment. After a few hours of training, I went out to sell door-to-door on my own.

On my first day, I totally butchered the presentation, but my sales were great. I thought, *wow I'm really good at this, I've got the magic. If I could do this every day, I'll be able to save for university in no time.*

Day Two: Didn't sell a thing. Day Three: No one was home, or they didn't have time to talk to me. Day Four: Still not good. I felt discouraged. The only thing accomplished: burning gas and wasting time. Hmmm, *maybe this wasn't such a good idea after all.*

But I remembered that first day, the sales were good. How could I get the magic back? I decided to keep going and not give up so easily. The next day proved a little better, clearly some days were good, and some were not, but I met lots of people, and over time made very loyal clients leading to ongoing success.

The moral of the story is: There is no magic, I needed to think about it differently. I studied books that taught me salesmanship which significantly influenced my thoughts and future. I learned, focused, practiced, and polished those basic success principles like vision, passion, and discipline.

Now I understand that it's the same with building relationships whether it be with a spouse, children, clients, or in any endeavor. We must persevere. Be genuine, honest, and work hard and usually great success will follow.

Mark Advises Us: Don't Chase Bears

My father, Herb Bishop, told me of an adventure when he and a friend, both thirteen years old, decided that they would ride a motorcycle from Raymond (a small town in southern Alberta) to Vancouver, BC. Circa 1938. Their excursion took place well before the Trans-Canada Highway or the Rogers Pass when few paved roads existed. The plan to visit the friend's sister proved not exceptionally well conceived. They strapped some gear to the 125cc Francis Barnett and headed west. Maps were not great, so they talked with fellow travelers and were directed from place to place They traveled through Montana, Idaho, and Washington State while on their way to the Pacific Coast of British Columbia. Their route took them over forestry, logging, and gravel roads of the era. They made it to Vancouver and returned the same general way a few weeks later.

A couple of years after my father's passing, I had some extra time and decided to recreate the trip in memory of my dad. So, in the summer of 2011, I headed west from Calgary to Vancouver on my BMW GSA motorcycle. Equipped with maps and a GPS, everything had been figured out. I decided to ride only on logging, forestry, and even power line roads. All of which can be exceptionally rustic. My intention focused on staying off pavement as much as possible.

Pretty early I began to wonder "What was I thinking?" This adventure included navigating sketchy river crossings, broken bridges, washed-out deeply rain-rutted sections, and trees and debris from winter avalanches. Getting to the Pacific coast represented three days of full-body pucker. I felt completely out of my element with this great big motorcycle piloting through that scraggy landscape solo.

The terrain got increasingly technical until my descent down the west side of the Coastal Range into the Frazer Valley. I crossed a rustic bridge made of logs three to four feet in diameter, covered with cross planks and dirt, without any side rails. It stretched forty or fifty feet across a chasm of sheer rock walls above an emerald-green river that flowed robustly down the mountains. The span had been used by logging trucks, so for me to go across it was a no-brainer. Crossing over, I came to a T-Intersection and headed south.

The road proved fantastic, and I felt like a conqueror for finishing something I'd never heard of anybody doing. Except, of course, two thirteen-year-olds who pioneered it in 1938. I started down the gentle descent on a pristine, dust-controlled gravel road. Thrilled to be near the west terminus of my adventure, I became a little daring and started drifting the motorcycle around some corners. Pavement-like, the gravel road had a little layer of sand on it. Amazingly good for a back country road; so much fun to be riding quickly once again.

Sliding around a corner, I saw up ahead of me, a hundred feet or so, the jiggling back end of a bear. A large, mature grizzly about four feet high and four feet wide, running down the road away from me. With my conqueror attitude, I thought quickly and I'm sure erroneously, he knows I'm at the top of the food chain and he's running away, I'm a hero and even this bear knows it.

I started to close the gap on him. As it ran down the road, I began to push it along by getting a little closer. The bear got tense; the muscles in his hindquarters were now defined. It didn't jiggle anymore. Running at around seventy kph or so, this giant made a full-speed left-hand turn, like he had engaged his Go-Go Gadget Go Claws and ran down towards the rushing creek.

Mere moments later, I passed the spot where it veered off the road and disappeared into the forest. The total time I engaged the bear, to the time of its Exit Stage Left, lasted less than ten seconds. A few moments of bad judgment that could have had a tragic finale.

My reaction surprised me. I thought that I would say to myself, look at that, I chased a grizzly and won. Instead, after a head scratch, I thought, *are you kidding me, what did you do, that's so ridiculous. A love tap from that monster could have done you in. I wasn't acting like the Boss or even a low-level manager of my Thinker.*

I began the short, eight-hour trip home on the Trans-Canada and started to reminisce about all the events that had transpired over the past few days. Thoughts were launched and an internal dialogue ensued.

> *You know it's a bad idea to chase grizzly bears.*
> *What were you thinking?*
> *Bears kill people!*

How many times do we flirt with situations that could damage us or someone we care for? Do we ever play with potentially devastating temptations? Whether it's overeating, substance abuse, bingeing on screens, or anything that could injure our souls. Do we chase bad habits?

How about actions that could severely hurt or even kill us emotionally or spiritually?

Do we chase those kinds of *BEARS?*

What are our individual weaknesses, our Achilles Heels? It's probably a good idea to identify our personal grizzlies and then commit to not chasing them!

"Flirting with our known vulnerabilities is a very bad idea. It's sabotage of the worst kind: self-sabotage."

—M. S. STARK

Moral to the story: It's never a good idea to flirt with disaster. Don't chase bears, no matter what they look like.

Low Clouds Hovering Over Fish Creek

When individuals are experiencing gloomy circumstances, our genuine smiles or kind words can help others find spectacular hope. "What do we live for if it is not to make life less difficult for each other?"

— GEORGE ELIOT

CHAPTER 12

SEIZE RESPONSIBILITY

Own It!

We really admire a fabulous family in our Utah neighbor-hood: the Mortensons. They have a family motto: Own It. It means to take responsibility. Not only for one's words or actions, but if anyone sees something out of place, put it where it belongs even if it's not yours. There are numerous applications for this directive. Let's teach our children and ourselves to 'Own It!' Take responsibility for our thoughts or our actions, and the results, good or bad.

We can have confidence and resilience. Nurture an 'I can' attitude. Try this experiment. Right now, let's raise our hands over our heads as high as we can. Okay, hold them there for a few seconds. Now, raise them another inch. Did we find that we raised them higher? Isn't it interesting what we could do when we thought we were as high as we could go? Seldom in life are we maxed out even though we may think we are. Try new things and believe we can do more.

Let's love ourselves. Know who we are (or are working to become) and what we believe. We can create, and regularly refer to, a personal Creed on how we will act, and diligently strive to live by it. It's powerful to line up our actions and words with our beliefs and values. We need to understand our ideals and then follow them as closely as we can and be honest with ourselves when we fail. Don't make excuses, blame others, justify, or say we can't help it if we feel a certain way. Take full responsibility for all our thoughts, words, emotions, and actions. Own it. Then we can change it if necessary.

We can accept that we have strengths and be grateful for them. Also, acknowledge our weaknesses and use them to set goals to become more like we envision. Remember, don't judge our past self and actions by our present self. Hopefully, we are better and will act, speak, and think differently now.

Thinking in a Healthy way is a skill we get better at with practice. When we find ourselves repeating a particular problem over and over, STOP. Think about it and find a solution. Decide specifically how to not have that occur again. For example: I don't have the problem of losing my keys because I've decided where they live and that's where they stay.

Skills

There are some skills we can develop that make being responsible easier. The foundation of being naturally responsible improves our self-image. For Mark and I, understanding we have a divine origin and then aligning what we think, say, and do with the values we espouse creates within us a strong sense of harmony. Knowing we are children of a Heavenly Father; we will be comfortable with ourselves and grow to like who we are. We won't have a reason to make excuses for our behavior because we understand we are a work in progress, and we have evidence that we are truly striving to improve.

We can all learn not to blame others because we realize that we are each on our own journey and we are seriously concerned about taking the right path. That will make us willing to take responsibility for all our thoughts, words, or actions because we know *that* is where our power lies.

We will refrain from justifying poor actions because we won't settle for subpar behavior from ourselves. We don't want those limits anymore. Our goal is to be all we can be.

Bad things have probably happened to all of us, after all, we live in a world inhabited by normal human beings with frailties and weaknesses. We can forgive or forgo and escape those bonds that bind us. Instead of harboring hurt, anger, sorrow, or feelings of revenge or self–pity, we yearn to heal. We desire to remove the cloak of a broken soul and emerge strong, confident, and whole.

Let's study empathy, compassion, and how to have happy relationships. We become more responsible when we can speak openly and honestly. We let go of any inclination to overpower others or be overpowered. When we remind ourselves there may well be an underlying story to another's poor behavior, we can develop compassion and charity that will free us to not only be responsible for our own feelings but also allow others to not feel harshly judged.

Some skills may not seem to be related to responsibility but the more secure we are and the better we practice and align with our values, the more mentally healthy and responsible we will be. Here are some ideas and skills that will help us be more responsible.

- Set goals.
- Do the right thing, at the right time, for the right reason.
- Learn to analyze and challenge our thoughts.
- Discover how to be a cheerful, pleasant person, and not only when others are around.
- Have an 'I can do it' attitude.
- Be grateful for our resilience.
- Look for the Good, Be Positive.
- Do not get stuck in a funk.
- Even amid great trials we can find things to be grateful about and shift our focus.
- Don't forget to be thankful for our strengths.
- Being strong and staying happy through hard times does not diminish the adversity but makes it manageable.

We CAN do hard things without falling into a depressed state. Let's put some time into learning and practicing these vital principles and turning them into essential habits.

We will actively work on becoming who we truly desire when our focus is not staring in a mirror with a self–absorbed reflection but viewing the world through a window. Soak in our humanity. Then we lose the stress of needing to be perfect, or juggle comparisons, or worry about what others may think of us. We have freedom to make the world a better place. When we are comfortable within, and live in the moment, we banish anxiety.

Excuses and Blame

Making excuses is unhealthy and irresponsible. It also doesn't work. We can't get away with lying to ourselves; we know we messed up. Own it and move on. Otherwise, we will be dragged into the game of making another excuse when we realize the first is lame, and then an even bigger excuse, until soon it will all be ridiculous.

Once when my son, Josh, was really young, all the furniture in the family room had been moved, cushions were scattered over the floor, and he hopped wildly in a large circle from piece to piece. I told him to put the room back together and stop climbing on the furniture like that. When I returned to the room later, he leaped from the sofa to the chair and then to a table. He expressed his excuse for not obeying by saying that there were alligators all over the floor and he had to stay away from them. I pointedly gazed around the room slowly, looked at him with raised eyebrows, and said, oh yeah? Well, alligators need water. I don't see any. He quickly answered, "These are very sweaty alligators."

It's a bad idea to try to fool ourselves or others. Come clean. It feels so much better.

If we view our errors as someone else's fault, we surrender the ability to change. We give up our power in those circumstances and we are in essence, out of control. We can also learn how to be respectful and stop belittling and demeaning others to build ourselves up. Because that is what we do when we blame someone for our mistakes.

Instead, let's be confident in our ability to change, and recognize our part in situations—regardless of what someone else may have contributed. When we read an article on what a good spouse does and hand it to our better half, we may be shifting blame, instead of reading it with the purpose of self-improvement.

When Marissa was little, I went to check out the alarming quiet from her bedroom. I walked in to see elaborate crayon drawings covering one whole wall from about three feet down. Facing towards the large, colorful new mural, stood a line of her stuffed animals and dolls, all with an incriminating crayon in their hand or posed on their paw. She immediately pointed at her 'babies' and firmly stated, "They did it." She still had to scrub 'their' misdeed.

Justification

Perhaps we're angry because a person hurt our feelings; so, we falsely justify our temper with weak thoughts like *anyone would be angry.*

That's simply not true. We have no idea what would make someone else angry. I have had someone overhear a conversation with me and another individual and tell me later what the other person said would make them angry, and I must be mad. It had not even occurred to me it would be something that would make anyone even a little upset.

Our self-talk is very important. It's essential that if we get annoyed, we take responsibility for that feeling. One way to do that is by questioning *why* this is upsetting us. Is this making us feel like we're not good enough? Is this reminding us of something that we're not talented at and so we feel inferior? Do we think this person is demeaning us? Is there a memory from our past that makes us feel uncomfortable?

Once we can understand why it makes us angry, we can challenge our thoughts and have a healthier reaction.

Some people say that there are only two primary emotions: love and fear. If we're feeling angry, do we think that's coming from love or fear? For example, we may become angry at our child who isn't paying attention in a parking lot and a car nearly hits them. It's very likely the anger is coming from fear that our child could have been hurt because we love the child. Isn't it interesting that we may not react in a loving, kind, compassionate, and concerned manner, but we let fear take over so that it quickly transfers to the emotion of anger, and we yell at the child? Let's try to react from love, not fear.

It would be so helpful if we would read, study, and learn how to control our thoughts that lead to unhealthy emotions and be fully responsible for them.

Not Perfect

I think it's interesting how often we hear people say comments like, 'My kids are really good, I mean they're not perfect, but they're good kids.' Why do we put the disclaimer in there? There wasn't any question whether the kids were perfect. We can end this unhealthy hang-up over perfection.

It's alright for us to say we accomplished something, and it turned out good, we learned a new skill or hobby, or we had a good day at pickleball. It isn't necessary to add, 'Of course I'm not perfect,' because everyone already knows that and, it's sort of like a waiver that we add to soften anything good we do, so we don't appear too proud of ourselves. Why can't we realize we're all working on improving and that's all we need to do. We don't need to be concerned about being perfect; simply strive to be better. If we improve, that's enough.

Honestly Stepping Up

For some of us, it's hard to take full responsibility for our actions because unfortunately, we've become very good at blaming others and twisting the truth. We are incredibly invested in accusing others. Otherwise, all the horribleness is our fault and that's a heavy burden to bear.

If we know we did wrong, but do not make any restitution whatsoever, make no effort to overcome the issue, and soon do it again, it is selfish and damaging. Being able to admit we have a fault, studying and looking for help to develop the skills to overcome it, and then diligently working on it is vital to our health. Not taking action to change a problem or simply letting a difficult situation happen over and over is NOT being honest with ourselves or those around us. We must accept responsibility; it is an important part of our mortal journey.

Light and Shadows

We can trust when we see shadows that light is present. "*Trust is the glue of life. It's the most essential ingredient in effective communication. It's the foundational principle that holds all relationships.*"

— STEPHEN R. COVEY

CHAPTER 13
LOVING RELATIONSHIPS

Close, healthy relationships reduce stress, anxiety, and unhealthy thoughts. The condition of our associations even affects our physical well-being. If we are in positive relationships, there's evidence we are less likely to get sick after exposure to flu and colds. Research also shows we may experience faster recoveries.

Our self-image is vital to living the life we choose rather than being doomed to react to negativity. The more we like ourselves (which results when we live our principles) the happier we are with others. A good self-image also attracts individuals to us and can inspire them to reach their potential. When our relationships remain strong, our health is better, we're happier, and we feel more motivated.

Love is important in our lives. It is not only being involved in a romantic relationship. We can love ourselves. We can love our family. We can love dogs. We can love our friends. We can love chocolate. We can love laughter. We can love trees or rocks or oceans or bikes. If we love something, we enjoy it fully. Let's find things we love, and love 'All In.' And we'll have lots of love in our life, but *chief* is being lovable.

We usually love our spouse, but we may not like everything they do. When we also choose to *like* them, we will learn to enjoy their quirks. Eventually, we will acquire the uncanny ability to anticipate their Crazy and even adore it. Personalities are not cafeteria style. We don't get to pick and choose, because the person is a package deal. It's what makes them who they are. If they want to change something about themselves, it is their job, not ours.

> *"Everyone I see today will be blessed by me—*
> *with my smile, my comforting presence,*
> *my cheerful countenance, and my kind spirit."*
>
> **—M. S. STARK**

Mark and I believe there is an order in building a romantic relationship. If we switch the order, there's often a problem. We think it's a good idea to first spend enough time to be friends, then eventually best friends, and then move into romance.

Mark had been a widower for a few years, and I was a recent widow when we met. We'd both previously made lists of what we wanted in a partner (not surprisingly, they matched), and we knew our deal breakers (also a match, so no problem). Neither of us would have compromised those traits we knew we needed; they were vital to us.

Mark is from Calgary, Alberta, Canada, and I had recently moved to St. George, Utah, USA. Though we were able to be together a lot, we spent almost half of our three-and-a-half-year courtship long-distance—in two different countries! We even wrote and edited some of this book from afar. We invested incredible amounts of time each day on the phone and became acquainted with each other very well. We talked a lot and had no secrets. Our attraction was not shallow, many long discussions made it deep and lovely, and quite magical. We totally accept each other for who we are, adore our time together, and we don't like being apart.

Our relationship is total bliss and oneness. We laugh and chat and have a ridiculous amount of fun no matter what we're doing. We work together seamlessly and with mutual beliefs, we are amazed at how easy it is to be together, especially since we were both married before and know how different it can be. Our close unity and immense love make it feel like one soul in two bodies. We adore each other all the time. Mark loves my curiosity and eagerness to try new things. I surprised him once when I asked if we could please go on a walk—at 1:00 a.m. in a temperature 47 degrees below zero with gentle snow falling. Pleased I didn't fear Canada's famous winter, he enthusiastically agreed. It felt magical walking through the woods in the muffled silence of deep snow brightly illuminated by the cloud cover's reflection (fortunately we had great equipment). I love his playful nature, exuberance, kindness, and wisdom.

Agreements

To avoid a lot of disagreements, focus on *agreements* first—well before making a long-term relationship commitment. If you are already in a serious relationship, try to agree on principles as often as possible. Let's choose a good partner for *us*. It is probably the most important decision we'll ever make. We must be honest with ourselves during the process. Don't ignore 'red flags.' Let's be authentic and transparent when we date, with our eyes wide open. Take your time. Enjoy it.

*"When someone shows you who they are,
believe them the first time."*

— MAYA ANGELOU

To assess our long-term compatibility, we must go through deliberate, essential considerations such as: are we a match intellectually, spiritually, emotionally, and physically?

Some people spend more time purchasing a pair of jeans than choosing a partner. If denims are too short or too tight or too wide or narrow or even the wrong color, we keep looking. During the dating stage is the time to be 'fussy.' Determine what is necessary in a companion for your happiness. Will your future be harmonious and balanced with this individual? The most important traits will vary by person. Having similar goals, values, morals, beliefs, and ideas about some common marriage deal-breakers like money, family, interests, intimacy, recreation, how time is spent, and selfishness, may be crucial areas of agreement for relationship success.

Other matters may not be so pivotal such as appearance, ambition, social tendencies, sense of humor, political views, religion, or skills like cooking or handyman repairs. Although if something on that list is super important to you, weigh it carefully. Don't make assumptions; talk about these areas. Talk to each other a lot, make sure there are no issues you avoid discussing, and don't make excuses for someone's alarming behavior.

Understand that mental health issues or addictions will make a healthy relationship difficult to maintain. The rate of divorce in those cases is extremely high for a reason. Mental stability and emotional maturity are vitally important. A stable person can work with you to make your many dreams come true, but a person who struggles to maintain sobriety, control a bad temper, or is unstable will cause you to have *one* overriding dream—a healthy relationship.

Also, if you have been married before, especially if there are children (regardless of age), research blended families. Know what you are getting into.

Give yourself an excellent chance to be successful in a relationship. Good decisions come from good information. And good information regarding interpersonal relationships takes time. Before making a long-term commitment, be scrupulously honest with yourself, and invest in togetherness in a variety of situations and experiences. Pay attention. 'She's very pretty and affectionate,' or 'He's funny and drives a cool car' is unlikely to be enough. An essential combination is someone with a strong sense of **responsibility** and **kind empathy** that you **trust** and **respect**. These are all vital foundations for a strong, long-lasting relationship. Hopefully, the person is The Boss of their Thinker.

Disagreements

We must always keep our promises, so make them carefully. In healthy relationships, we all know that if we say we're going to do something—or not do something—then we're committed. If anything changes and we want to make other arrangements—regardless of the reason—we must renegotiate first. If we make plans together, we change plans together. We think we can't really trust if one of us doesn't do what we said we would or would not do. It is important to be able to implicitly trust each other.

Most arguments in a relationship are not over the issue but in trying to assign who is right and who is wrong. It is usually two different opinions, neither of which is wrong or right. Just different. Our body may feel tense, and we may feel attacked or that we are not good enough. That does not mean we are under a terrible and huge assault. There isn't a need to overreact and equate how we may feel in our body with how mean we interpret the other person is being. They may kindly and simply disagree with us.

Feelings/Opinions are not facts.

If we have told ourselves that if we are disagreed with, that means we are being criticized, then we may overreact. However, if deep inside we believe strongly that we have lots of opinions and they differ from other peoples' ideas, when someone disagrees with us, that's fine. For example, we like blue, and they like yellow.

Our favorite colors are only preferences. Blue is not better it is only what we may prefer. Our other opinions should be no more divisive than any of our preferences. It's nothing sinister. So, to contend over what color is right is ridiculous. Since there are two primary emotions, love, and fear, if we enter fear, we become contentious or angry. And if we become contentious because of a difference of opinion, perhaps we're afraid that our opinion is not as valid as what we think it is and we get angry to defend it. It's kind of silly. Or maybe we take it to a more personal level and think it's not looking at any opinion at all but they're contending against *us*. And that makes us feel like *we* are what's wrong. And themz fightin' words!

"Love can only be found through the act of loving."
— **PAULO COELHO**

Perhaps if we decide to feel the emotion of love instead, we will become accepting, understanding, and tender towards our partner. There's no need to fight. To argue over opinion is absurd. We reason that it simply means that they see it in a different way based on their past experiences and things that they've learned or incorporated into their thinking.

If we are overreacting, we might ask ourselves, what is this making me think? What meaning am I attaching to it? Is it making me feel worthless, or afraid, or like I'm losing? If that's the case, we might need to spend some time thinking about how healthy and normal it is to have different experiences than someone else. It's all right to accept their various opinions instead of twisting it and deciding that it means we are being attacked. There is no reason to feel enraged or like we MUST make the other person agree with us. Or think if they would only see our point better, then they would agree, and all would be well. It is not about reaching consensus; it is about coming to an understanding.

Explore Rather Than Argue

So, when somebody disagrees with our opinion, maybe a healthy, loving way to respond is to become curious as to what experiences they have had to bring them to that opinion. That would change it to an exploration of why they think that, as opposed to an argument.

Don't get caught up in seeking drama, excitement, or feeling more alive when there is a fight. We may not even be conscious of this thought process. That is not a healthy way to invite thrills into our lives. Sometimes when our thoughts are unhealthy, we often feel sad or insignificant. We may think our drab life is so boring we unconsciously seek to rev it up with a strong emotion like anger. Instead, seek exhilaration in life through great interactions with others, or fun hobbies, or being outdoors, or engaging in exciting activities.

Our relationships do not need conflict. When we are comfortable with ourselves, we don't need approval of others by forcing them to declare our opinions are the right ones. We don't need to think we won, and it does not make us feel better. If our opinion is valid, there is no need to fight about it. Even if the other person is insistent that their opinion is THE right one. Realize they need some 'thought therapy.' Let it go.

But they do not respect us, we say. Then let's respect ourselves; that's enough. Fighting over opinions does not make us a winner, it is shallow, silly, and childish. We didn't win anything. We are not the appointed judge of what is right or wrong. Remember, some things matter, most things don't. Fighting is fear-based, let's choose love.

Remember: Temper is our enemy; humor is our friend.

When we are in a relationship, if we start looking for things that irritate us, we're probably going to find them. But if we think about looking for the good and minimizing things that bug us, or even decide we can like those things, we'll be more content. For example, Mark is a biking fanatic. I can choose to be annoyed and resent the time and money he spends on it. Or I can choose to like the fact that he has this passion in life that he's very good at. He's had lots of adventures doing it, it's great exercise outdoors, and it's something fun and healthy that we can do together. I've learned to love it too. Sometimes he goes alone on trails too scary for me or with one of his many Biking Brothers. We all need friends. That attitude and way of thinking make a better relationship. Of course, Mark keeps a healthy balance and I know for sure that I am number one in his life, as he is in mine.

Made-Up Rules

Sometimes, we make up 'The Rules of Life" and then become bitterly disappointed when someone breaks one. A rule *we* made up and *they* know nothing about. We falsely assume EVERYONE knows these statutes, agrees with them, and is bound to keep them. When we decide something should be done a certain way, at a certain time, etc. and then insist that everyone follow these 'Rules of Life' it sets us up for unrealistic expectations and can lead to unjust judgment and frustration. The rules are usually simply the way we like things.

We can have rules for ourselves, but we need to understand that these are not THE RULES for everyone. The problem comes when we assume that there is a right way and a wrong way to do things, and our way is the right one. Most of the time, these hard, fast rules are simply an opinion or a pref-erence, or the way our mom did it. No more and no less. If we can accept this, relationships will be easier, and we will suffer far less disappointment and offense. And we'll Live Happily Ever After.

Sometimes we inherit these Life Rules from another, like a parent, and adopt them and pass them on without realizing it is only one opinion. It usually does not hold true for every-one. Plus, people have many opinions and just because they are different than ours doesn't make them wrong. Rules we make up and expect everyone to follow—even though we may think they're wonderful—may not serve us well, but instead, can make us sad victims or cause a battle of wills (Mark calls it a high-volume conversation). Decide rules for ourselves and allow others to make rules for themselves unless it is a marriage or relationship rule, then we make them together. 'How to fold socks' is not an example of a marriage rule but 'call if you're going to be late' might be.

For example, we invite a couple over for dinner. It's a fun evening; we like them and look forward to a budding friendship. They express thanks and we're happy. Now our rule comes in. It is their turn to invite us, and we can't have them over again until after that happens. OUR rule. Weeks go by and no invitation arrives. Slowly, we not only grow resentful, but their very character begins to change in our minds. We may now obsess that she didn't offer to help with dishes again after we refused her first offer. Maybe we don't want to be friends with them. After all, we now know because they aren't following Our Rule for Friendship, they are simply rude. Not true at all.

It can cause more problems too. For example: the man has that rule, but his wife doesn't know about it. A couple of weeks after the dinner, they run into the other couple again and they talk about how much fun they had and say, "We should do that again."

The wife says, "Are you busy this Friday?" They answered that they were not, and they'd love to come over.

Afterwards, as the man and his wife get in their car, the man angrily asks, "Why did you invite them again? You know it's their turn!"

The wife responds calmly, "What do you mean, it's their turn? It's okay if we invite them over. For some people it's scary to have someone come to their house and be responsible for dinner and hosting an evening; it makes them nervous wrecks. It may seem easier after we get to know each other better."

"But it's their turn! They're taking advantage of us!" fumes the man. "What is wrong with you?"

"Wrong with *me*? You're the one ...." And so, it begins.

'Rules' over how to load the dishwasher, how to sweep the floor, when to decorate for Christmas, the man mows the lawn and the wife cooks, what colors match, or how to make the bed, etc., can make marriage uneasy or even erupt into a full-blown fight. Our spouse may not follow the rules as written in *our* Book of Life that we were sure everyone received a copy of at birth.

For instance, we frequently hear we need closure after a difficult circumstance. So, we falsely assume everyone needs closure or at least the same way we do and feel resentful when we are urged to move on after a disappointment without the ritual or designated time frame we are expecting.

Or do we think it is a rule that we need a written apology when someone hurts our feelings? We can become very easily offended because other people don't follow our rules. Happy doesn't live there.

One wife had a rule on which feet her husband must wear his *tube* socks. He thought either foot would work but soon found out it proved to be a big deal to her, and he unfortunately often wore them 'wrong.'

One woman decided she would never talk to her sister anymore. When Jane posted pictures of her kids online, Mary always 'liked' the post. But soon she noticed that sometimes Jane didn't like all the kid shots Mary posted and she became very angry. Jane inadvertently broke Mary's rule.

I say you look handsome, now you need to tell me I look pretty. Or I told you I love you, now you need to say it back.

One woman walked next to her new boyfriend, and he pushed her back behind him. He angrily insisted she showed a lack of respect for him by daring to walk side by side. "Everyone knows the man leads!" he declared. He got quite upset that she didn't know the rules. She grew confused and alarmed. Wow! She wondered where he learned those rules. But thanks for the HUGE waving red flags.

A woman exclaimed, "I can't believe she doesn't do her eyebrows right; I mean they look awful. I don't know how she can go out in public with her eyebrows like that!"

Let's not worry if someone is keeping our rules; realize others may not have any idea what our rules are. We will be better children, parents, workers, spouses, neighbors, or friends if we understand that we don't get mad when somebody is not obeying *our* rules. Who does that make sense to? Of course, there are laws of the land that we adhere to as well as common manners and courtesies (although those may differ). Be gracious and remember that others may not have the same rules.

Life Can Be So Amazing

Let other people be themselves. They're on their own path and they may not have progressed as far in one area as us. Keep in mind though, they may be miles ahead of us in another way. We're not here to compete with others. Plus, it makes our life grand and happier if we're not always being offended.

In a relationship, we must take responsibility for the relationship. If it is not good for both, it is not good. We know our partner's buttons. Don't push them. A loving relationship can be so wonderful, and all parts of our lives will feel blessed because we think about life in a healthy, beneficial, happy, unoffended way.

It may not even be *our* problems that teach us and strengthen us but instead by observing someone else's difficult journey. We may get inspired by watching movies or reading books about the Holocaust or other difficult times in history. Would we have been brave enough to risk our lives to save people who were being treated so unfairly?

Challenges can help form a fabulous connection between people. When I still had active, horrible CRPS, people would often say they were inspired to see me happy and cheerful, and handling it so well. Others said when they thought about a minor problem in their life, they thought of me and decided not to complain.

Russ bravely sojourned through his cancer and people sought his advice on how to cope with life. They valued the perspective of one who suffered with great pain and faced death. When our last oncologist broke the news that Russ only had a few weeks left and placed him in hospice, the doctor became visibly shaken and cried, while Russ comforted him.

When Nola received similar news, she said, "Actually it's kind of exciting."

"Exciting?" Mark said, looking for understanding.

"It's like a brand-new adventure, and it looks like I'm going first," she replied.

Viewing the Beautiful Struggle of someone dealing with adversity in a way that is noble, and even elegant, is an inspiring lesson. It also closes the space, so we connect with other people.

I've noticed when I've been going through a hard time, I tend to want to be left alone and suffer through, but other people wish to be around, they desire to help and be a part of it. I feel the same when I see someone suffering. I think, *please let me help you.* It is an honorable and incredibly strengthening value of humanity that we want to reach out; we seek to help each other. No doubt there are those praying for our welfare. Think about that. Try to feel those prayers and the love conveyed. It doesn't matter if you believe in prayer.

That's what is good about human beings. When we have healthy thoughts, we want to unite. We become more compassionate, more tender, more loving, and more kind, and we reach out to help other people. We can see in these struggles something good for all humanity.

When we forge ahead alone, it's like saying we don't want others to be more kind, compassionate, and charitable. Or we don't want to connect with other human beings, this is my deal, go away. We may desire to serve others, but we don't want it the other way around.

Sometimes we have such fierce pride and independence. What about encouraging *interdependence*, a synergy where we work together to make things happen? We can form an alliance with others to get through difficult times. Interdependence is the best part of humanity.

Can we learn to love someone different than us? Of course, and let's be Soft with those we love, Hard hurts.

The Gift of Feedback

First of all remember, 'Some things matter, most things don't.'

In most interactions, but especially in an intimate relationship, it is very important that both are free to express their feelings and work together. For committed couples, let's recognize for the good of the relationship that the day we marry we give up thinking that everything is about 'me'— regardless of how many years we've been alone. No longer do we get to decide everything or only rely on *our* feelings or opinions. We must truly understand that now many things affect both of us. So, BOTH need to be fully involved. In a happy marriage, the individuals have learned to put the marriage's best interest above their own. Being open to feedback to overcome issues shows humility.

If we won't allow feedback and refuse to even listen, or consider other opinions, it is stifling. To silence our spouse is controlling and manipulative behavior. It limits our ability to see alternatives and grow. If we are giving feedback, be kind and gentle. Let's strive to be equal partners. We can help our companion feel respected, listened to, and acknowledged as a valuable partner—outside a Hallmark card once or twice a year.

If we get upsetting feedback, we have options.

1. Stay calm and on topic. Remember our Creed. Stay on the journey we have decided for ourselves. Think clearly about who we are.

2. Avoid the temptation to counter with a complaint or point out something we don't like to 'even the score.' Listen to understand how the other person feels and thinks. Ask questions to explore why and how they think. Do not use questions to make your partner feel the need to defend themselves. Focus on truly seeing their point.

3. Then ask ourselves, is it true? (It may not be what we *want* to hear, but maybe what we *need* to hear.)

4. We can calmly explain if what we said or did was misunderstood.

5. If it was not a misunderstanding, but true, with maturity and courage take full responsibility for our part. Respond with love and kindness. Show the integrity of our character. Think about how knowing this and changing it can bring more harmony into the relationship.

6. Be grateful you have shown your partner you can be trusted. Thank them for bringing it to your attention in a kind way. This is important to ensure issues are quickly settled while small and calm.

7. If necessary, apologize sincerely and quickly.

8. Ask if there is something that would make it better, some way we can fix any damage done. Follow up later to show your commitment to change.

9. If it is not something we feel the need to change, then explain why and work to end in agreement.

OR

We can refuse to listen, get mad, blame, justify, and throw a freaking fit or storm out. And then we WILL deal with it again. Our reaction may be worse than the offense. This is not smart or loving. It makes it hurtful and sets a terrible precedence.

"If there is a disagreement,
think of it as a time for Discovery, not Defense."
— M. S. STARK

Simply talk over a problem. Clarify by asking questions, don't argue. Explain our emotions, don't act out, and we will open the door to solutions instead of arguments. If we're not a very mature and healthy thinker, listening to somebody explain themselves could be upsetting and make us feel like we must defend ourselves. Or perhaps it sounds like they are telling us that we are wrong because they are throwing around what they think is evidence. If we start to hear it that way, we could get offended. However, if we're listening to understand and we don't make it about us, we can find a solution. Seeing another point of view is powerful. We already know what we think and now we get to add a whole other brain's worth to it.

Let's be capable of expressing ourselves with respect, honesty, empathy, and kindness as we move toward resolution and understanding. Keep in mind that feedback is meant to be helpful, not hurtful. Listen, think, and act in a way that is true to our proclaimed values. No emotional theatrics. Allow a conversation where both can be heard and felt understood. In talking, are our words focused on the purpose of making things better? Do our words and tone of voice show we are speaking to someone we love, or do they sound more like we consider this person our enemy?

Everyone receives feedback. Don't be afraid of it. No one is perfect; we should expect and even hope for feedback so we can grow from it. It is a sign of emotional maturity to deal with it in a healthy, open-minded, curious way.

Sometimes we may deal with a person who feels broken. They can't make a mistake; they can't handle being human because they are so afraid of not being good enough. Tread softly with broken souls. We can believe that with what we've all been through and learned up to this point, it is very likely that we are the best we can be. We are enough. For now. If we are sincerely trying to get better—we will. Self-improvement is a constant endeavor. Give grace.

Focus on today instead of looking back and beating ourselves up. If we made a mistake yet still feel bad five years later even though we've made amends and never done that thing again, that's ridiculous. If we learn to forgo or at least, forgive, and offer that gift to others, let's kindly extend it to ourselves and realize that we make mistakes because we're human beings but we're trying to be better. Year after year, we get better and better. It's okay if we make a mistake, fix it to the best of our ability and try not to do it again.

"Feedback is the breakfast of champions."
—KEN BLANCHARD

There are numerous quotes about how successful people value feedback, even ask for it, and how it should be viewed as a gift. Don't be crushed by it, get defensive, or retaliate. Don't fight it, instead examine why we can't be objective about it.

It could be that another has misunderstood us. Remember to start with the discovery process when we think there may be a problem. I recall asking my nearly deaf, elderly mother-in-law if she would like a glass of water and she answered. "There's a flyswatter hanging by the back door." Misunderstandings happen. It's okay. You may be misunderstood, or you may be the one who is misunderstanding. Remember that.

When I lived in Canada, we often saw bobcats, deer, foxes, coyotes, geese, beavers, owls, and so much more. Later when borders closed and we were limited to phone calls between our two countries, Mark and I often talked about all the wildlife around our house which backs up to a large provincial park full of woods, meadows, hills, and a large creek. He would report the activity of the critters and let me listen to owls hooting or often, coyotes howling and yipping across the valleys.

One day we were on the phone, and he was out at Sunset Point, and said there was a bobcat down at the bottom of the hill. "Cool!" I remarked.

"Yea, it's moving rocks."

"Why would a bobcat be moving rocks?" I asked, very puzzled and trying to picture this in my head.

"I think they're making a new trail," Mark replied casually.

"What!" This seemed so weird to me. "Why would a bobcat be moving rocks to make a trail?"

"It's just gravel."

I felt so confused. "Is he picking it up with his mouth and moving it?"

Mark burst out laughing. And then it hit me. Not an animal bobcat but a front-end loading excavation machine. Thinking about how in the world a furry bobcat would be picking up gravel to move it and realizing how vastly different the image in our heads must have been, we laughed in delight.

Though usually tightly connected on the same wavelength, we thought it all so funny. The humor of our misunderstanding made Mark anxious to share the story with his friends. I may be famous in Calgary now.

Then a few days later, after a rain, Mark called and said he had found some tracks in the woods. And he would send a photo. He wanted to test me to see if I could tell what it could be. I knew the imprint most animals made and eagerly clicked on the text. There in the mud lay the heavy-tread tire marks of the bobcat machine. Sometimes, Mark thinks he is so funny. Actually, we both laughed. Mark is very kind and loving towards me and would never laugh *at* me. But we tease and laugh together often, easily, and loudly.

But sometimes it's not a misunderstanding, perhaps the person intentionally did it. Even then, I think carrying a grudge means that we are not willing, or able, to talk it through and resolve it and let it go. Maybe it's the other person who doesn't want to talk about things, fearing it makes them look bad or that they were wrong, and they can't deal with that. Before we try to solve the issue, we may need to clear up that misconception.

I think a lot of people who carry a grudge have a reason for it and they are focused on 'this person did me wrong.' It was real, we didn't misunderstand, it happened. Maybe it's upsetting to us because we haven't been able to deal with it, and they won't talk about it. They won't accept the fact they did it. They won't apologize and they're carrying a grudge too. But do we stop and ask ourselves, does holding on to this make my life better or worse? If there's nothing else we can do, it's probably not going to get fixed, ask—and be completely honest—is being in this disturbed, agitated state the way we want to live?

One woman carried a grudge attitude for a long time. It probably stemmed from the fact that she had a very strong aversion to thinking someone would take advantage of her, and she would have to endure it. She didn't want to appear weak or be a victim. She hated the idea of that happening so much, that whatever offense, even a small slight, that someone did to her gave her enough fury to ensure they were going to pay for it dearly. Yet it hurt *her* so much more. But that worry was drilled into her so strongly for some reason, that she had a hard time letting go of anything and thinking of it in a healthier way.

One man could never be wrong. He had made many serious mistakes and felt like such a failure that subconsciously, one more mistake would tip him over the edge, and he couldn't face it. Even when he did something terrible to someone, he had this overwhelming guilt and exploded in rage. Instead of apologizing, he tried to find an excuse for it, so it looked like he wasn't in error. Lame excuses like, he had a headache or didn't get enough sleep. Or he twisted it and blamed anyone else. Lying to ourselves never works—we know the truth—so the justifications continue and can get quite absurd. Remember, own it.

Abuse

Let's say it takes a while to accept responsibility for regrettable actions or words due to ridiculous attempts to justify, make excuses, or trying to transfer blame. Then on top of that, we cause our partner emotional suffering by engaging in lengthy stonewalling and withdrawal. By then, even if we eventually apologize, it's not cool. Procrastination is generally not an effective way to live. To delay repairing issues in a close relationship—even for a few minutes—is one of the worst ways to procrastinate. The faster we get back to love, the better.

Stonewalling is cruel. We must not abandon our loved ones. Stonewalling is like saying you are so unimportant to me; I'm not even going to talk to you. I'm not even going to acknowledge you exist. That's a hurtful thing to do to somebody, especially someone who has vowed to love us.

Perhaps someone says they're sorry for the same things over and over and over and over. (Hopefully, we are The Boss of Our Thinker and don't do this.) Then they do nothing to prevent it or to learn the skills to react in a better, more appropriate way next time. They seem to have this idea that they can do whatever and 'sorry' always fixes it. Real repentance has more to do with 'go and do no more' than the word 'sorry.' Their 'thanks for putting up with me' is hollow. They take us for granted, and maybe they think since they got away with it, they can keep doing it. But the truth is, they really didn't get away with it, and now they feel bad about themselves.

We totally get that they don't know how to do things differently. But refusing to learn how to change is not an effective way to live.

> *"Progress is impossible without change, and those who cannot change their minds cannot change anything."*
> **— GEORGE BERNARD SHAW**

We can have emotional abuse without physical abuse, but we can't have physical abuse without emotional abuse too. Having someone—whom we love and who loves us—hitting us does not only hurt the body but also the mind and soul. Bruises on the skin heal more easily than the ones on the heart. There are degrees of physical/emotional abuse. The loss of self-respect from enduring the abuse is a form of personal emotional abuse. All abuse forms are damaging, so comparisons are pointless. If it is an issue in your life, please keep your distance and seek help immediately. Abuse may cause death.

Empathy

What is empathy? Empathy is a deep understanding of another and how they feel. Be kind. We've made mistakes so who are we to make big judgment calls? It's not our place to condemn others; that's what human beings do; they make mistakes. Let's learn to be tolerant and patient. Focus on our own 'stuff.' How are we doing on behaviors we'd like to improve?

If we are not acting as we would like to be treated, or in the way we think is right, then STOP IT! Be aware of what we are doing and saying, the tone we use, and why we are acting so out of control. Apologize and don't keep doing it. Is that really who we want to be? Don't we all want to Live Happily Ever After?

We can develop empathy by listening to others and trying to understand another point of view. We may even have the opportunity to listen to someone who lives a very different life than we do or has radically opposing views. We don't need to be defensive or change our views, because it's not about agreeing, it's about being open-minded and understanding.

Helping Children Develop Empathy

I believe that a strong sense of responsibility and deep empathy are the foundations of mental health. I focused on these traits for my children knowing it would be a gift in their futures. When my children were growing up, I wanted them to develop empathy for others, especially their siblings. If they misbehaved, I would have them write about it. Before they were old enough to write, we talked it through. However, writing involves more of our brain, so it makes a bigger impact on our thinking.

I would ask them to write the answers to these questions:

- What did I do?
- How did it make me feel?
- How did it make others feel?
- What could I do better next time?
- How would that make me feel?
- How would that make others feel?

This exercise helped them examine their words and actions, and their feelings as well as the feelings of others. It also made them more aware of the impact of their actions. It helped them to take responsibility for what they did in a more empathetic way. Notice that I did not ask them why they did it or about what anyone else did. I didn't want to turn the discussion to excuses, blame, or justification. I wanted to simply emphasize *responsibility* and *empathy*, the essentials of mental health.

It made them think deeply about an incident and it took time. I felt the time for thinking and writing was better used than simply having them sitting in the corner or being sent to their room.

This exercise also works with adults. It is the very essence of the Golden Rule.

Light it Up

Light and beauty can happen during a grey day. Joy, peace, and happiness are available even in the midst of grief, adversity, or sorrow. "Very little is needed to make a happy life; it is all within yourself, in your way of thinking."
—MARCUS AURELIUS

CHAPTER 14

GRIEF

Mark and I have had times of grief in our lives like most people. The loss of a spouse, child, parent, sibling, or a close relative or friend is significant. We both had our spouses die from cancer, so we are very familiar with that world. Of course, it is sad and challenging, but grief can also be a Beautiful Struggle. It can soften us and help us develop more compassion and empathy for others.

> *"I heard a widow complain that life will never be the same. Well, it never is. Life changes."*
>
> **— M. S. STARK**

Some may say we've earned the right to be bitter and angry when we lose our spouse for example, but does that make things better? Let's see it as a time to earn the right to become a better person, to be stronger, to see the world through new eyes, and to be more compassionate. We can be healthier depending on our response to loss.

We can seek healing from our grief and from the pain it causes us, or we can wallow in misery. It's a choice. Two great ways to assist our healing are gratitude and providing service to others.

Tears are Liquid Love.

Each of us will face loss and sadness. We each grieve in our own way but let's ask ourselves: is this a healthy way to do it or an unhealthy way? For example, I know a man who has very harmful thoughts which has often made life complicated for him and those around him. He was on a plane rushing to arrive before his father died. But he didn't make it. The man became crazy furious making a huge scene at the airport and security had to be called.

Hours later, he remained so angry that when his wife tried to talk calmly to him, he physically attacked her. How could anyone see that as wholesome grief? We are not free to grieve *however* we want; and though it's a common saying, it's simply not true. Of course, nobody can stop us from grieving that way so I guess I should say if we want to be healthy and not pile up awful regrets on top of sadness, or if we want to truly grieve and even honor and show respect to the person who has died, we'll try to grieve in a noble way.

Since we can choose, let's choose a healthy way. Especially when we're in grief we don't need to make it harder for ourselves. Mark and I have heard the opinion that 'there is no wrong way to grieve' but we don't believe that. Let's not turn adversity into deeper tragedy. We think a better choice is to think in terms of healthy or unhealthy ways. We can determine this by asking ourselves if it makes things better or worse. Clearly, if a grieving person committed suicide or became so angry that they lashed out and seriously hurt someone, we could describe that as an unhealthy way to grieve.

Remember when we face the challenge of losing a spouse or another serious trial, let's ask ourselves, "Is how I'm dealing with it making my life better or worse?"

Grieving destructively is not a right, so why would we tell people that it's okay, that *however* we grieve is fine? Instead, we can Be the Boss of our Thinker. By using healthy thoughts, we dissolve our harmful emotions. There are complicated feelings around death often based on the relationship itself. Other times, it is influenced by our beliefs about death.

Unhealthy thinking does not bring our spouse back and it makes a terrible experience worse. Why would we do that? It is not God, our mother-in-law, our neighbor, or anyone else doing it to us. We think for ourselves. It may be difficult to change habitual thoughts because we begin to go to those dark places with little conscious awareness. It takes intentional, courageous thoughts to break away from destructive and negative ones.

We may go into the Cave of Sorrows, but we shouldn't live there.

Examining our thoughts when we are grieving may seem harsh. We may not want to examine our feelings at such a difficult time and in such a pragmatic way. We may feel it needs to be discussed with emotion, passion, and tragic drama because it is so horrible.

Mark and I are not trying to shame anyone for their method of grieving, or create any anger, guilt, or hurt feelings. We hope that if we examine our thoughts and think honestly, and perhaps in a different, healthier way about it, our suffering may be eased.

That does not mean we forget our loved ones. It does not mean we are not sad they are gone. It does not mean we don't have sudden, random waves of intense mourning, perhaps even years later. It does not mean we don't love them, or we won't miss them. It means we want to honor them (and ourselves) by living a full and healthy life with purpose, emotional strength, and fulfillment. Life is exquisite when we are emotionally, spiritually, mentally, and physically healthy.

We certainly don't have any delusions that healthy thoughts will suddenly erase the grief and sorrow either. Death, especially of a dear loved one, is daunting indeed.

After a deep loss, it may be hard to think clearly. It may not be a great time to make important decisions. Let's give ourselves space to think. Get into the habit of responding to whatever somebody asks with, "Oh, let me think about it and I'll get back to you" so we're not committing ourselves to something that we are not comfortable doing yet.

Don't let other people tell us what to do or make decisions for us. Sad does not equate to incompetent. For example, others may say we must get rid of our loved one's clothing, (or car or golf clubs or the house or whatever). Or they may suggest we should stop wearing our wedding rings. If we don't want to yet, let them know that we'll need a little more time before we're ready to deal with that. If they continue telling us what they think we should do, simply repeat it, "I'm not ready for that; I need more time." Or you may ask, "Why do you need me to do that?"

Sometimes we may feel hesitant to talk about the deceased person because it's so painful. Other times we may want to talk about them, and talk about them, and talk about them. That's fine too. Let's be aware that for some people listening to us talk about our late spouse may make them uncomfortable because they're not sure how they're supposed to respond. Find those people that will let us talk about our loved one, and maybe they will share some stories of their own if that makes us feel better.

Widow and Widower

Prolonged self-pity is not the answer. For example, Mark and I know widows, who even years later, complain bitterly because a married couple are holding hands where they may witness it. They feel like the couple is being insensitive and hurtful to them. Why? Do we wish others to suffer too? A loving couple can't hold hands because it hurts us. Really? Why would we make that act be about *us*? Do we twist things to be a martyr? Are we seriously suggesting that couples not hold hands to make a widow or widower feel better? Did we restrict all public displays of affection before our spouse died? How about seeing handholding and using it as a trigger to bask in fond memories of affection with our late spouse? Or are we only triggered in a negative way? Remember: Better not bitter.

When we judge others harshly who are unintentionally 'hurting' us, the truth is, we are hurting ourselves with our unhealthy thoughts of interpreting their actions of love as bad or taking their actions personally. Why would we seek out more suffering?

We don't need to work at being a bigger victim by thinking our challenge beats out trials others may face. Mark and I don't think it is healthy to view our individual suffering as the most horrible or feel it diminishes the suffering of others. Though it certainly ranks way up there, I don't believe being a widow or widower is the worst thing. Unfortunately, there are horrible things out there. Suffering is not a contest.

It's not that becoming a widow or widower isn't difficult, but the hyperbole that whatever happens to us is the worst, is false, and does not make us feel better. Let's watch our thoughts and subsequent speech.

Remember the suggestion that hardships happen *for* us. It may be loathsome and perhaps even seem insulting that our profound loss is in some way *beneficial.* I'm not saying we should hope it happens, or be glad that it occurred, but since it has and we can't change that, what if we tried to see how this could aid our personal growth? Or see what new insights and characteristics, like empathy, it may help us develop. Perhaps it may guide us to good experiences we never would have had otherwise. It could even lead to events that make us, or our children, stretch and even flourish. Mark and I don't think personal growth is disrespectful to our late spouse or shows we don't love them.

We don't think we came here to Earth just to grieve. We believe we came to learn, develop our minds and characters, grow into our best selves, create joy, render service, and make the world a better place.

Sometimes we hear or read things that increase our misery. For example, we may hear that when a spouse dies, we've lost all our future hopes and dreams. It is very likely that we change our countless hopes and dreams many times in our lives for numerous reasons besides death. Future hopes have never been promised to anyone and our expectations in life seldom turn out to be the way we anticipated. Plus, it seems small-minded that ALL we ever dreamed or hoped for was to stay married for a long time. A stark reality is that everyone dies, and we all know that. It is not a secret. There isn't a guarantee of when that may occur. Losing a spouse is not unique or unavoidable, about half of us will suffer that loss. Yes, our marital relationship is important, but let's not increase our sorrow by exaggerating our language or the reality of our situation.

And we never lost our future. It is still looming before us. Without our spouse, our life may not be like what we thought it would be, and their death *is* a great loss, but we didn't lose *everything*. 'All or Nothing' thinking is not healthy or true. Hyperbole can make us feel worse than necessary. If we have a 'why me, poor me' attitude, we shrink. Yes, we need to give it time, but don't hold still.

> *"Expecting a trouble-free life because we are a good person is like expecting the bull not to charge you because you're a vegetarian."*
> **—JEFFREY R. HOLLAND**

As a new widow, I was told that "the second year is much harder." I did not find that to be true and wondered why I would be 'set up' like that. Often, I spoke to widows who heard that many times, so they dreaded the second year, long before it happened. If hardships can be a time for us to grow and refine ourselves, perhaps the second year—with a new, stronger character—could be a bit easier to handle. Unless we've bought into a misguided message or neglected the effort to become better.

Life experiences are very much personal and depend on so many factors such as our age, previous experiences, our support system, our personality, our beliefs, etc. A 'one size fits all' approach can lead to making a situation more challenging than it needs to be. We don't want to become stuck or suffer more than necessary to fulfill someone's demoralizing prediction. We can decide how we deal with problems.

That means that an understanding of possible issues that may come up for us in a situation can help us with common feelings. Then we can seek help since many others have also experienced those emotions.

We may also want to consider that defining an unhealthy reaction as a virtue, then clinging to it can be self-destructive. For example, after we shared that we cried off and on the first few months, then hearing several widows or widowers describe hours of crying every day for years, we may believe they are better at grieving because they mourned deeper and longer. Sobbing, in and of itself, is neither a virtue nor vice nor the definitive sign of mourning. It can be easy for some to mistakenly assign it righteousness.

Don't be too ready to buy into a declaration. It was simply something someone said one time. Quotes can inspire or cause us to think, but question whether it is true for us. For example, let's again look at a common one, 'When a spouse dies the widow or widower loses their future.' Yes, we may not have the future we envisioned or be able to do things exactly as we expected, but let's be brutally honest, we still have a future. Don't embellish hardships. And keep in mind, no one has a guaranteed future. Yes, it may be different, and we may not like parts, but unhealthy grief can rob us of our life today—and well into the future.

Life happens, and we will *always* experience change. Plus, sometimes changes can be for the better. Be careful not to stop living, engaging in glad anticipation, planning, having goals, or being happy, etc. just because our future changed.

Stages of Grief Redefined

Sometimes we hear something and take it for an absolute fact that surely fits every situation including ours. For example, we may be told that there are five or six or seven stages of grief (depending on what we read) and we must go through them. We may not find this realistic at all, we may feel some steps are legitimate for us and others don't apply whatsoever.

This may lead us to try to grieve in the 'correct' way. Or wonder what is wrong with us if we miss a stage. Don't confuse opinions with facts. These 'stages' can set us up for more grief, or confusion about what we are 'supposed' to be doing. There are several philosophies of what those stages are. Don't worry about breaking one of the rules. They are arbitrary. If we don't go through the 'anger' stage, it doesn't mean anything is wrong with us, even though we'll probably be told that everyone gets angry. No, they don't.

The steps don't go in any order, and we may visit one several times even after we think we've got that one dealt with. There may be others that we skip altogether. It's alright; don't let anyone—despite the letters behind their name—tell us that we must have each one of these stages. We don't.

Grief can be a Beautiful Struggle. Deep sorrow can soften us so we can grow to be more aware and authentic with people who may be suffering. Perhaps there is a way to live through grief besides the more traditional, negative stages: intense sorrow, anger, denial, guilt, bargaining, depression, and acceptance. Perhaps we could orchestrate deliberate, healthy stages.

Healthy Grief Stages

Compassion	Empathy	Service
Gratitude	Reflection	Patience
Nature	Peace	

Here are some examples of this new set of Stages: COMPASSION. I felt moved to tears of love as I experienced increased compassion towards me after my late husband died. People were so kind and sweet to me it made me more aware that I didn't suffer alone. While others may be facing a job loss, a wayward teen, or a health issue instead of death, I could choose to unite with fellow humans with an outpouring of compassion. I noticed that some who had dealt with losing a spouse were particularly empathetic. I vowed to reach out to others, especially widows. We can gain sincere EMPATHY since we have experienced a similar loss, even though each situation is different. We can become a strong resource to others.

We can go through the SERVICE Stage and determine who we can help each day. Our acts of kindness bless us as well as others. It helps us look beyond our problems with the understanding and acceptance that challenges are a part of *every* life. Helping others makes the world a better place.

Or the GRATITUDE Stage when we may choose to write a thank you note daily to someone who has been a blessing in our life. The Gratitude Stage does not mean we are grateful a spouse or other dear person died. But there are always aspects in our lives that merit our humble thanks. As we actively and intentionally look at the good in our lives, let's not stubbornly refuse to acknowledge any blessings to claim bigger victimhood. Death is a normal part of every life, not a means to adopt a wounded status.

In the REFLECTION Stage, we can realize we are now facing a new beginning (even though it may not be our choice). We can reflect on our former lives and intentionally decide what parts we want to keep and which areas we would like to modify. We may feel a renewed energy in moving in a new direction. It may be our style to start with small changes and then eventually take on larger endeavors. Or we may boldly decide to embark on a brave new journey with greater strength than ever. Perhaps the best reflection is seeing the world through a window not a mirror. Let's not allow tragedy to make us self-absorbed.

PATIENCE is needed as we make changes and face the consequences of what has happened. We must be patient with ourselves when we need time to adjust to our new and unexpected life, and with others when maybe they say or do something, usually with good intentions, that could feel hurtful. It will unlikely be all better right away. Let our days unfold at a natural pace. There is a great lesson in nature. Just like a flower opens in its time, we can't yank a bud open early and expect a beautiful rose.

NATURE teaches us a healthy flow and makes us feel better. The wonder and awe of being outside on a beautiful, sunny day or a calm, tranquil night brings us peace and expands our thoughts to a wider view well beyond our life or this one day. The dead of Winter is always followed by the new life of Spring.

These new Healthy Stages will also infuse PEACE throughout and help us calmly arrive at a peaceful place. They certainly supported Mark and me. Adding a big dose of NATURE helps immensely. Be open to ALL possibilities for growth. Be purposeful about traveling through kinder, gentler, and healthier approaches to grief. We can compose our own Happily Ever After.

When I became a widow, I made an intentional decision to not get caught up in society's expectations for me. I chose my own beliefs. I will not cling to sadness or misery. My situation is not unique or unusual. I am not a victim. I am not a Star in a Hollywood drama. If I grieve the most, I don't win a prize. Life is full of experiences, and I knew I could learn from each one. The more I learn, the more I can improve and the happier I can be. My life had changed but was not over. I felt an obligation to appreciate life more and live it to the fullest. How could I explain to Russ that because he lost his life to cancer, I gave up on mine? He wanted to live; I need to want to live as much as he did. Really. Fully. Live.

"Everyone dies, but not everyone lives."
— **PRINCE EA**

We must believe our healthy thoughts. No option is better than to do what we think is right, at the right time, in the right place, for the right reason.

Choose to Not Be Offended

Sometimes people say the wrong thing. When we're grieving, we may be overly sensitive. That may be part of it or maybe they do say something inappropriate. We may not know how to respond. Let's think about what we could say next time when someone says, "Oh, you'll be fine, you're so strong." Our response could be, "Yes, I think usually I am a pretty strong person, however right now I'm not feeling very strong."

What if someone says at the funeral, "You'll be fine, you'll probably remarry." Our answer could be, "I don't know what my future will hold. I'm not thinking about remarriage right now, I just lost my husband; I'm thinking about him." Or "The idea of remarriage right now is not something that sounds like it's going to make everything all better."

Try to validate what other people say and then we could perhaps add our thoughts. For instance: Someone says, "All things will work out." We can say, "Yes, I can see in my life that things have worked out even though it was different than I expected. I appreciate your concern for me, but right now I'm having difficulty seeing how things are going to work out and I need some time before I'm to that point." We have validated what they said and acknowledged their concern, but we haven't necessarily agreed with them.

We don't have to be strong or stalwart for others. Sometimes we feel like we're being pushed into that role. Let them know, be honest and open, say, "Right now I'm feeling very weak" or "very vulnerable" or "very sad" or "very emotional" (express how we feel) and let them know that while we appreciate their concern, we need to be alone, or we'd like to be with people, or we don't feel up to hosting a group of people, or anyone for that matter at this point.

This helps people understand that maybe some of the things they're saying—platitudes they may have heard from someone else, are not really what we want to hear right now but we can give them grace for what they're trying to do. Because they intend to help us. Keep in mind they're in a difficult position (yes, we are the new widow or widower and are in a very difficult position, but we can still exercise empathy). We've probably been in their shoes in the past when *we* didn't know quite what to say. And even the right thing to say to one person may not be correct or appropriate or welcome, for someone else.

Let them know that we appreciate that they are thinking about us and trying to comfort us. We can see they are trying to say something that will make the situation better even though there's probably very little they can say right now that's going to make it better. We can still say something like, "Thanks for your concern, but right now I'm grieving, and I don't feel fine and it's difficult for me." But remember to give them grace in the fact that they are trying, and their intentions are most likely compassionate, loving, and kind.

Don't try to win the 'I had someone say this awful thing to me' contest. I had someone once tell me after losing a baby, "I know how you feel, last week I lost my cat." I didn't feel offended. This woman had never been married, never had children, and had this cat for fifteen years. This cat to her was her family. She had been devastated and sad when the cat died; to her, it did seem like a fair comparison. So, I chose not to be offended; I took it in the vein of her good intentions. And I thanked her and even expressed condolences for her cat.

People tend to want to fix things. It's also awkward for them and they may be uncomfortable when they see we are hurting. They want us not to hurt anymore so they try to say something that they hope will stop that. Even though there's nothing that they can say that's going to fix it. But their acts of love are beautiful things. See them for what they are.

Someone may very well say something that seems super inappropriate, but if we recognize they had good intentions, there is no reason to blast them. Could our elevated emotions possibly make us a bit oversensitive? Or maybe we are unfortunately dealing with someone who struggles to be kind. Let's not squander our internal Peace. Place your thoughts someplace beautiful. Instead, we can give them grace and pray we are never like that. We will feel better showing compassion, not anger. Being in a brokenhearted condition, let's not decide to be offended on top of it all.

A widower told me once that someone said to him, "Oh yeah, my dog died last week; I know what it's like." Even if someone lost their spouse recently, they still don't know exactly how *we* feel about it. But instead of being critical of the person, keep in mind that we have all experienced loss. That is all they are trying to say, so don't take it as they know exactly how we feel about this death.

When my late husband died, I wasn't sure how *I* felt about it all. My feelings changed a lot, and I felt many different emotions. It was a confusing experience for me. This reflection gave me empathy and compassion when others talked to me. After all, if I was stressed and feeling confused, I understood that they were also.

When others struggle with what to say, cut them some slack. Does being judgmental help? Did we know what to say in sad times? Maybe simply saying, "I don't know what to say to you. I'm so sorry for your loss and I'm here for you. I love you and I care about you'" Or maybe just a hug.

Advice from Mark and me: GO OUTSIDE!!!!!!! If we want to increase our happiness, spend more time in nature.

Although we think it's wonderful at any time, especially when we are experiencing grief, being outside and in nature can provide great comfort. Nature brings solace, it calms our souls, and it can even make us feel like maybe there's a bigger world out there than this immediate problem. It can be a healing balm. Take advantage of it.

Our Earth's environment is a beautiful teacher; it brings great hope. Being outside gives us the opportunity to observe nature's great example of how things change, how things come full circle, how the natural world heals itself, and how animals, plants, and weather all interact. It teaches harmony. It shows life's flow.

Sometimes the fact that we've transcended hard things gives us faith in ourselves. Being able to say, 'I can do hard things' is something that can bring us solace, strength, and calmness during difficult times.

Maybe think about that when we see someone else grieving, not wait until we're in the midst of it ourselves. Don't expect other people to behave, to say, or act, or do, or help in particular ways. Again, like we've talked about before, don't make up rules. For example, even a rule like: 'I helped this lady by going over and taking her meals and visiting with her for weeks after her husband died, now she owes that to me; she should do the same thing.' She may not help us at all. It may bring up memories that are too painful and remind her of her own situation and pull her back into a grieving period and she may avoid us. Don't feel like she's breaking the rule or a bad friend. She may be doing the best she can.

Don't make up rules that people should say or do certain things, or that we must be able to grieve a certain amount of time, and everybody will agree. Their opinions are fine—but so are yours.

Men and women often grieve differently. Sometimes men (or women) are very uncomfortable grieving with tears or even showing emotion around others. That does not mean they are not grieving. Maybe we need to talk. Some seem to be good listeners and allow us to say whatever we need. Seek out those people. Or maybe we're not ready to talk about it yet. Then don't.

Sometimes there are rituals that might help; perhaps we want to give away the clothing and personal items of a loved one to certain people. That act of giving it to them and connecting may be very healing to us. Or perhaps we need to hold onto their belongings but packing them away seems disrespectful to our loved ones. Neither of those methods is more correct than the other. They are both fine. Don't judge someone who does it differently. Maybe planting a tree as a remembrance of our loved one and watching it grow may be helpful—or not.

Guidelines for Healing

When we provide service, it is healing. Service to others helps them have a better experience, not just us. After the death of my father-in-law, I gathered the blooms on the grave a few days later and took them home to dry. Then I filled beautiful glass jars with flowers and decorated them with lace, ribbon, and beads and gave one to each of his daughters and one to my mother-in-law. They are lovely, cherished memorials.

After her father was murdered, a creative woman took a few of his old shirts and made stuffed teddy bears for her sisters. I still have mine.

Grief can be exhausting. Be tolerant of our limits. Don't overschedule. Don't think we have to keep busy; sometimes we use busyness to avoid and escape our feelings; eventually we will need to face them. Do things that help renew us physically, emotionally, mentally, and spiritually. Let's try to get as much sleep as we can. We can cut back on unhealthy foods and spend more time eating those things that would be good for our body. It is physically draining to grieve. If we don't want to do something because we're tired or maybe we didn't sleep well, learn to say no gracefully, and take a nap.

If we realize that we're doing things that are making it harder for us, stop it! We may feel we need professional help; that we're floundering or drowning in our grief and we're not able to be the Boss of our Thinker. Let's show ourselves love and compassion. If we need help, asking for it is not a sign of weakness. It is a sign that we're ready to be strong again.

We may hear that we have a situation that is too difficult to handle. We may even think we can't handle it. Honestly, the truth is: we *are* handling it. If we're lying in our bed, crying all day and it's been months or even years, *that* is the way we are handling it. We have no choice but to handle it. It's happened and now we must decide how we react.

There are healthy approaches for handling it and unhealthy. Healthy principles that are going to make us feel better faster versus techniques that may keep us drowning in deep grief for much longer than necessary. We don't always have to make decisions immediately but even doing nothing is a way of handling it. It may not be the final solution, it's a process. Some days, we may need to take a break from it. We can begin again tomorrow.

Grief and Guilt

I think guilt is a very difficult response to grief. We may feel that if we express a lot of guilt, it is showing a kind of humility. I think that most of us did the best we could at the time, as a widow or widower we can't dwell on something we did maybe early in our marriage because we were a different person at that time. If we are engulfed in thoughts that are not helping us, let's please stop it. Replace those thoughts with healthy, healing ones.

When our grief starts to subside, we may feel guilty worrying that it might look like we didn't love our spouse that much. Or we may feel guilty we are still alive. Trying to live our life fully even though something very sad has happened to us is nothing we need to apologize for. It is not shameful. Don't worry if others might judge us as a bad widow or widower or may think we're not mourning hard enough or long enough or too long. It's our life and we know how we feel. Let's be true to ourselves.

If someone else says something to us that's judgmental or hurts us, remember we are the Boss of our Thinker. We can decide how we interpret what someone else says and what it means. If we don't agree, don't worry about it anymore, put it out of our mind, don't dwell on it, don't torture ourselves, don't revisit it again and again with others, let it go—that is going to be a healthier response. Seek out those that will encourage us to be our best selves.

We can try to be aware of our emotions and focus on them. Do we feel sadness, fear, hope, determination, grace, gratitude, anger... Why? Where does it come from? Shine the light of awareness on it.

Sometimes grief can overwhelm us. We may think we're doing better and we're past the point of sobbing our eyes out and then there's something that happens that brings grief back to us in an instant, and it may be incredibly unexpected.

I remember my baby Megan; she didn't live. It was very difficult for several months, lots of crying. Well, years went by and of course, though always sad about that situation, I wasn't sad every minute of my day. I had a peaceful feeling that she was in a good place and taken care of while she waited for me.

I thought I had recovered (not forgotten); it had been two decades. Then one day in a grocery store, I saw this darling little blonde girl with blue eyes, very similar to the coloring of my other children, and she was about two or three years old, and she seemed a handful!

She dashed away from her mother who kept telling her to get back here and finally, her mother said with exasperation,

"Megan, get over here!" Strangely, hearing that name, certainly not an uncommon name, one that I'd heard many times through the years, but in that moment, for some reason it touched my heart. Here I stood in a grocery store, standing in line behind this mother and this darling little girl, and I started to cry. We never know. It's okay. We don't need to apologize to anyone, and we don't need to be embarrassed. We don't have to explain ourselves or our feelings.

Sometimes if we have a belief in God and have tried to be a good person, we wonder why this happened to us. Why did God let them die? Why did God lead me here? Why did God do this to my children?

We may hear some very cliche responses such as it was God's will, she's in a better place, or God needs him more than we do. These phrases may not be helpful but it's okay, let it go. Don't dwell on words that make us sad or angry. Don't waste time asking our 'why' questions. Why my husband? Why my child? Why now? Why this way? Don't torture ourselves; it's very unlikely we're going to find answers. What has happened, has happened. It's healthier to think: What will I do now? That's a question we can answer. Keep asking until you have some ideas.

We will have good days and we may have days, hours, or moments that are very difficult. Don't think that if we've had three good days in a row the next day is going to be great. It may not. It's alright, keep taking steps forward, and let's be patient with ourselves.

We don't need to be brave; we don't need to cry, we don't need to 'move on,' we don't need to be sad. We don't need to do anything. Don't try to do what we think others expect us to do. Don't worry about being the proper widow or widower. Remember that the way we deal with our grief will be unique from anyone else because our relationship was probably quite different. It's not a contest; we don't need to compare ourselves with anyone else and feel inferior or superior.

Cooperation, not comparison, is a better way to think. I'm great, you're great. We're all great. Not great*er*.

Keep in mind that we don't have to do it alone. If we need help, ask for it. Don't be angry with other people because they're not fulfilling our needs. Often people are not sure what to do; they don't want to bother us. They may feel embarrassed, unsure, or afraid they may offend us because many people in this situation are easily offended. Or maybe they are deep in their own troubles.

When people say, if we need anything, call, they probably mean it. Take them up on their offer. Most people would be very happy if we would call and say what we need help with. I remember the unexpected volume of paperwork that had to be done after Russ died. Making numerous phone calls and saying the words, "My husband died" brought tears and my 'crying' voice. Sometimes I was so overcome with emotion, I simply hung up. Needing help doing that or even discovering the long list of 'widow business' felt daunting and made me feel sad. I put it off because I didn't want to bother anyone by asking for help. Don't be like me.

We can ask people if they can do grocery shopping, especially if it was something we did with our late spouse making it difficult and sad. We can ask people for help with meals, house cleaning, childcare, or errands. We can borrow a book or a movie. Maybe we want someone to come over for a little bit. Perhaps it's sad for us to eat dinner alone. Call a neighbor and say, "Hey it's kind of hard for me right now to eat dinner alone because I always ate with my spouse, would it be possible maybe tomorrow for me to come over and eat dinner with you?"

We don't need to say. "I'm fine" unless we do feel fine. Keep in mind that even though our world seems to have drastically changed, other peoples' worlds tend to go on and they have other issues in their life. Don't become angry, bitter, or vengeful if someone declines. It doesn't mean they don't love us; it doesn't mean they don't care, give them another opportunity to do it. If they said that they would love to but can't on that date, say, "It's alright, there may be other days I want to have dinner with someone." and then call them up later. Don't take it as a personal rejection.

After death or tragedy, at first, it may seem like we'll never laugh or even smile again, but eventually, we will and it's okay. We don't need to feel guilty about it. Surprisingly we may laugh a lot earlier than we think. It's okay, we're not a bad widow or widower, or a bad person if we laugh at something.

I can remember leaving the hospital after the loss of a baby and driving down the road and looking around and seeing people in other cars laughing or bobbing their heads to the music. I couldn't believe that life went on amid my tremendous sorrow. I thought, shouldn't the world stop? But it didn't. No one else seemed to be aware of this huge significant event that happened to me. They were simply driving by in their car, and it puzzled me that they seemed to be going on when something so big had happened; something so horrible.

Mortality is all about feeling all the feelings, which makes life deeper and richer. Sometimes the emotions of over-whelming grief or deep sadness or that idea of being alone or lost is appropriate. Even though it may seem painful or bring torrents of tears, embracing our feelings can be an incredibly beautiful and strengthening experience. I have found that those moods during times of great difficulty or grief can be very tender and prepare us to be incredibly compassionate as well as stronger people in the future. Not only caring for others but more importantly, being gentle to ourselves. A loss, even if it's a loss of a job, or health, or a friend, or whatever the loss may be, even if someone else has a similar experience, it's still not the same.

Mark Shares a Story of the Day After Nola Died

Nola succumbed to death after a relatively short struggle and she passed about fifteen minutes before midnight on a Friday night, December 4, 2015, from cancer. On Saturday morning I woke up with the realization I had a lot of things to do to notify people and prepare for her funeral. Yet, I had a raging headache and I thought *I don't want to deal with this headache, so I'm going to take something and get rid of it.* I had some headache pills in my hand, ready to take.

Then I had the impression *if you take that medication, you're going to be a little bit impaired.* I further thought *the reactions I'm experiencing would never happen again and I get one shot at it. If I do something to drown my emotions, it will also ruin my ability to fully receive those feelings and thoughts that are God-given.*

I decided to instead go about my day and deal with everything raw and unfiltered. I needed to face and deal with all those things without diminishing them. I experienced powerful thoughts and strong emotions which subdued the headache, and it soon faded away.

I kept busy and appreciated having full access to those God-given feelings, which I remember even today as a comfort and a blessing to me. I'm grateful that I followed the impression to embrace them.

I ended up with feelings of love and thankfulness, of comfort and peace from Heavenly Father telling me it would be okay. Gratitude filled my soul and my heart for the love of many and how my family came together and organized things. We spoke together, had meals together, and enjoyed each other's company. We wept together and even laughed together. We felt a surprising amount of joy and happiness, and even though it also felt sad and emotional, it reinforced the continuity of family.

The moral of the story is: Take it all in—every whit. It's exquisite in all ways.

Mark and I believe we are not meant to only feel Happiness in life. We want to experience ALL the emotions unimpaired and live life fully.

Pathway to the World

The whole wide world is accessible from this point.
We get to determine our direction. "I may not have gone
where I expected to go, but I think I have ended up right
where I'm supposed to be."

—M.S. STARK

CHAPTER 15
THERE IS ALWAYS HOPE

After a deep loss or disappointment, there is always hope. Every ending is a bright new beginning. The universe is not conspiring against us. Perhaps our plans were in opposition to God's plans. Don't try to take over for Him. Remember, a rosebud opens into a perfect rose at the perfect time, in no hurry, and not too soon. Let's allow our life to unfold naturally.

The sun is always there, sometimes it's just behind the clouds.

Depending on the type of loss we've experienced, we may want to join a support group, a singles group, a job-hunting group like LinkedIn, or a widow or widower group. Still, others don't want to join something like that, they want to join a book club, hiking group, a gym, or a bird-watching group to go in an entirely different direction. We can choose what we think will help us be healthier and happier to assist with our recovery. We don't need to make excuses to anyone about the choices we make.

We may find this a time to start a new hobby. Maybe we want to do some painting or spend some time either listening to music or playing an instrument. There have been fabulous poems and songs written about break-ups, or when we are facing a fork in the road, or as tributes to loved ones, or the proverbial dog that ran away. Maybe that's something we can do. We may want to write a story about our new situation, past times with our loved ones; or the feelings we're having in this period of our life.

Sometimes the best way to work our way through loss is by doing something with purpose. After losing our partner, it could be doing something to honor our loved one like planting a tree or donating to a cause or charity that they felt strongly about, maybe reading a book about grieving that is supposed to be comforting, or maybe serving someone else will help us feel better. If it's post–break–up, a job loss, or another disappointment, we can also look for purpose. We can try different things—but don't get caught up in frantic busyness to keep ourselves from facing grief. If we try something and it doesn't work, it's okay, stop and try something else.

We may want to send notes to someone. As a widow or widower, maybe write a letter to each one of our children to express how we feel about this special time or share tales of their other parent. After a divorce, we can also write letters to our kids to assure them it was not their fault. We can promise them we will work peacefully together with their other parent to take care of them or express our love and encourage them that it will be different, but all right. We can assure them we recognize they still love the other parent, and we won't make them choose. After a job loss, we can get in touch with friends or relatives who could help us in a new job search. Word of mouth is a great way to find a position or get some solid references.

We can decide to write about how we are doing each day. How we handled it, what our feelings or thoughts were, what were the difficult parts of that day, or what successes we had. In any situation, we can write things down privately in a journal without the intention of ever showing it to anyone else and that's fine too. If we write in a journal regularly, maybe at the end of each month we can go back and read what we've written. We might be surprised at the progress we've made. If there is an improvement, take note, be grateful for it, and be proud of ourselves.

Some of us have religious affiliations and this may be a time that we can lean on people in our congregation. Maybe a spiritual leader or professional therapist will be able to give us advice or counsel or simply listen to us. Guidance may be helpful—or may not.

No matter who the counselor is, we can still choose the advice to follow that is right for *us*. And that can change. If they suggest doing something right now, but we don't feel good about it, then don't do it. In a few months, we may start wondering if we would like to try it. We can always change our mind.

As we slowly start to edge back into normal life, when people ask, for example, if we want to go to a movie, don't automatically say no. If we are ready, say yes, get out, do things with others, don't lock ourselves away. Try to do what would be healthy for us and helpful to our emotional well-being. We don't have to do anything we're not ready for yet. But saying yes often leads to a healthier outlook because it means we're going to be with other people, and often being with others is a little better than spending a great deal of time alone mourning. So go for it, try things.

Even though this may be hard to think about, it could be one of those experiences that will prepare us for our future in ways we never thought possible. We could become more compassionate, more service-oriented towards others, and more understanding. I would hope we will be proud of ourselves for what we're doing; recognize we've grown through the process and realize we're a better person.

To live with purpose in our lives generally involves connecting with life, which implies we connect with others. We must keep going. Think about some project we've always wanted to do; maybe now is a good time for it.

"I lost someone I love but I didn't lose my ability to love."
—CHARLES SCRIPPS

Let's remember life is constantly changing, and we cannot control everything that happens. Few people are where they thought they would be ten years ago. This is probably a big change for us, but may have some positive dimensions to it, even though we may be sad about the circumstances that brought it. There's likely value in what we can learn from the situation. It can influence us to be more sensitive to others. Keep in mind there are ways our very difficult experiences can make us better people. It may even prepare us for challenges in the future.

Don't lose all the lessons and the growth that can come from it. All these things are a choice. We can take away from our loss, healthy or unhealthy views. We can choose to be better or bitter.

"In times of darkness, it would serve us well to trust that shadows only exist when light is near."
—M. S. STARK

We may even consciously plan to make our life happy. We can learn how to be more appreciative. Even saying to the cashier at the grocery store that she has beautiful eyes, or to other strangers, "You have such a cheerful smile" or "Hey, great shoes" or "I love the way your hair is styled." Those things not only make them feel better, but they make us feel better too.

Showing appreciation is a fabulous way to help us heal. Maybe something small like letting the person behind us in line go in front of us, makes us feel nice. It's a very small thing, not life-changing for us or them; but lots of small things certainly can make a difference.

There are some great books or movies that may help us navigate difficult times. Sometimes we might want to read a book that is specifically written for passing through our specific dilemma. Other times we prefer to watch a movie that has nothing to do with it; but it puts our mind in a different place in the world. Maybe there's an adventure that we can get lost in or maybe it's teaching us about a topic we've always wanted to know about. Or maybe if we're sad we want to read a book or watch a film that makes us laugh out loud. And that's acceptable.

Let's try to seek harmony, understanding, and peace with others; and not be offended. It's not healthy and it's upsetting to us and the other person.

Be careful to say true statements. For example: we didn't lose *everything*. Perhaps we lost someone extremely important to us. Let's be honest, we still have reasons to be grateful. We will undoubtedly have a different life than we thought we would, but we can still have a fabulous life.

"Hang on to hope. Get high on Hopeium."
— M. S. STARK

Mark and I leave you with our warmest wishes and heart-felt hopes for your success. And may we all live Happily Ever After.

ABOUT THE AUTHORS

Mark and Stephanni Myers Bishop have emerged from vastly different backgrounds—Mark hails from Alberta, Canada, and Stephanni from Utah, USA. Both lost their spouses to cancer and were tremendously blessed to be married in 2023 and divide their time now between both countries. They quickly discovered remarkable harmony, inspiring them to collaborate on this book, which encapsulates their personal insights, lessons learned, observations, and conclusions. Despite some serious hardships (a few shared in this book) they love life and are deliriously happy.

By encouraging individuals to become The Boss of Their Thinkers, the authors believe that together we will make the world a better place.

Once you have read our personal experiences in this book, you'll probably feel like you know us. So dear friends, to hear about our latest adventures, connect with us:

www.BetheBossofYourThinker.com

YouTube @BetheBossofYourThinker

Facebook @BetheBossofYourThinker

Instagram @BetheBossofYourThinker

For discounted bulk purchases of this book for
your company, association, or conference, please
email: Bishop@BetheBossofYourThinker.com

For speaking, consulting, or interviews with authors,
email: public@BetheBossofYourThinker.com